THE WORLD'S GREATEST CRICKET MATCHES

Norman Giller

OCTOPUS BOOKS

Published in 1989 by Octopus Books Limited
Michelin House, 81 Fulham Road,
London SW3 6RB

Typeset and designed
by Norman Giller Enterprises
Shoeburyness, Essex, England

First published in 1989

ISBN 0 7064 38957

Printed by Bath Press, England

CONTENTS

ACKNOWLEDGEMENTS

Editor Norman Giller picked a lot of brains before arriving at the list of matches featured in this book. He is making a donation to the Children In Need Fund in return for all the help received. Among the people to whom he would like to offer his sincere thanks for their co-operation during his compilation of the match reports are:

Dennis Amiss, Trevor Bailey, Alec Bedser, Ian Botham, Geoff Boycott, Mike Brearley, David Brown, Tom Cartwright, Brian Close, Denis Compton, Colin Cowdrey, Mike Denness, Ted Dexter, Basil D'Oliveira, John Edrich, Farokh Engineer, Godfrey Evans, Keith Fletcher, Mike Gatting, Sunil Gavaskar, Lance Gibbs, Graham Gooch, David Gower, Michael Holding, Kim Hughes, Sir Leonard Hutton, Ray Illingworth, Doug Insole, Imran Khan, Robin Jackman, Syed Kirmani, Alan Knott, David Larter, John Lever, Tony Lewis, Dennis Lillee, Ray Lindwall, David Lloyd, Brian Luckhurst, Rodney Marsh, Peter May, Colin Milburn, Keith Miller, Arthur Milton, Arthur McIntyre, John Murray, Alan Oakman, Jim Parks, Pat Pocock, John Price, Derek Randall, Peter Richardson, Derek Shackleton, David Sheppard, Bishop of Liverpool, Reg Simpson, Mike Smith, John Snow, Brian Statham, David Steele, Bob Taylor, Fred Titmus, Fred Trueman, Derek Underwood, Dilip Vengsarkar, Peter Walker, Doug Walters, Allan Watkins, Wasim Bari, Peter Willey, Bob Willis, Don Wilson, Bob Woolmer, Norman Yardley.

The Editor also thanks prince of photographers Patrick Eagar for his illustrative support, Michael Giller for his Apple-a-day computer skills, Leigh Jones for his design advice, and Piers Murray Hill and David Ballheimer for their motivating powers. Thanks also to the bible of cricket, *Wisden Cricketers' Almanack, The Wisden Book of Test Cricket* by statistical wizard Bill Frindall, and those marvellously informative magazines *The Cricketer* and *Wisden Cricket Monthly*, and, of course, master batsman Tom Graveney for his opening spell.

A ticket to paradise

Tom Graveney OBE

How do you judge which have been the greatest Test matches in post-war cricket? This was the poser facing my writing colleague Norman Giller when commissioned to edit this book. He decided to solicit the assistance of the people who should best know the answer: the players. Norman sent questionnaires winging around the world, and the catalogue of cricketers who searched their memories to help him select the matches to feature in the following pages reads like a Who's Who of Test cricket.

The players approached are listed on the facing page, and in return for their contributions Norman has made a donation to the Children In Need Fund.

The most memorable match in which I played is spotlighted—the final Test in the 1953 series when England regained the Ashes. You need to appreciate the depths to which English cricket confidence had sunk to understand the euphoria that surrounded our victory over Australia at The Oval. England had been buried out of sight by Don Bradman's 1948 wonders and it was 19 years since we had won the Ashes, the historic prize against which all our achievements were measured.

We were desperate for an Ashes victory to rid ourselves of an 'Aussie complex' that had been brought on by the magnificent tandem team of Ray Lindwall and Keith Miller and a procession of brilliant batsmen. Even more than 30 years on my spine tingles at the memory of that marvellous final Test when we clinched the Ashes triumph, the one and only Denis Compton sealing the victory with a characteristic sweep for four. The emotion-charged atmosphere at the ground was simply unbelievable and the country just about came to a halt as people gathered around their television and wireless sets to watch and listen to the final day's play. The Australians were marvellous in defeat and I recall foggily how both teams celebrated at a party afterwards during which skipper Lindsay Hassett showed the unerring accuracy of all Australian fieldsmen by hitting the clock on the wall with a half-pint mug. The match finished at three o'clock in the afternoon. I arrived home at three o'clock the next morning. Ah, happy days!

All this was brought back to me when I read the report in this book on the 1953 Test. I was lucky to play in or see several of the matches highlighted, but the game for which I would most liked to have had a grandstand seat was the first ever tied Test, between Australia and West Indies in Brisbane in 1961.

To have seen this and all the other post-war matches featured in the following pages would have been like getting a ticket to paradise.

Tom Graveney

1946-47 Double centuries by Barnes and Bradman sink England

Match: Australia v England, Second Test
Venue: Sydney **Date:** December 13, 14, 16, 17, 18, 19

THE SETTING: When skipper Walter Hammond won the toss and elected to bat in this six-day Test at Sydney, England hopes were high of avenging the crushing defeat in the First Test at Brisbane where Australia won by an innings and 332 runs.

The pitch looked benign, and the Aussies were without their No 1 pace bowler Ray Lindwall who was suffering from chicken pox. The sight of master batsman Don Bradman limping with a torn thigh muscle on the first day sharpened England's vision of victory.

England went into the match prepared for pace on a Sydney wicket that was traditionally as hard as concrete, and they included only one specialist spinner—Doug Wright—in their attack. Australia's selectors clearly knew something that had escaped England's intelligence network, and they picked three merchants of spin—George Tribe, Colin McCool and Ian Johnson—and in medium-pacer Ernie Toshack they had a bowler who could be naggingly accurate on any pitch taking spin.

THE MATCH: England made a disastrous start when in the second over of the first day Fred Freer —Lindwall's replacement playing in his only Test match—bowled opener Cyril Washbrook for one. Len Hutton and Bill Edrich dug in on a pitch that was encouraging the spinners as early as the first hour and their stand of 78 gave England a solid foundation, but wicket-keeper Don Tallon held three catches in the space of 25 minutes soon after lunch and England were struggling at 99 for four. It was the spin of Johnson (six for 42) and McCool (three for 73) that was baffling the England batsmen and only a stubborn stand between Edrich and Jack Ikin saved a complete collapse.

England were all out for 255 early on the second day which was reduced to just 93 minutes play because of torrential rain. Scorching sunshine on the Sunday rest day transformed the pitch and it was a perfect batting strip by the time Australia resumed their innings on the third day that was dominated by opener Sidney Barnes. He batted all day, gathering runs at almost snail-like pace while building an innings that slowly but surely put the match beyond England's reach.

Doug Wright bowled with style and guile but without any luck whatsoever, and it was plucky paceman Edrich who took three of the four wickets to fall before the close of the third day's play with Barnes and a limping Bradman together at 252 for four.

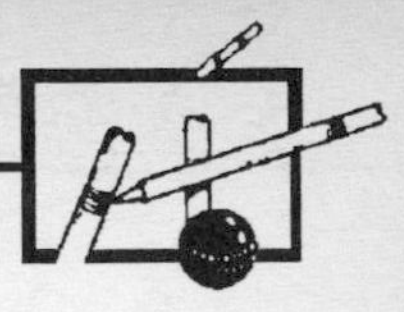

It was twenty minutes to six the following day when England at last broke the Barnes-Bradman stand, but not before they had established an all-time record fifth-wicket partnership of 405. They were finally dismissed in successive overs and with identical scores of 234 runs each. Barnes was at the crease for ten hours forty minutes, and his 200 in 570 minutes was the slowest double-century in first-class cricket. Bradman, fighting off a gastric problem and having to play nearly all his shots off his back foot because of his thigh injury, harvested his runs in six and a half hours and hit 23 fours.

Bradman finally declared 25 minutes before lunch on the fifth day with the total at 659 for eight, the highest Test total by an Australian side playing at home. An outstanding feature of England's performance was the wicket-keeping of Godfrey Evans. Playing in his first Test against Australia, he did not concede a single bye during their marathon innings—the highest Test total that does not include a bye.

Hutton opened England's second innings with a fierce attack and he raced to 37 before unluckily hitting his wicket when facing the last ball before lunch. He drove powerfully at a ball from Keith Miller but as he followed through the handle of the bat slipped through his glove and clipped the bails.

Edrich, England's man of the match, shared a century stand with his Middlesex 'twin' Denis Compton and he was still at the wicket at the close of play with the total at 247 for three. He completed his first century against Australia the following morning before being bowled by McCool, whose five wickets took his match aggregate to eight for 182.

Australia clinched their resounding innings and 33 runs victory at 3.15 pm on the final day when the last England wicket went down with the total at 371.

THE WITNESSES: Don Bradman: 'I was in quite a lot of pain while batting, but Sidney Barnes was going along so well that to have brought on a runner for myself might have interrupted his concentration. Anyway, I've never been comfortable with a runner. I felt we won because we had the better balanced side able to adjust to the changing conditions.'

Bill Edrich: 'I consider Sydney a happy hunting ground and was happy with my personal performance—particularly my century. But I knew we could be in trouble when the pitch started taking spin so early. We just did not expect that in Sydney where we have always been accustomed to a rock-hard surface. Johnson and McCool were spot-on with their spin bowling, and were given the runs to play with by Barnes and Bradman.'

FOR THE RECORD: It was the first time this century that England had been defeated twice by an innings in successive Test matches. The match attracted an aggregate attendance of 196,253 spectators. The Third and Fourth Tests were drawn (there had not been a drawn Test in Australia since 1881-82), and Australia won the final Test by five wickets.

Australia v England, Second Test, 1946-47

ENGLAND

L. Hutton	c Tallon b Johnson	39	— hit wkt b Miller	37
C. Washbrook	b Freer	1	— c McCool b Johnson	41
W.J. Edrich	lbw b McCool	71	— b McCool	119
D.C.S. Compton	c Tallon b McCool	5	— c Bradman b Freer	54
W.R. Hammond*	c Tallon b McCool	1	— c Toshack b McCool	37
J.T. Ikin	c Hassett b Johnson	60	— b Freer	17
N.W.D. Yardley	c Tallon b Johnson	25	— b McCool	35
T.B.P. Smith	lbw b Johnson	4	— c Hassett b Johnson	2
T.G. Evans†	b Johnson	5	— st Tallon b McCool	9
A.V. Bedser	b Johnson	14	— not out	3
D.V.P.Wright	not out	15	— c Tallon b McCool	0
Extras	(B 4, LB 11)	15	— (B 8, LB 6, W 1, NB 2)	17
Total		**255**		**371**

AUSTRALIA

S.G. Barnes	c Ikin b Bedser	234
A.R. Morris	b Edrich	5
I.W. Johnson	c Washbrook b Edrich	7
A.L. Hassett	c Compton b Edrich	34
K.R. Miller	c Evans b Smith	40
D.G. Bradman*	lbw b Yardley	234
C.L. McCool	c Hammond b Smith	12
D. Tallon†	c and b Wright	30
F.W. Freer	not out	28
G.E. Tribe	not out	25
E.R.H. Toshack		
Extras	(LB 7, W 1, NB 2)	10
Total	(8 wickets declared)	**659**

AUSTRALIA	O	M	R	W	O	M	R	W
Miller	9	2	24	0	11	3	37	1
Freer	7	1	25	1	13	2	49	2
Toshack	7	2	6	0	6	1	16	0
Tribe	20	3	70	0	12	0	40	0
Johnson	30.1	12	42	6	29	7	92	2
McCool	23	2	73	3	32.4	4	109	5
Barnes					3	0	11	0

ENGLAND	O	M	R	W
Bedser	46	7	153	1
Edrich	26	3	79	3
Wright	46	8	169	1
Smith	37	1	172	2
Ikin	3	0	15	0
Compton	6	0	38	0
Yardley	9	0	23	1

FALL OF WICKETS

Wkt	E 1st	A 1st	E 2nd
1st	10	24	49
2nd	88	37	118
3rd	97	96	220
4th	99	159	280
5th	148	564	309
6th	187	564	327
7th	197	595	346
8th	205	617	366
9th	234	—	369
10th	255	—	371

*Captain
†Wicketkeeper

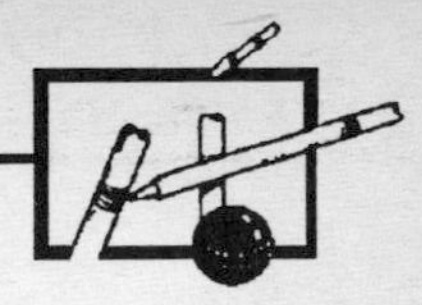

1947 Compton and Edrich beat Springboks at the double

Match: England v South Africa, Second Test
Venue: Lord's **Date:** June 21, 23, 24, 25

THE SETTING: Denis Compton and Bill Edrich—the 'Terrible Twins'—claimed squatters' rights on just about every wicket they invaded during the golden summer of 1947. Their road show with Middlesex and England was one of the most exciting sights ever seen on the cricket circuit, and wherever they played they lured massive crowds while plundering runs in devastating style.

Compton was the pacemaker, batting with a spirit and a sparkle that brought him an army of hero-worshippers of all ages. He finished the season with a record aggregate of 3,810 and an incredible average of 90.85. His glittering run collection included 18 centuries, which remains a record for one season.

Edrich followed his partner's lead in the run riot, and he finished the season with an accumulation of 3,539 runs at an average 80.43 and he contributed 12 centuries. They saved some of their most savage assaults for the Test matches against the touring South Africans, touching the peak of their power in the second Test on their home county ground at Lord's.

THE MATCH: Compton joined Edrich at the wicket midway through the afternoon session on the first day with the score at 96 for two. At the close of play three hours 10 minutes later they were still together and 216 runs had been added to the England total. Edrich had completed his first Test century in England and Compton had scored his second in successive Test innings against South Africa.

They continued the torment of the South African bowlers on the second day and it was not until 20 minutes after lunch that the partnership was at last broken. Edrich showed a rare lapse of concentration and was bowled by bespectacled left-arm spinner 'Tufty' Mann for 189. The England total was 466 for three and Compton and Edrich had shared a record third-wicket stand of 370.

Edrich, who survived a stumping chance when 47, struck a six and 26 fours. Compton followed him to the pavilion after going on to his first double century in Test cricket. He was at the wicket for five hours 50 minutes and his 208 included 20 boundaries before he was caught by Athol Rowan off the bowling of Len Tuckett. The score was then 515 for four and skipper Norman Yardley eventually declared at 554 for eight after 111 runs had been added in a 65-minute blitz.

Openers Alan Melville and Bruce Mitchell gave a solid start to South Africa's reply before Compton came into the attack with his left-arm chinamen and broke the stand when he had Mitchell stumped by Godfrey Evans with the score at 95. Skipper Melville went on to make 117, his fourth hundred in consecutive innings spread over a time span of eight years. The former Oxford University and Sussex captain added 118 in a third-wicket stand with Dudley Nourse before mis-hitting a long hop from Eric Hollies into the safe hands of Alec Bedser at backward short leg. Kent leg-break artist Doug Wright broke the back of the South African innings when he trapped Nourse leg before eight runs later and then in a spell of 22 balls clean bowled Athol Rowan, Len Tuckett and 'Tufty' Mann. South Africa followed on 227 runs behind and, after being introduced to King George VI, batting hero Edrich showed he could also strike with the ball as he knocked back the stumps of Melville and Ken Viljoen in a fierce opening spell.

There was stubborn resistance from Mitchell and Nourse, but their hopes of saving the match were shattered with the first ball on the final day when that man Edrich sent Nourse's bails flying. Mitchell and Ossie Dawson put on 72 for the fourth wicket before Mitchell's brave stand was ended after four hours 15 minutes by an acrobatic slip catch by—yes, of course—Bill Edrich.

Edrich was still not finished with his one-man spectacular. He produced an equally magnificent catch to dismiss Dawson off the bowling of his running partner Denis Compton.

Doug Wright claimed another five wickets to bring his match aggregate to 10 for 175, but the beleaguered South Africans at least had the satisfaction of making England bat again. Len Hutton and Cyril Washbrook knocked off the required 26 runs for victory without any problems.

THE WITNESSES: Alan Melville: 'Edrich and Compton were a continual thorn in our side. We tried every tactic we could to dislodge them, but they would have gathered runs no matter who was bowling. They were just untouchable.'

Norman Yardley: 'I felt privileged to captain a team including Edrich and Compton in such magnificent form. We all remember what they achieved with the bat during their glorious summer, but it tends to be forgotten that they both also did an extremely useful job with the ball. They were an inspiration to us all.'

Denis Compton: 'When I joined Bill at the wicket on that first day I said to him, "We're at home...let's enjoy ourselves." Lord's was just like home to both of us and there could not have been a more fitting setting for us to share a record stand. We were both seeing the ball as big as a football throughout that summer. I was thrilled to notch a double century because there were some people who suspected that I could not concentrate long enough to get a really big score. I even wondered about that myself!'

FOR THE RECORD: Edrich and Compton hounded the South Africans throughout the summer of '47. Between them they scored 2,057 runs—1,187 off the bat of Compton. England won the second, third and fourth Tests, with the first and last drawn.

England v South Africa, Second Test, 1947

ENGLAND

L. Hutton	b Rowan	18	— not out	13
C. Washbrook	c Tuckett b Dawson	65	— not out	13
W.J. Edrich	b Mann	189		
D.C.S. Compton	c Rowan b Tuckett	208		
C. J. Barnett	b Tuckett	33		
N.W.D. Yardley*	c Rowan b Tuckett	5		
T.G. Evans†	b Tuckett	16		
G.H. Pope	not out	8		
A.V. Bedser	b Tuckett	0		
D.V.P. Wright				
W.E. Hollies				
Extras	(B 2, LB 10)	12		
Total	(8 wickets declared)	**554**	(0 wicket)	**26**

SOUTH AFRICA

A. Melville*	c Bedser b Hollies	117	—b Edrich	8
B. Mitchell	st Evans b Compton	46	—c Edrich b Wright	80
K.G. Viljoen	b Wright	1	—b Edrich	6
A.D. Nourse	lbw b Wright	61	—b Edrich	58
O. C. Dawson	c Barnett b Hollies	36	—c Edrich b Compton	33
T. A. Harris	st Evans b Compton	30	—c Yardley b Compton	3
A.M. B. Rowan	b Wright	8	—not out	38
L. Tuckett	b Wright	5	—lbw b Wright	9
N.B.F. Mann	b Wright	4	—b Wright	5
J.D. Lindsay†	not out	7	—c Yardley b Wright	5
V. I. Smith	c Edrich b Pope	11	—c Edrich b Wright	0
Extras	(LB 1)	1	(B 3, LB 4)	7
Total		**327**		**252**

SOUTH AFRICA	O	M	R	W	O	M	R	W
Tuckett	47	8	115	5	3	0	4	0
Dawson	33	11	81	1	6	2	6	0
Mann	53	16	99	1	3.1	1	16	0
Rowan	65	11	174	1				
Smith	17	2	73	0				

ENGLAND	O	M	R	W	O	M	R	W
Edrich	9	1	22	0	13	5	31	3
Bedser	26	1	76	0	14	6	20	0
Pope	19.2	5	49	1	17	7	36	0
Wright	39	10	95	5	32.2	6	80	5
Hollies	28	10	52	2	20	7	32	0
Compton	21	11	32	2	32	10	46	2

FALL OF WICKETS

	E	SA	E
Wkt	1st	1st	2nd
1st	75	95	16
2nd	96	104	28
3rd	466	222	120
4th	515	230	192
5th	526	290	192
6th	541	300	201
7th	554	302	224
8th	554	308	236
9th	—	309	252
10th	—	327	252

1948 Lindwall express brightens a sad farewell for the Don

Match: England v Australia, Fifth Test
Venue: The Oval **Date:** August 14, 16, 17, 18

THE SETTING: Donald Bradman, one of the greatest accumulators of runs the game of cricket has ever seen, announced that this would be his final Test match, and The Oval was packed every day as English fans gathered to say a fond farewell to a player who had earned their lasting respect and admiration while destroying a procession of England bowling attacks.

What they witnessed was one of the greatest bowling performances of all time, a total humiliation for England's batsmen and a heart-stopping final Test innings by the immortal Bradman.

'The Don' was skipper of an all-conquering Australian team that had won three of the first four Tests, with theThird Test drawn after rain at Old Trafford had ruined England hopes of a possible victory. Rain also threatened to interrupt the final Test, and The Oval ground was patched with mounds of sawdust when the match got off to a delayed start. Norman Yardley won the toss and it was just about all that England managed to win over the next four days of dramatic action.

THE MATCH: England's batsmen found Ray Lindwall's express deliveries just about unplayable on the rain-affected pitch, and they were shot out in their first innings in less than two and a half hours for 52. It was the lowest England total of the century and their second lowest in Test history. Lindwall wrecked England with a lethal spell of 8.1 overs after lunch during which he snatched five vital wickets for eight runs. He finished with figures of six for 20 off 16.1 overs, his final ball of the innings claiming the wicket of Len Hutton, who was the only England batsman to offer any real resistance. The Yorkshire opener battled to 30 runs before being caught brilliantly by wicket-keeper Don Tallon, who dived to his left to hold a delicate leg glance.

Lindwall clean bowled four victims and his variations of pace and direction had the England batsmen looking as bemused and confused as if they were batting in the dark.

There was a stark contrast when the Australians opened their innings. Sidney Barnes and Arthur Morris played comfortably and smoothly, moving easily to 117 runs before Barnes was caught by wicket-keeper Godfrey Evans off the bowling of spinner Eric Hollies for 61 runs. The stage was now set for Bradman to put the seal on his majestic career by finishing with a Test average of 100.

Bradman got a standing ovation

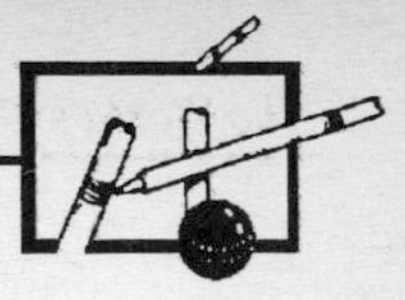

as he walked to the wicket shortly before six o'clock. Norman Yardley greeted him with a warm handshake and then called for three cheers from the England players. The crowd joined in and Bradman was visibly moved by this impromptu expression of affection for a man who had delighted England supporters even when he was carving their heroes to pieces with a bat wielded with the skill of a surgeon's scalpel. For once Bradman's famous composure and concentration deserted him and he failed to read a second ball from Hollies that was a googly which turned sharply past his bat and broke his wicket. He returned in stunned silence to the pavilion for the last time as a batsman with a duck alongside his name. Just four runs would have taken his Test aggregate to 7,000 and his average to exactly 100.

Left-handed Morris shared a third-wicket stand of 109 with Lindsay Hassett and steered Australia into a commanding position before being eighth man out four runs short of a double century. Hollies was rewarded for a bowling marathon of 56 overs with five wickets for 131.

England needed 337 runs to make Australia bat again, and this looked like a mountain from the moment John Dewes was bowled by Lindwall with the score at 20. There were aggravating interruptions because of bad light and rain, and early on the third day Bill Edrich had his stumps knocked down by a corker of a ball from Lindwall.

There then followed the only England stand of any consequence when Hutton and Compton put on 61 runs before Lindwall made a smart catch at slip to remove Compton off the bowling of Bill Johnston.

Hutton, who was on the field for all but the last 57 minutes of the match, batted for just over four hours with a variety of panicking partners before falling to a catch behind by Tallon off Keith Miller's erratic but productive bowling. England's hopes of saving the match disappeared with Hutton's dismissal and they were all out 149 runs short of making Australia bat again.

THE WITNESSES: Don Bradman: 'I was extremely moved by the reception given to me by the spectators and the England players, but I would not dream of taking anything away from Eric Hollies. He hoodwinked me with an excellent ball and deserved his wicket. It was a pity to end my Test career with a duck but it is the unpredictability of cricket that makes it such a fascinating game.'

Denis Compton: 'It was sad that The Don had to finish with a duck, but in a way it was more memorable than if he had made a big score. It was an incredibly dramatic moment, and it was so silent in the ground when he walked back to the pavilion that you could almost hear the sound of his footsteps.'

FOR THE RECORD: Bradman's full career record was 28,067 runs (average 95.14) in 338 innings, 117 of which were centuries. He topped 200 on 37 occasions and passed the 300 mark six times, with a personal best of 452 not out against Queensland in 1929-30.

England v Australia, Fifth Test, 1948

ENGLAND

L. Hutton	c Tallon b Lindwall	30	— c Tallon b Miller	64
J.G. Dewes	b Miller	1	— b Lindwall	10
W.J. Edrich	c Hassett b Johnson	3	— b Lindwall	28
D.C.S. Compton	c Morris b Lindwall	4	— c Lindwall b Johnston	39
J.F. Crapp	c Tallon b Miller	0	— b Miller	9
N.W.D. Yardley*	b Lindwall	7	— c Miller b Johnston	9
A.J. Watkins	lbw b Johnston	0	— c Hassett b Ring	2
T.G. Evans†	b Lindwall	1	— b Lindwall	8
A.V. Bedser	b Lindwall	0	— b Johnston	0
J.A. Young	b Lindwall	0	— not out	3
W.E. Hollies	not out	0	— c Morris b Johnston	0
Extras	(B 6)	6	— (B 9, LB 4, NB 3)	16
Total		**52**		**188**

AUSTRALIA

S.G. Barnes	c Evans b Hollies	61
A.R. Morris	run out	196
D.G. Bradman*	b Hollies	0
A.L. Hassett	lbw b Young	37
K.R. Miller	st Evans b Hollies	5
R.N. Harvey	c Young b Hollies	17
S.J.E. Loxton	c Evans b Edrich	15
R.R. Lindwall	c Edrich b Young	9
D. Tallon†	c Crapp b Hollies	31
D.T. Ring	c Crapp b Bedser	9
W.A. Johnston	not out	0
Extras	(B 4, LB 2, NB 3)	9
Total		**389**

AUSTRALIA	O	M	R	W	O	M	R	W
Lindwall	16.1	5	20	6	25	3	50	3
Miller	8	5	5	2	15	6	22	2
Johnston	16	4	20	2	27.3	12	40	4
Loxton	2	1	1	0	10	2	16	0
Ring					28	13	44	1

ENGLAND	O	M	R	W
Bedser	31.2	9	61	1
Watkins	4	1	19	0
Young	51	16	118	2
Hollies	56	14	131	5
Compton	2	0	6	0
Edrich	9	1	38	1
Yardley	5	1	7	0

FALL OF WICKETS

	E	A	E
Wkt	1st	1st	2nd
1st	2	117	20
2nd	10	117	64
3rd	17	226	125
4th	23	243	153
5th	35	265	164
6th	42	304	167
7th	45	332	178
8th	45	359	181
9th	47	389	188

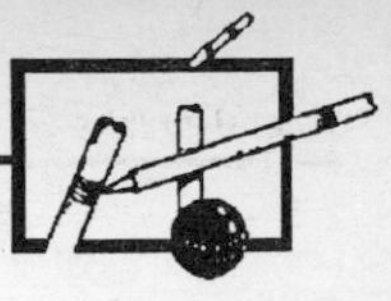

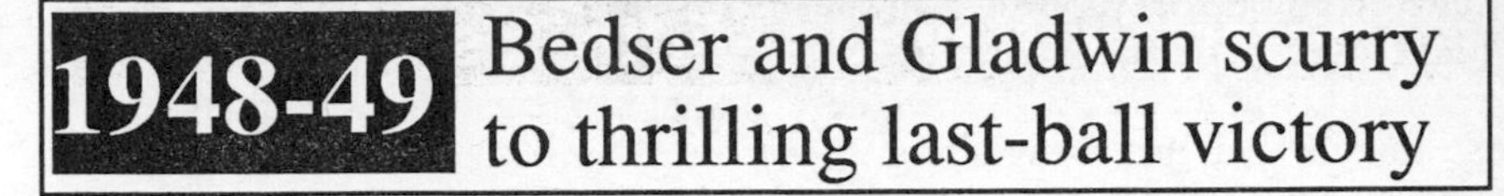

1948-49 Bedser and Gladwin scurry to thrilling last-ball victory

Match: South Africa v England, First Test
Venue: Kingsmead, Durban **Date:** December 16, 17, 18, 20

THE SETTING: There has rarely been a more exciting and dramatic climax to a match than that produced by South Africa and England in the first Test between the countries on South African soil for ten years.

Both captains insisted on playing on through incessant drizzle on the final day in the search for a positive result, and they were rewarded for their adventurous attitude with an epic, nail-biting finish.

With three balls left and England's ninth-wicket pair out in the middle any one of four results remained possible, with a draw or a tie as much on the cards as a victory for either side. The unforgettable match was eventually decided off the last ball.

THE MATCH: Springboks' skipper Dudley Nourse won the toss and, aware of thunderstorms forecast for the second day, elected to bat on a wicket that was, to say the least, unpredictable. The humid atmosphere suited the swing bowling of Alec Bedser (4-39) and Cliff Gladwin (3-21), and South Africa folded to a first innings total of 161. Wicket-keeper Godfrey Evans and Denis Compton, at backward short leg, held five catches between them, but the catch that turned the match came from Allan Watkins. He broke South Africa's only stand of real significance when he dived to his right at short leg to hold a magnificent one-handed catch off a solid shot from Nourse after he had put on 51 in a third-wicket partnership with Bruce Mitchell.

Openers Len Hutton and Cyril Washbrook gave England a sound start of 84 runs between rainstorms that caused continual delays on the second day. But on a dramatic third day, with the pitch crumbling at both ends, the bowlers were in complete command. England collapsed against the spin of Tufty Mann (6-59) and Athol Rowan (4-108). An uncharacteristic funeral-pace 72 by Denis Compton—scorer of a triple century in 181 minutes against North-East Transvaal in his previous innings—boosted the total to 253.

Heavy rain and bad light brought further hold-ups, and the South Africans went into the final day two runs behind and with six wickets left. Spirited middle-order knocks by Billy Wade (63) and Denis Begbie (43) filled the Springboks with sudden hope of not only saving the game but of possibly snatching victory.

England needed to make 128 in 135 minutes to win, but this looked a difficult target on a wicked wicket that made every stroke a challenge. A sharp shower suddenly made the pitch more suitable for pace than spin and 19-year-old Cuan McCarthy marked his Test debut with a hostile 85-minute spell that brought him six wickets for 33 runs in ten overs and lifted South Africa to within sight of victory. With an hour to go England were six wickets down with only 70 runs on the board.

Bowling colleagues Bedser and Gladwin were together for the final eight-ball over as ninth-wicket partners. The light was appalling and there was drizzling rain, but nobody considered calling off the enthralling action.

Bedser brought the scores level with a single off Len Tuckett's sixth delivery. One run needed for victory.

Gladwin swiped at but missed the seventh ball.

The two batsmen held a mid-wicket conference and decided they would run regardless of what happened off the last ball.

Again Gladwin swung and missed. The ball thudded into his thigh and bounced two yards away from him towards Tufty Mann at short leg. Bedser was coming down the wicket like a wing-threequarter and Gladwin scurried off towards the other end.

Mann pounced on the ball but could not break the wicket before Bedser hurtled to safety to clinch an incredible last-ball victory for England.

Players from both sides were chaired off the pitch by excited spectators who could hardly believe what they had witnessed. Many of the England players in the pavilion missed the winning run because they could not bear to watch.

THE WITNESSES: Alec Bedser: 'Cliff and I agreed that no matter what happened we were going to run once the final ball had been sent down. I don't think I have ever run so fast in my life!'

Cliff Gladwin: 'It was a nightmare pitch to bat on because you never knew at what height the ball was going to come through. One minute it would lift and the next shoot through scarcely an inch off the ground. The light was so bad that you could hardly see the ball, but there was no way that we were going to appeal. I have never known such a tense finish to a match.'

George Mann: 'I was making my debut in Test cricket and also as England skipper, so it's a match I'll never forget. It was a heart-stopping finale. We won the game because of our superior fielding. Some of our catches were out of this world.'

FOR THE RECORD: The second, third and fourth Tests in this series were drawn, and the fifth and final Test at Port Elizabeth produced a finish almost as dramatic as that at Durban. England were set 172 runs to win in 95 minutes, and they reached their target with just one minute to spare. Hutton and Washbrook were parted after putting on 58 in 53 minutes. The run chase cost seven wickets before Jack Crapp clinched victory by collecting ten runs off three successive balls in Tufty Mann's final over. Skipper George Mann laid the foundation for England's three-wicket victory with an undefeated maiden Test century in the first innings.

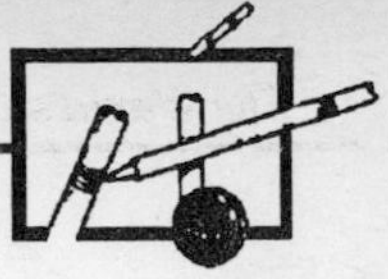

South Africa v England, First Test, 1948-49

SOUTH AFRICA

E.A.B. Rowan	c Evans b Jenkins	7	— c Compton b Jenkins	16
O.E. Wynne	c Compton b Bedser	5	— c Watkins b Wright	4
B. Mitchell	c Evans b Bedser	27	— b Wright	19
A.D. Nourse*	c Watkins b Wright	37	— c and b Bedser	32
W.W. Wade†	run out	8	— b Jenkins	63
D.W. Begbie	c Compton b Bedser	37	— c Mann b Bedser	48
O.C. Dawson	b Gladwin	24	— c Compton b Wright	3
A.M.B. Rowan	not out	5	— b Wright	15
L. Tuckett	lbw b Gladwin	1	— not out	3
N.B.F. Mann	c Evans b Gladwin	4	— c Mann b Compton	10
C.N. McCarthy	b Bedser	0	— b Jenkins	0
Extras	(B 3, LB 2, NB 1)	6	— (B 1, LB 5)	6
Total		**161**		**219**

ENGLAND

L. Hutton	c McCarthy b A. Rowan	83	— c Dawson b Tuckett	5
C. Washbrook	c Wade b Mann	35	— lbw b Mann	25
R.T. Simpson	c Begbie b Mann	5	— c E. Rowan b McCarthy	0
D.C.S. Compton	c Wade b Mann	72	— b McCarthy	28
A.J. Watkins	c Nourse b A. Rowan	9	— b McCarthy	4
F.G. Mann*	c E. Rowan b A. Rowan	19	— c Mitchell b McCarthy	13
T.G. Evans†	c Wynne b A. Rowan	0	— b McCarthy	4
R.O. Jenkins	c Mitchell b Mann	5	— c Wade b McCarthy	22
A.V. Bedser	c Tuckett b Mann	11	— not out	1
C. Gladwin	not out	0	— not out	7
D.V.P. Wright	c Tuckett b Mann	0		
Extras	(B 2, LB 12)	14	— (B 9, LB 10)	19
Total		**253**	(8 wickets)	**128**

ENGLAND	O	M	R	W	O	M	R	W
Bedser	13.5	2	39	4	18	5	51	2
Gladwin	12	3	21	3	7	3	15	0
Jenkins	14	3	50	1	22.3	6	64	3
Wright	9	3	29	1	26	3	72	4
Compton	2	0	5	0	16	11	11	1
Watkins	3	0	11	0				

SOUTH AFRICA	O	M	R	W	O	M	R	W
McCarthy	9	2	20	0	12	2	43	6
Dawson	3	0	16	0				
Tuckett	6	0	36	0	10	0	38	1
A.M.B. Rowan	44	8	108	4	4	0	15	0
Mann	37.4	14	59	6	2	0	13	1

FALL OF WICKETS

Wkt	SA 1st	E 1st	SA 2nd	E 2nd
1st	9	84	22	25
2nd	18	104	22	49
3rd	69	146	67	52
4th	80	172	89	64
5th	99	212	174	64
6th	148	212	179	70
7th	150	221	208	115
8th	152	247	208	116
9th	160	253	219	—
10th	161	253	219	—

1950 Ramadhin and Valentine start a calypso carnival

Match: England v West Indies, Second Test
Venue: Lord's **Date:** June 24, 26, 27, 28, 29

THE SETTING: Sonny Ramadhin and Alf Valentine, untried and untested 20-year-old spin bowlers, had each played only two first-class matches before arriving in England with the 1950 West Indian tourists. By the time the second Test at Lord's was over their names were on the lips of cricket followers around the world and on the to-be-avoided lists of the England batsmen.

Valentine had given notice of his potential with 11 wickets in his Test debut against England in the drawn match at Old Trafford. Slim and bespectacled, he was deadly accurate with his left-arm spin and could turn the ball viciously on even the most docile pitches.

In contrast the tiny, 5ft 4in right-armed Ramadhin relied as much on sleight of hand as making the ball work off the pitch. He camouflaged his deliveries and England's batsmen struggled to detect whether he was going to send down an off-break or a leg-break.

Individually, Ramadhin and Valentine were dynamic. Together at Lord's, they were almost unplayable.

THE MATCH: Skipper John Goddard won the toss and decided to bat on a wicket expected to take spin following heavy overnight rain. Yorkshire spinner Johnny Wardle trapped opener Jeff Stollmeyer lbw for 20 with his first ball in a home Test match, but it was one of the few moments for celebration for England in a match in which they were outplayed in all departments.While Allan Rae carefully carved a century, Frank Worrell and Everton Weekes took it in turns to accompany him with a range of thundering shots to all points of the compass. At 233 for two, the West Indians looked on their way to a mammoth total, but after Alec Bedser had bowled Weekes leg-break specialist Roley Jenkins had an inspired seven-over spell during which he sent back Clyde Walcott, Rae and Gerry Gomez. West Indies finished the first day sitting comfortably at 320 for seven.

England rattled through the West Indies tail in the first ten minutes of play on the second day, and the total of 326 looked well within their range when Len Hutton and Cyril Washbrook gave them a solid send-off with an opening stand of 62. There was a hint of what was to come when first Hutton and then Washbrook got themselves stumped by Walcott when being tempted out of their ground by cleverly flighted balls. Ramadhin (five for 66) and Valentine (four for 48), the new calypso kings of cricket, took complete control and between them bowled England out for 151.

Only the free-hitting Wardle faced the spin twins with any real confidence and he hammered six fours before running out of partners.

An immaculate undefeated 168 by Walcott (the third of the famous 'three Ws'), during which he shared a sixth-wicket stand of 211 with Gomez, enabled skipper John Goddard to declare the West Indies second innings at 425 for six. It left his spin twins a day and a half in which to wrap the match up.

Washbrook (114) and debutant Gilbert Parkhouse (48) put a brake on the West Indian victory march, and England had outside chances of saving the game when they started the last day with six wickets left and 383 runs required to win.

But those hopes quickly died when Ramadhin yorked Washbrook before he had added to his overnight score. The last six wickets fell for 46 runs, with Ramadhin the hero. He included 43 maidens in his marathon spell of 72 overs, and was rewarded with six wickets for 86 runs and a match analysis of 11 for 152. Valentine was just as accurate, sending down 47 maidens in his 71-over stint. His match figures were seven for 127.

This first West Indies victory in a Test match in England triggered a joyful pitch invasion by an army of calypso-singing spectators who brought the sight and sounds of a Caribbean carnival to the headquarters of cricket. Lord's had never seen or heard anything like it.

A calpyso record featuring 'those two little friends of mine, Ramadhin and Valentine' became one of the hit songs of the year.

THE WITNESSES: Sonny Ramadhin: 'That was the greatest time of my career. It was like a dream come true to take 11 wickets on the most famous ground in cricket. Frank Worrell was a great help to me. He kept stressing that I should be patient and that the wickets would come.'

Alf Valentine: 'The batsmen gave us a lot of runs to play with and Sonny and I knew that if we just kept plugging away we would eventually get the breakthrough. What I remember most about the match is the wonderful atmosphere. We had so many supporters in the ground that it was almost like playing at home.'

Len Hutton: 'Nobody had heard of Ramadhin and Valentine when they first arrived in England, but it wasn't long before the buzz was going around the cricket circuit that they were something special. We eventually learned how to read them, but not before they had given a lot of our batsmen some very harrowing times.'

FOR THE RECORD: Ramadhin and Valentine took 59 wickets between them during the four-match Test series. Valentine was the chief wicket taker with 33 victims, which was a long-time West Indies record. Ramadhin took 26 wickets at an average 23.23. West Indies won the second, third and fourth Tests after the draw at Old Trafford. The outstanding performance in the fourth and final Test was an unbeaten double century by Yorkshire opener Hutton, who has the distinction of being the only England batsman to carry his bat in a completed Test innings against the West Indies.

England v West Indies, Second Test, 1950

WEST INDIES

A.F. Rae	c and b Jenkins	106	— b Jenkins	24
J. B. Stollmeyer	lbw b Wardle	20	— b Jenkins	30
F.M.M. Worrell	b Bedser	52	— c Doggart b Jenkins	45
E.de C. Weekes	b Bedser	63	— run out	63
C.L. Walcott†	st Evans b Jenkins	14	— not out	168
G.E. Gomez	st Evans b Jenkins	1	— c Edrich b Bedser	70
R.J. Christiani	b Bedser	33	— not out	5
J.D.C. Goddard*	b Wardle	14	— c Evans b Jenkins	11
P.E. Jones	c Evans b Jenkins	0		
S. Ramadhin	not out	1		
A.L. Valentine	c Hutton b Jenkins	5		
Extras	(B 10, LB 5, W 1, NB 1)	17	— (LB 8, NB 1)	9
Total		**326**	(6 wickets declared)	**425**

ENGLAND

L. Hutton	st Walcott b Valentine	35	— b Valentine	10
C. Washbrook	st Walcott b Ramadhin	36	— b Ramadhin	114
W.J. Edrich	c Walcott b Ramadhin	8	— c Jones b Ramadhin	8
C.H.G. Doggart	lbw b Ramadhin	0	— b Ramadhin	25
W.G.A. Parkhouse	b Valentine	0	— c Goddard b Valentine	48
N.W.D. Yardley*	b Valentine	16	— c Weekes b Valentine	19
T.G. Evans†	b Ramadhin	8	— c Rae b Ramadhin	2
R.O. Jenkins	c Walcott b Valentine	4	— b Ramadhin	4
J.H. Wardle	not out	33	— lbw b Worrell	21
A.V. Bedser	b Ramadhin	5	— b Ramadhin	0
R. Berry	c Goddard b Jones	2	— not out	0
Extras	(B 2, LB 1, W 1)	4	— (B 16, LB 7)	23
Total		**151**		**274**

ENGLAND	O	M	R	W	O	M	R	W
Bedser	40	14	60	3	44	16	80	1
Edrich	16	4	30	0	13	2	37	0
Jenkins	35.2	6	116	5	59	13	174	4
Wardle	17	6	46	2	30	10	58	0
Berry	19	7	45	0	32	15	67	0
Yardley	4	1	12	0				

WEST INDIES	O	M	R	W	O	M	R	W
Jones	8.4	2	13	1	7	1	22	0
Worrell	10	4	20	0	22.3	9	39	1
Valentine	45	28	48	4	71	47	79	3
Ramadhin	43	27	66	5	72	43	86	6
Gomez					13	1	25	0
Goddard					6	6	0	0

FALL OF WICKETS

Wkt	WI 1st	E 1st	WI 2nd	E 2nd
1st	37	62	48	28
2nd	128	74	75	57
3rd	233	74	108	140
4th	262	75	146	218
5th	273	86	199	228
6th	274	102	410	238
7th	320	110	—	245
8th	320	113	—	248
9th	320	122	—	258
10th	326	151	—	274

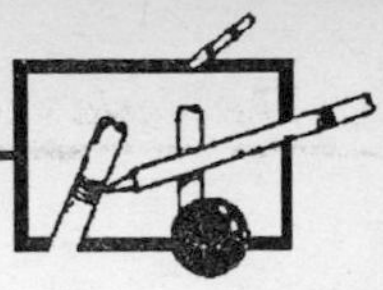

Nourse goes through a pain barrier to end the famine

Match: England v South Africa, First Test
Venue: Trent Bridge **Date:** June 7, 8, 9, 11, 12

THE SETTING: South Africa went into the first Test at Trent Bridge on a run of 28 Tests without a single victory, a disastrous sequence that covered 16 years. The fact that they ended their famine at Nottingham was due amost entirely to an astonishing innings by their skipper Dudley Nourse.

Three weeks before the Test Nourse had broken his left thumb during a game with Gloucestershire, and he played in the Test against medical advice. Nourse won the toss and chose to bat on a placid pitch that offered little encouragement for bowlers.

The South Africans made a solid start and were 107 for two when Nourse came to the wicket to start an innings of a lifetime.

THE MATCH: The South African medical officer tried to persuade Nourse to have a pain-killing injection before he went to the crease, but he refused because he felt that his timing would be affected by a numb hand. He stayed at the wicket for a marathon innings that lasted nine and a quarter hours, and all the time he was out in the middle he defied the pain of a thumb that had swollen to three times its normal size by the end of his memorable knock.

Nourse accumulated 208 runs while steering the South Africans to a total of 483 in an innings that stretched across most of the first two days. He declared soon after being run out to become the ninth man dismissed. A naturally aggressive batsman with huge forearms, Nourse had to rely on stroking the ball and he square cut and drove his way to 25 fours. When the doctor inspected his thumb after his dismissal he barred him from taking any further part in the match.

Eric Rowan took over the captaincy, and led the tourists in to the field for the final five minutes of play that were left on the second day. In the final over, Geoff Chubb—making his Test debut at the age of 40—claimed the wicket of England opener Jack Ikin with his second ball when Cuan McCarthy dived to take a smart catch at short fine-leg.

A fine anchor innings by Len Hutton (63) and centuries by Reg Simpson (137) and Denis Compton (112) helped push the England reply to 419 for nine before skipper Freddie Brown declared with two hours to stumps on the fourth day.

Thundery weather had made batting conditions difficult and eight fielders surrounded the bat when Alec Bedser opened the bowling in South Africa's second innings. Spinner Roy Tattersall operated from the opposite end and the batsmen, missing the steadying influence of reluctant spectator Nourse, were forced into making elementary errors. England transformed the match by snatching five wickets for 99 runs before the close.

Bedser raced through the tail on the final morning, taking three of the remaining wickets in 40 minutes for the addition of just 26 runs. Only Jack Cheetham (28) and Clive van Ryneveld (22) showed any resistance as the South Africans slumped to a total of 121. Bedser finished with match figures of nine for 159.

England, seeking 186 runs in a little over five hours, now looked poised for a comfortable victory. But they struggled to score runs and had only 25 on the board for the loss of Len Hutton in the 65 minutes leading up to lunch. The ball started to turn on a drying wicket after lunch and Athol Rowan (five for 68) and Tufty Mann (four for 24) tied the England batsmen into terrible tangles. They collapsed from 57 for three to 84 for eight and only some savage hitting by Johnny Wardle kept victory hopes flickering.

Wardle took the attack to the bowlers, but his whirlwind innings of 30 was ended when he skied a catch to substitute Roy McLean. It was the last England wicket to fall, and the total of 114 left them 71 runs short of South Africa.

Watching from the players' balcony, match hero Dudley Nourse raised his hands high in triumph as he celebrated something that only cricket followers with a long memory could recall—a South African victory.

THE WITNESSES: Dudley Nourse: 'We had to play cautiously in our first innings because our confidence was low after an uncertain start to the tour. I felt pain in my thumb every time I hit the ball, but it has all proved worthwhile. This victory will do wonders for our morale. I thought Eric Rowan captained the team brilliantly in my absence. He put the pressure on England and forced them into making mistakes.'

Denis Compton: 'I'm afraid we threw the game away. We had the South Africans down and virtually out going into the final day, but our batting just went to pieces in the second innings. I have always prospered well against the Springboks, and so I cannot grumble about the result. It's about time they had some luck. Dudley Nourse's innings was a magnificent display of determination and character. He was a marvellous inspiration to his team-mates.'

FOR THE RECORD: England won three of the remaining four Tests, with the fourth Test at Headingley drawn after Eric Rowan had scored a record 236 in South Africa's first innings. Bedser was the star of England's nine-wickets victory in the third Test, with match figures of 12 for 112. Jim Laker bowled England to a victory by four wickets in the final Test at The Oval. He finished with match figures of ten for 119. It was the final Test for Nourse and the Rowan brothers. The son of English-born South African batting stalwart Dave Nourse, Dudley finished with a Test average of 53.81 including seven centuries against England.

England v South Africa, First Test, 1951

SOUTH AFRICA

E.A.B. Rowan	c Evans b Brown	17	— c Ikin b Bedser	11
J.H.B. Waite†	run out	76	— c Ikin b Tattersall	5
D.J. McGlew	b Brown	40	— st Evans b Bedser	5
A.D. Nourse*	run out	208	— absent hurt	—
J.E. Cheetham	c Ikin b Bedser	31	— b Bedser	28
G.M. Fullerton	c Compton b Tattersall	54	— c Brown b Tattersall	13
C.B. van Ryneveld	lbw b Bedser	32	— c Hutton b Bedser	22
A.M.B. Rowan	b Bedser	2	— c Evans b Bedser	5
N.B.F. Mann	c Tattersall b Wardle	1	— b Tattersall	2
G.W.A. Chubb	not out	0	— not out	11
G.N. McCarthy	not out	1	— b Bedser	5
Extras	(B 3, LB 17, NB 1)	21	— (B 4, LB 9, NB 1)	14
Total	(9 wickets declared)	**483**		**121**

ENGLAND

L. Hutton	c Waite b A. Rowan	63	— c and b A. Rowan	11
J.T. Ikin	c McCarthy b Chubb	1	— b Mann	33
R.T. Simpson	c Waite b McCarthy	137	— c and b A. Rowan	7
D.C.S. Compton	c Waite b McCarthy	112	— lbw b A. Rowan	5
W. Watson	lbw b McCarthy	57	— lbw b Mann	5
F.R. Brown*	c Fullerton b Chubb	29	— c McCarthy b A. Rowan	7
T.G. Evans†	c sub. b Chubb	5	— c Van Ryneveld b Mann	0
J.H. Wardle	c Fullerton b Chubb	5	— c sub. b A. Rowan	30
T.E. Bailey	c Fullerton b McCarthy	3	— c Waite b Mann	11
A.V. Bedser	not out	0	— b McCarthy	0
R. Tattersall			— not out	0
Extras	(B 4, LB 3)	7	(LB5)	5
Total	(9 wickets declared)	**419**		**114**

ENGLAND	O	M	R	W	O	M	R	W
Bedser	63	18	122	3	22.4	8	37	6
Bailey	45	13	102	0	2	0	10	0
Brown	34	11	74	2				
Tattersall	47	20	80	1	23	6	56	3
Wardle	49	21	77	1	4	3	4	0
Compton	2	0	7	0				

SOUTH AFRICA	O	M	R	W	O	M	R	W
McCarthy	48	10	104	4	8	1	8	1
Chubb	46.2	12	146	4	6	2	9	0
A.M.B. Rowan	46	10	101	1	27.2	4	68	5
Mann	20	5	51	0	24	16	24	4
Van Ryneveld	3	0	10	0				

FALL OF WICKETS

Wkt	SA 1st	E 1st	SA 2nd	E 2nd
1st	31	4	12	23
2nd	107	148	20	41
3rd	189	234	24	57
4th	273	375	52	63
5th	394	382	87	67
6th	465	395	98	80
7th	467	410	103	83
8th	476	419	106	84
9th	482	419	121	110
10th	—	—	—	114

1952 Trueman the newcomer unnerves Indian batsmen

Match: England v India, Third Test
Venue: Old Trafford **Date:** July 17, 18, 19

THE SETTING: England's long, frustrating search for a successor to Harold Larwood as a bowler of pace and fire ended during the 1951 Test series against India with the startling emergence of 21-year-old Yorkshireman Freddie Trueman.

Motivated by an aggressive spirit that was to make him one of the most competitive of all cricketers, Trueman announced his arrival as a formidable force with seven wickets in the first Test and eight in the second.

But it was in the third Test at Old Trafford that he produced the sort of devastating speed and hostility that set him apart as a bowler of outstanding quality.

THE MATCH: Len Hutton, who in the first Test of the series had become the first professional to captain England, won the toss and decided to bat in damp, overcast conditions that restricted play to a total of just over seven hours on the first two days. A painstaking century from Hutton and powerful knocks by Peter May (69) and Godfrey Evans (71) enabled England to declare at 347 for nine early on the third day after more delays because of the unfriendly weather. It was an uninspired batting performance by England until the swashbuckling Evans came to the wicket. He hammered his 71 runs out of 84 in two rain-disrupted periods while spending a total of an hour and ten minutes in the midde.

It was then curtain up on Trueman's spectacular show. With a strong wind at his back and making the ball kick and rear off the unpredictable pitch, he had the Indian batsmen—in pre-helmet days—ducking and defending as if in fear of their lives.

It was Bedser who claimed the first Indian wicket with four runs on the scoreboard when his Surrey colleague Tony Lock quickly marked his Test debut with a blinding catch at short-leg.

Then hurricane Trueman struck, taking the next six wickets while the Indians managed to add just 47 runs. Bedser interrupted the Trueman show by bowling Vijay Hazare, and then Freddie—bowling to an 'umbrella' field that contained three slips, three men in the gully, two at short-leg and a short mid-off— finished off the Indian innings to take his haul to eight wickets for 31 runs off 8.4 overs. It is an analysis that remains the best by an English bowler in Tests against India.

The Indian total of 58 equalled their lowest score in Test cricket, registered against Australia at Brisbane in 1947-48. Only Hazare and Manjrekar reached double figures.

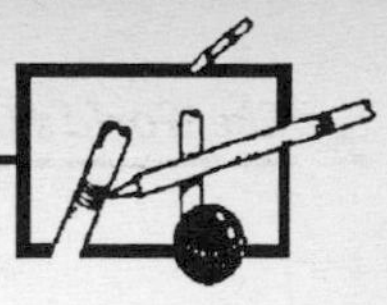

Trueman started India's collapse when they followed on needing 289 runs to make England bat again. Luckless opener Pankaj Roy, failing to score for a second time in the match, was caught by Jim Laker.

When Trueman was rested after eight overs, the shell-shocked Indian batsmen tumbled against the accurate bowling of Bedser (five for 27) and Lock (four for 36). The last seven Indian wickets fell for 27 runs—including four tail- enders down for one run— and they were all out for 82, leaving England winners by an innings and 207 runs.

The two Indian innings' had lasted a total of only three and three-quarter hours, and they had the unenviable record of being the only Test team ever dismissed twice in one day. In all, 22 wickets fell on the extra-ordinary third day.

Trueman finished with a match analysis of nine wickets for 40 runs in 16.4 overs. Bedser bowled with exceptional accuracy and was rewarded with seven wickets for 46 runs in a total of 26 overs.

THE WITNESSES: Freddie Trueman: 'I would have liked to have wrapped that wicket up and carried it around with me. It was a beauty to bowl on. I really let rip and some of the Indian batsmen had no idea how to handle the sort of pace I was able to generate. My line and length was exactly right from the first ball that I bowled and there was so much bounce that the batsmen quickly became demoralised.'

Tom Graveney: 'Freddie terrorised the Indian batsmen. They were used to the slow, placid pitches of India and could not believe that anybody could bowl so fast. Several of them were out even before Freddie had started his run-up. I swear that one of their established players was so frightened that he was walking towards the pavilion before the ball had reached him. Freddie was helped by the conditions, but the pace at which he bowled clearly signalled that England had discovered a quick bowler to stand comparison with the best in the world. No Indian would have argued with that assessment.'

Pankaj Roy: 'This is a match we would rather forget. The conditions were against us, and we were just not accustomed to the sort of pace produced by Trueman. It was the fastest bowling that many of us had ever faced, and we were unable to cope with it.'

FOR THE RECORD: Trueman made a sensational start to his Test career against India at Headingley. India lost the first four wickets in their second innings without scoring a single run. Three of the wickets fell to Trueman in just eight balls and he missed a hat-trick by a whisker. He finished the four-Test series with 29 wickets. England won the first three Tests and were robbed of a certain whitewash when rain forced a draw in the final Test at The Oval. England declared at 326 for six and then Trueman and Bedser took five wickets each as India collapsed to 98, losing their first five wickets for six runs. Hutton enforced the follow-on, but rain washed out the rest of the play before India could start their second innings.

England v India, Third Test, 1952

ENGLAND

L. Hutton*	c Sen b Divecha	104
D.S. Sheppard	lbw b Ramchand	34
J.T. Ikin	c Divecha b Ghulam	29
P.B.H. May	c Sen b Mankad	69
T.W. Graveney	lbw b Divecha	14
A.J. Watkins	c Phadkar b Mankad	4
T.G. Evans†	c and b Ghulam	71
J.C. Laker	c Sen b Divecha	0
A.V. Bedser	c Phadkar b Ghulam	17
G.A.R. Lock	not out	1
F.S. Trueman		
Extras	(B 2, LB 2)	4
Total	(9 wickets declared)	**347**

INDIA

V.M.H. Mankad	c Lock b Bedser	4	— lbw b Bedser	6
P. Roy	c Hutton b Trueman	0	— c Laker b Trueman	0
H.R. Adhikari	c Graveney b Trueman	0	— c May b Lock	27
V.S. Hazare*	b Bedser	16	— c Ikin b Lock	16
P.R. Umrigar	b Trueman	4	— c Watkins b Bedser	3
D.G. Phadkar	c Sheppard b Trueman	0	— b Bedser	5
V.L. Manjrekar	c Ikin b Trueman	22	— c Evans b Bedser	0
R.V. Divecha	b Trueman	4	— b Bedser	2
G.S. Ramchand	c Graveney b Trueman	2	— c Watkins b Lock	1
P. Sen†	c Lock b Trueman	4	— not out	13
Ghulam Ahmed	not out	1	— c Ikin b Lock	0
Extras	(LB 1)	1	(B 8, NB 1)	9
Total		**58**		**82**

INDIA	O	M	R	W
Phadkar	22	10	30	0
Divecha	45	12	102	3
Ramchand	33	7	78	1
Mankad	28	9	67	2
Ghulam Ahmed	9	3	43	3
Hazare	7	3	23	0

ENGLAND	O	M	R	W	O	M	R	W
Bedser	11	4	19	2	15	6	27	5
Trueman	8.4	2	31	8	8	5	9	1
Laker	2	0	7	0				
Watkins					4	3	1	0
Lock					9.3	2	36	4

FALL OF WICKETS

	E	I	I
Wkt	1st	1st	2nd
1st	78	4	7
2nd	133	4	7
3rd	214	5	55
4th	248	17	59
5th	252	17	66
6th	284	45	66
7th	292	51	66
8th	336	53	67
9th	347	53	77
10th	—	58	82

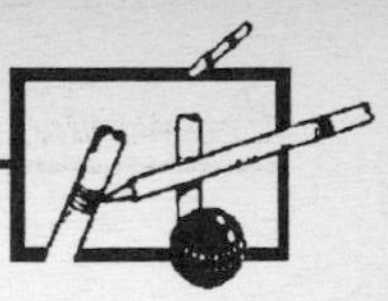

1953 Compton's sweep for four brings back the Ashes

Match: England v Australia, Fifth Test
Venue: The Oval **Date:** August 15, 17, 18, 19

THE SETTING: Australia had held the Ashes for a record period of just one week short of 19 years when they faced England in the fifth and final Test at The Oval with the series all square after the first four matches had been drawn.

It was a climax to a summer when English passions and patriotism were at a peak, stoked up by the Queen's coronation, the ascent of Everest, the first Derby victory by new knight Gordon Richards and the 'Stanley Matthews FA Cup final' at Wembley.

Rarely, if ever, has a Test series so captured the imagination and interest of the nation. The rubber attracted a record aggregate attendance of 549,650, and there were complaints from manufacturers that industry was being hit because so many workers were taking time off to tune in to the wireless commentaries and to the limited television coverage.

England's heavily criticised selectors at last got the bowling balance right by calling in the young Yorkshire tiger Freddie Trueman to share the new ball with the old warhorse Alec Bedser, and in Surrey spin twins Jim Laker and Tony Lock they had two bowlers who knew the Oval turf like the back of their artistic hands.

There were groans across the nation when it was learned that skipper Len Hutton had lost the toss. It was the fifth time that the call had gone against him and statisticians were quick to point out the gloomy fact that no captain had ever led a side to victory after losing every toss in the series. Aussie skipper Lindsay Hassett elected to bat for the fourth time in the rubber.

THE MATCH: The Test was scheduled for six days, so the Australian batsmen knew they could afford to show patience but Hassett—opening with the left-handed Arthur Morris—signalled that any loose ball would be punished by hammering Bedser's second delivery of the day to the long-leg boundary. The Australian openers were just getting themselves cemented when Alec Bedser deceived Morris with a swerving ball that trapped him leg before wicket. It was the fifth time in the series that Bedser had dismissed the left-handed Morris, and the 18th time in 20 Test matches.

Trueman, making his debut against the Australians, opened with a hostile five-over spell in which he conceded just 12 runs and was time and again just a coat of paint away from taking a wicket. Then Trevor Bailey, England's dogged hero in the first four Tests, sent the potentially dangerous Keith Miller back to the pavilion for just one after he had padded up to the ball and was given out lbw.

Australia were 98 for two at lunch, but sharp showers during the interval and early in the afternoon session brought sudden life to a placid wicket. In the face of some dynamic bowling from Bedser, Trueman and Bailey the Aussies collapsed to 160 for eight before some savage late-order hitting by Ray Lindwall (62) brought some respectibility to the scoreboard. The tourists were finally all out for 275, and England's openers Hutton and Bill Edrich were left to face two awkward overs from Lindwall and Miller before bad light ended the first day's play 13 minutes early. Hutton was lucky to survive Lindwall's fifth ball, which was a vicious bouncer. The sharply rising ball struck the handle of Hutton's bat and knocked off his cap which fell just inches from the stumps.

Hutton contributed a masterly 82 on the second day, but after Peter May's exit for 39 the skipper got little support and by the end of play England were still 40 runs behind the Australian total with three wickets remaining. The battling 'Barnacle' Bailey (64) defied the Australians on the third morning—as he had throughout the summer—and his last-wicket stand of 44 with Bedser lifted England to a surprising lead of 31 runs.

The turning point of what had been an evenly balanced match —turning being the operative word— came on the afternoon of the third day when Laker and Lock suddenly sent the Australians spinning. They crashed from a comfortable 59 for one to a panic-propelled 85 for six, with four of the wickets falling in a remarkable spell of just 14 minutes during which only two runs were scored.

Laker (four for 75) started the decay when he had Hassett leg before with the last ball of his first over during which he twice completely hoodwinked the Aussie captain. Lock (five for 45) carried on the destruction from the pavilion end, clean bowling Neil Harvey for one and trapping Arthur Morris lbw. Keith Miller was caught by Trueman off Laker for a duck, and suddenly half the Australian team was out for just 61 runs. Ron Archer (49) and Alan Davidson (21) swung the bat in a desperate bid to hit Australia out of trouble, but once Lock had eliminated them both England were within sight of a memorable victory.

It took England only two hours 45 minutes to dismiss the Australians for 162 runs, leaving England requiring just 132 for victory.

The tourists did not have a spinner in the Laker-Lock class to take advantage of the conditions, and England reached their target for the loss of two wickets at seven minutes to three on the fourth afternoon with, fittingly, the 'Terrible Twins' of Middlesex, Bill Edrich and Denis Compton, together at the wicket.

Of the thousands of shots Compton played during his glorious career none brought him greater satisfaction than his sweep for four off the friendly bowling of Arthur Morris.

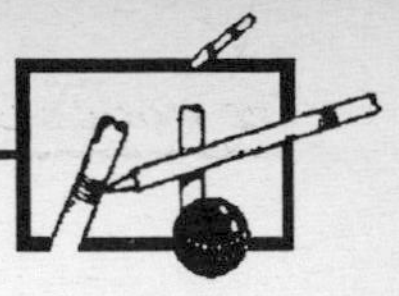

The shot clinched an eight-wicket victory and brought the Ashes back to England for the first time since 1932-33. Celebrating fans swarmed across the ground to heap their congratulations on Edrich—unbeaten on 55—and Compton, who came running towards the pavilion with his bat held high like a knight waving his sword at the end of a victorious duel.

THE WITNESSES: Len Hutton: 'That victory meant so much to us because it restored pride in English cricket. It was a wonderful climax to a great series in which the Australians battled us every inch of the way. We were fortunate to have such outstanding spin bowlers as Laker and Lock to take full advantage of the conditions on the third day. I cannot possibly refer to the series without mention of the parts played by Alec Bedser and Trevor Bailey. They gave England every ounce of their effort and enthusiasm throughout the series, and they must take a great part of the credit for the fact that we regained the Ashes.'

Denis Compton , a hero for all seasons

Lindsay Hassett: 'It was a magnificent series that swung first one way and then the other, and I considered it a privilege to have taken part in it. England won on merit in the final Test, but we might have made more of a fight of it had we been able to call on Laker or Lock. Both could be close to unplayable on any wicket offering the slightest encouragement.'

FOR THE RECORD: Alec Bedser ended the series with a record collection of 39 wickets. He finished with match figures of 14 for 99 in the first Test, eight for 182 in the second, seven for 129 in the third, seven for 160 in the fourth and three for 112 in the final Test. Len Hutton led England to victory on the same ground where he scored his then world record 364 in 1938—the last time that England had beaten Australia in a home Test. Lindwall was Australia's top bowler with 26 wickets. There were six centuries scored—Hassett (115) in the first Test, Hassett (104), Hutton (145), Miller (109) and Watson (109) in the second Test and Harvey (122) in the third. Trevor Bailey rivalled even Alec Bedser for the unofficial 'Man of the Series' title with a succession of gritty performances. His top score was 71 in the second Test , but it was the time he occupied the crease as much as the runs he scored that made him such an immoveable menace to Australia.

England v Australia, Fifth Test, 1953

AUSTRALIA

A.L. Hassett*	c Evans b Bedser	53	— lbw b Laker	10
A.R. Morris	lbw b Bedser	16	— lbw b Lock	26
K.R. Miller	lbw b Bailey	1	— c Trueman b Laker	0
R.N. Harvey	c Hutton b Trueman	36	— b Lock	1
G.B. Hole	c Evans b Trueman	37	— lbw b Laker	17
J.H. de Courcy	c Evans b Trueman	5	— run out	4
R.G. Archer	c and b Bedser	10	— c Edrich b Lock	49
A.K. Davidson	c Edrich b Laker	22	— b Lock	21
R.R. Lindwall	c Evans b Trueman	62	— c Compton b Laker	12
G.R.A. Langley†	c Edrich b Lock	18	— c Trueman b Lock	2
W.A. Johnston	not out	9	— not out	6
Extras	(B 4, NB 2)	6	— (B 11, LB 3)	14
Total		**275**		**162**

ENGLAND

L. Hutton*	b Johnston	82	— run out	17
W.J. Edrich	lbw Lindwall	21	— not out	55
P.B.H. May	c Archer b Johnston	39	— c Davidson b Miller	37
D.C. S. Compton	c Langley b Lindwall	16	— not out	22
T.W. Graveney	c Miller b Lindwall	4		
T.E. Bailey	b Archer	64		
T.G. Evans†	run out	28		
J.C. Laker	c Langley b Miller	1		
G.A.R. Lock	c Davidson b Lindwall	4		
F.S. Trueman	b Johnston	10		
A.V. Bedser	not out	22		
Extras	(B 9, LB 5, W 1)	15	(LB 1)	1
Total		**306**	(2 wickets)	**132**

ENGLAND	O	M	R	W	O	M	R	W
Bedser	29	3	88	3	11	2	24	0
Trueman	24.3	3	86	4	2	1	4	0
Bailey	14	3	42	1				
Lock	9	2	19	1	21	9	45	5
Laker	5	0	34	1	16.5	2	75	4

AUSTRALIA	O	M	R	W	O	M	R	W
Lindwall	32	7	70	4	21	5	46	0
Miller	34	12	65	1	11	3	24	1
Johnston	45	16	94	3	29	14	52	0
Davidson	10	1	26	0				
Archer	10.3	2	25	1	1	1	0	0
Hole	11	6	11	0				
Hassett					1	0	4	0
Morris					0.5	0	5	0

FALL OF WICKETS

	A	E	A	E
Wkt	1st	1st	2nd	2nd
1st	38	37	23	24
2nd	41	137	59	28
3rd	107	154	60	—
4th	107	167	61	—
5th	118	170	61	—
6th	160	210	85	—
7th	160	225	135	—
8th	207	237	140	—
9th	245	262	144	—
10th	275	306	162	—

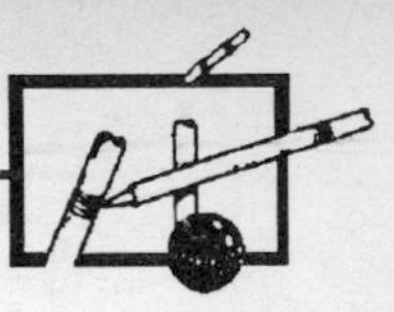

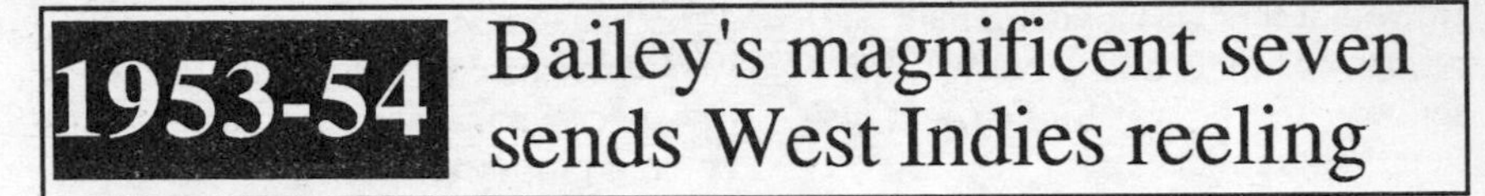

1953-54 Bailey's magnificent seven sends West Indies reeling

Match: West Indies v England, Fifth Test
Venue: Sabina Park, Kingston **Date:** March 30, 31, April 1, 2 , 3

THE SETTING: As in the 1953 home series against Australia, Len Hutton had no luck with the toss during the 1953-54 tour of the West Indies. When he called wrong for a fourth time before the final Test in Kingston the experts considered it was England's death knell.

They were trailing 2-1 in the series, with one match drawn. But all odds were on the West Indies when skipper Jeff Stollmeyer chose to bat first on what seemed a perfect batting strip and on a ground where they had never experienced a defeat. It was the same pitch on which the West Indians had trounced England by 140 runs in the first Test, and it again looked full of runs for a home team that was giving a debut opportunity to a 17-year-old spin bowler called Garfield Sobers.

England were without injured Brian Statham, their naggingly accurate fast bowler and the job of sharing the new ball with Fred Trueman fell to vice-captain Trevor Bailey. Somebody seemed to forget to tell Trevor that the pitch was considered a batsman's paradise.

THE MATCH: Bailey gave just a hint of what was to come when with his fifth ball he had John Holt brilliantly caught at short-leg by Tony Lock for a duck. Most onlookers put it down to a wicket that belonged to the amazing reflexes of Lock rather than the swing bowling skill of Bailey. But when 40 minutes later West Indies were four wickets down for 13 runs Bailey had earned the respect of everybody witnessing his incredible performance on a pitch offering no assistance whatsoever. The Essex all-rounder had taken three of the wickets for five runs, including the clean bowling of the formidable Everton Weekes before he had troubled the scorer. Freddie Trueman, for once playing a supporting role, claimed the other wicket when he had Frank Worrell caught by Johnny Wardle for four.

Clyde Walcott tried to lead a resistance movement with a beautifully carved half century, but nobody could stay around to support him against the swinging seam bowling of Bailey. He finished with best-ever Test figues of seven for 34 off 16 overs as the shell-shocked West Indies tumbled all out for 139.

Bailey went straight from his exceptional bowling stint to his role as opening partner to Hutton as England started their reply in the last session of the first day. He gave sound support to the England skipper and together they put on 43 before Bailey became the first of Gary Sobers' 235 Test victims. Trevor knew that this was a young man booked for fame and a quarter of a century later he was Sir Garfield's official biographer!

By the end of the second day England—curbed by some fierce bowling from Frank King—were 55 in the lead with half their wickets gone. But Hutton, batting with grim determination and occasional flashes of genius, was still there and on the third day he shared century stands with Godfrey Evans and Johnny Wardle on his way to a majestic double century. It was the first 200 scored by an England captain in an overseas Test. He was at the wicket just under nine hours and struck 23 fours and also hoisted the young Sobers for a six. It was Hutton's 19th Test century.

West Indies feared an innings defeat when they lost four wickets—three of them to a full-steam Trueman—for 123, but Walcott saved their face with a fighting century before falling to Jim Laker, who took four wickets as West Indies battled their way to 346 all out. Sobers, batting at number nine, scored 26 to add to his 14 not out in the first innings. England were left needing just 72 runs for victory.

A sharp shower just before the end of the West Indies innings brought sudden life to the wicket and when Tom Graveney opened the batting with Willie Watson he was bowled in the first over by King.

Peter May and Watson then survived all efforts to blast them out and they steered England to a comfortable victory by nine wickets and with a day to spare.

THE WITNESSES: Trevor Bailey: 'I was as amazed as everybody else by my success on a wicket notorious for being a graveyard for bowlers. I was lucky to have the support of some magnificent fielding and this gave me tremendous encouragement. All of us were then, of course, inspired by Len Hutton's glorious double century. Considering all the pressures and responsibilities on his shoulders as captain it was an absolutely incredible knock.'

Garfield Sobers: 'I was very nervous because it was my first Test match, and I just couldn't believe it the way we collapsed in the first innings. I had grown up believing we were unbeatable at Sabina Park. Trevor bowled beautifully and got just enough movement with the ball to make it risky for our batsmen to try to make any strokes. I will always remember the game because I took my first wicket when I had Trevor caught behind. He has since been kind enough to say that he is proud to have been my first victim! But I wish it had been Len Hutton, because his innings won the match for England after Trevor's brilliant performance with the ball.'

FOR THE RECORD: England had been two matches down in the series, losing the first two Tests. They won the third Test at Georgetown, a match marred by a bottle-throwing riot when spectators objected to a run-out decision. A feature of England's win was an innings of 169 by Hutton. Clyde Walcott scored 220 in the second Test and Everton Weekes notched 206 in the fourth Test.

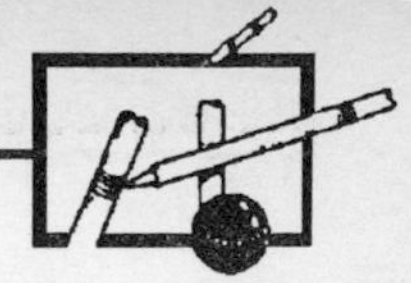

West Indies v England, Fifth Test, 1953-54

WEST INDIES

J.K. Holt	c Lock b Bailey	0	— c Lock b Trueman	8
J.B. Stollmeyer*	c Evans b Bailey	9	— lbw b Trueman	64
E. de C. Weekes	b Bailey	0	— b Wardle	3
F.M.M. Worrell	c Wardle b Trueman	4	— c Graveney b Trueman	29
C.L. Walcott	c Laker b Lock	50	— c Graveney b Laker	116
D. St E. Atkinson	lbw b Bailey	21	— c Watson b Bailey	40
G.E. Gomez	c Watson b Bailey	4	— lbw b Laker	22
C.A. McWatt†	c Lock b Bailey	22	— c Wardle b Laker	8
G. St A. Sobers	not out	14	— c Compton b Lock	26
F.M. King	b Bailey	9	— not out	10
S. Ramadhin	lbw b Trueman	4	— c and b Laker	10
Extras	(LB 1, NB 1)	2	(B 4, LB 3, W 1, NB 2)	10
Total		**139**		**346**

ENGLAND

L. Hutton*	c McWatt b Walcott	205		
T.E. Bailey	c McWatt b Sobers	23		
P.B.H. May	c sub b Ramadhin	30	— not out	40
D.C.S. Compton	hit wkt b King	31		
W. Watson	c McWatt b King	4	— not out	20
T.W. Graveney	lbw b Atkinson	11	— b King	0
T.G. Evans†	c Worrell b Ramadhin	28		
J.H. Wardle	c Holt b Sobers	66		
G.A.R. Lock	b Sobers	4		
J.C. Laker	b Sobers	9		
F.S. Trueman	not out	0		
Extras	(LB 3)	3	(B 12)	12
Total		**414**	(1 wicket)	**72**

ENGLAND	O	M	R	W	O	M	R	W
Bailey	16	7	34	7	25	11	54	1
Trueman	15.4	4	39	2	29	7	88	3
Wardle	10	1	20	0	39	14	83	1
Lock	15	6	31	1	27	16	40	1
Laker	4	1	13	0	50	27	71	4

WEST INDIES	O	M	R	W	O	M	R	W
King	26	12	45	2	4	1	21	1
Gomez	25	8	56	0				
Atkinson	41	15	82	1	3	0	8	0
Ramadhin	29	9	71	2	3	0	14	0
Sobers	28.5	9	75	4	1	0	6	0
Walcott	11	5	26	1				
Worrell	11	0	34	0	4	0	8	0
Stollmeyer	5	0	22	0				
Weekes					0.5	0	3	0

FALL OF WICKETS

Wkt	WI 1st	E 1st	WI 2nd	E 2nd
1st	0	43	26	0
2nd	2	104	38	—
3rd	13	152	102	—
4th	13	160	123	—
5th	65	179	191	—
6th	75	287	273	—
7th	110	392	293	—
8th	115	401	306	—
9th	133	406	326	—
10th	139	414	346	—

1954-55 'Typhoon' Tyson blasts through Aussie batsmen

Match: Australia v England, Third Test
Venue: Melbourne **Date:** December 31, January 1, 3, 4, 5

THE SETTING: Australia went into the final day of the third Test against England needing 165 runs for victory and with eight wickets in hand.

The series was evenly balanced at 1-1, Australia hammering their way to an innings and 154-run victory in the first Test and England winning the second by just 38 runs.

Fast bowler Frank Tyson had been the match winner in the second Test, taking six Australian second innings wickets despite an egg-size bump on his head after being flattened by a Ray Lindwall bouncer while batting.

Skipper Len Hutton tossed the ball to Tyson at the start of the last day of the Melbourne match. A 'Typhoon' was about to hit the Aussies as the Northamptonshire schoolteacher raced in to begin one of the most devastating bowling spells in Test history.

THE MATCH: A masterly innings by Colin Cowdrey had saved England from a complete collapse in their first innings on the opening day of a match played in stiflingly hot conditions. He carefully collected 102 runs out of a total of 191. It was the first of the man of Kent's 23 hundreds in Tests. England's score was the lowest total in the Ashes series to contain a century, a record Cowdrey shared with Don Bradman who scored 103 out of 191 in 1932-33. The pitch started to crack up on the first day and the ball that eventually dismissed Cowdrey was delivered by off-spinner Ian Johnson. The ball deviated two feet off a crack on the pitch outside the off-stump and bowled Cowdrey behind his legs as he padded up.

The irrepressible Keith Miller, shrugging off the pain of a strained knee, ripped the heart out of England's early order with vintage-style bowling before lunch when he snatched three wickets for five runs in nine overs that included eight maidens.

Wicket-keeper Len Maddocks (47), coming in with the score at 115 for six, was Australia's top scorer in a reply of 231 against some sharp, unerring bowling from Brian Statham (five for 60) on a pitch that it was alleged had been watered during the rest day when temperatures soared to 108 degrees.

Peter May struck a procession of blinding straight drives on his way to 91 in England's second innings to boost the total to 279 and to make Australia's victory target 240 runs. Trevor Bailey held up one end for two and three-quarter hours while first Godfrey Evans and then Johnny Wardle hit out at the Australian bowlers of whom Bill Johnston

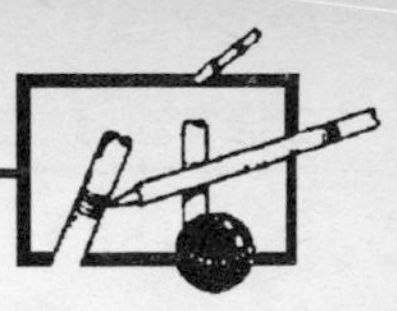

claimed five wickets for 85. The stubborn Bailey was undefeated on 24.

At the close of play on the fourth day, the Aussies stood at 79 for two with both openers back in the pavilion. Arthur Morris fell to a catch by Cowdrey off an excellent delivery by Tyson, and Bob Appleyard bowled his partner Les Favell. The controversial pitch was looking worn again and the prediction was that the final day would develop into a duel between the batsmen and England's spinners Appleyard and Wardle. But Tyson made the slow bowlers redundant with a stunning performance that left Australia's batsmen and their supporters nonplussed. Making the ball rocket through the air and getting the most from the unpredictable bounce of the pitch, Tyson demolished the opposition by taking six wickets for 16 runs in just 51 balls.

The crisis began for Australia when acrobatic wicket-keeper Godfrey Evans made a superb leg-side diving catch to dismiss Neil Harvey. It was the first of eight wickets to fall for 34 runs as Tyson worked up a devilish pace that had the batsmen struggling to see the ball, let alone play it.

He was given the finest possible support at the other end by the deadly accurate bowling of the always reliable Statham who in a six-over spell took two wickets for 19 runs. Tyson was also aided by some excellent close fielding, particularly from the effervescent Evans. Australia were all out in three hours five minutes for 111, leaving England the winners by 128 runs. Tyson's final figures were seven for 27 off 12.3 overs.

THE WITNESSES: Frank Tyson: 'Let me be the first to admit that it was a freakish performance that flattered me. Brian Statham bowled every bit as well, if not better, than me but without the luck that I had. I wish I had Brian's consistency and accuracy. The scorebook shows that I took seven wickets, but I could not have done it without some marvellous fielding support. '

Godfrey Evans: 'It's pointless asking Frank to talk about his performance. He plays it down as if it was nothing, but as the man standing behind the stumps I can tell you that he bowled faster than anybody I had ever seen. It's an exaggeration to say we had close fielders. The ball was coming off the bat so quickly that we all had to stand back at least five yards deeper than usual.'

FOR THE RECORD: England retained the Ashes by winning the fourth Test in Adelaide by five wickets. It was a combination of Tyson's speed and Appleyard's spin that was the match winning factor. They both took six wickets in the match, and Appleyard claimed three for 13 off 12 overs in the second innings when Australia were once again shot out for the 'Nelson's' total of 111. Heavy rain washed out the first three days' play in the final Test at Sydney. Tom Graveney was selected to open with Len Hutton and scored a century that put England firmly in command. Wardle (five for 79) was the most successful England bowler as the Aussies narrowly failed to avoid the follow-on. They clung on for a draw at 118 for six in their second innings.

Australia v England, Third Test, 1954-55

ENGLAND

L. Hutton*	c Hole b Miller	12	— lbw b Archer	42
W.J. Edrich	c Lindwall b Miller	4	— b Johnston	13
P.B.H. May	c Benaud b Lindwall	0	— b Johnston	91
M.C. Cowdrey	b Johnson	102	— b Benaud	7
D.C.S. Compton	c Harvey b Miller	14	— c Maddocks b Archer	23
T.E. Bailey	c Maddocks b Johnston	30	— not out	24
T.G. Evans†	lbw b Archer	20	— c Maddocks b Miller	22
J.H. Wardle	b Archer	0	— b Johnson	38
F.H. Tyson	b Archer	6	— c Harvey b Johnston	6
J.B. Statham	b Archer	3	— c Favell b Johnston	0
R. Appleyard	not out	1	— b Johnston	6
Extras	(B 9)	9	(B 2, LB 4, W 1)	7
Total		**191**		**279**

AUSTRALIA

L.E. Favell	lbw b Statham	25	— b Appleyard	30
A.R. Morris	lbw b Tyson	3	— c Cowdrey b Tyson	4
K.R. Miller	c Evans b Statham	7	— c Edrich b Tyson	6
R.N. Harvey	b Appleyard	31	— c Evans b Tyson	11
G.B. Hole	b Tyson	11	— c Evans b Statham	5
R. Benaud	c sub. b Appleyard	15	— b Tyson	22
R.G. Archer	b Wardle	23	— b Statham	15
L.V. Maddocks†	c Evans b Statham	47	— b Tyson	0
R.R. Lindwall	b Statham	13	— lbw b Tyson	0
I.W. Johnson*	not out	33	— not out	4
W.A. Johnston	b Statham	11	— c Evans b Tyson	0
Extras	(B 7, LB 3, NB 2)	12	(B 1, LB 13)	14
Total		**231**		**111**

AUSTRALIA	O	M	R	W	O	M	R	W
Lindwall	13	0	59	1	18	3	52	0
Miller	11	8	14	3	18	6	35	1
Archer	13.6	4	33	4	24	7	50	2
Benaud	7	0	30	0	8	2	25	1
Johnston	12	6	26	1	24.5	2	85	5
Johnson	11	3	20	1	8	2	25	1

ENGLAND	O	M	R	W	O	M	R	W
Tyson	21	2	68	2	12.3	1	27	7
Statham	16.3	0	60	5	11	1	38	2
Bailey	9	1	33	0	3	0	14	0
Appleyard	11	3	38	2	4	1	17	1
Wardle	6	0	20	1	1	0	1	0

FALL OF WICKETS

	E	A	E	A
Wkt	1st	1st	2nd	2nd
1st	14	15	40	23
2nd	21	38	96	57
3rd	29	43	128	77
4th	41	65	173	86
5th	115	92	185	87
6th	169	115	211	97
7th	181	134	257	98
8th	181	151	273	98
9th	190	205	273	110
10th	191	231	279	111

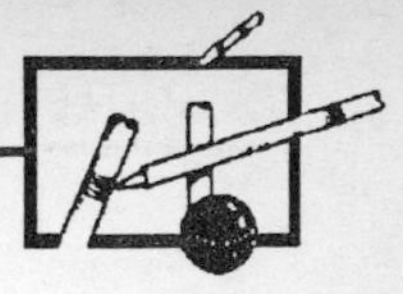

1956 Australians are Lakered on a deadly Old Trafford pitch

Match: England v Australia, Fourth Test
Venue: Old Trafford **Date:** July 26, 27, 28, 30, 31

THE SETTING: There had not been a definite result between England and Australia at Old Trafford since 1905, many of the matches being washed out by the almost traditional rainy weather at Manchester. There was a threat of rain in the air again when the teams went into the fourth Test level at one-all in the 1956 series with one Test drawn. For Australia, the storm clouds were gathering.

Peter May won the toss for England and elected to bat first on what looked a sound pitch, so sound in fact that when Australian team official, the great Sir Donald Bradman, met Jim Laker in the pavilion before a ball had been bowled he told him: 'This is just the sort of wicket for which we've been waiting.'

THE MATCH: The wicket certainly seemed tame enough when England batted and they accumulated 459 runs in 491 minutes, with Peter Richardson and David Sheppard—now the Bishop of Liverpool—each emerging as century-makers. Colin Cowdrey (80) and Peter May (43) made substantial contributions, and wicket-keeper Godfrey Evans joined in the run harvest with a lustily hit 47 runs in 29 minutes on a pitch that on the second day started to kick up clouds of dust. They were the sort of conditions Jim Laker would have given his right arm for, and he took the stage with the most successful spell of Test bowling there has ever been.

Colin McDonald and Jim Burke gave Australia a composed start to their first innings, steadily pushing the score to 48 without loss before Laker switched to the Stretford End from where he produced the stunning performance that was to win him a lasting place in the record books. McDonald was the first of Laker's procession of victims when Lock held a smart catch, and without addition to the score Laker bowled Harvey for a duck with a wickedly spinning ball that would have dismissed any batsman in the world.

The Australians were 62 for two at tea on the second day. At the close they were following on at 51-1 in their second innings!

Laker had destroyed them by taking seven wickets for eight runs in 22 balls. Tony Lock claimed his only wicket with his first ball after the tea interval, and from then on it was all Laker. Australia's last eight wickets in their first innings fell in 35 minutes. Laker's analysis was nine for 37 off 16.4 overs.

Following on 375 behind, Australia lost opener McDonald when a jarred knee forced his retirement with the score at 28 without loss. Neil Harvey replaced him and was out first ball for a pair when he uncharacteristically mis-hit a rare loose full toss from Laker into the hands of Colin Cowdrey at short mid-on.

Australia finished the day at 51 for one in their second innings, and there were angry accusations from the tourists during the evening that the Old Trafford wicket had been doctored to suit England's spinners. This was flatly denied by the Lancashire authorities.

Heavy rain restricted play to just three-quarters of an hour on the Saturday during which Australia lost the wicket of Burke—caught Lock, bowled Laker—for the addition of six runs to their overnight score. McDonald resumed his innings and proceeded to give a demonstration of how spin bowling could be played with the right application and regardless of the conditions.

Australian hopes of saving the match grew when there was non-stop rain on the Sunday rest day. Only two sessions of play were possible on the Monday, the first of 45 minutes and the second of 15, and the Australians took their total to 84 for two.

Play resumed only ten minutes behind schedule on the fifth and final day, and McDonald and Ian Craig carefully steered the score to 112 without further loss before lunch.

The sun shone through the heavy cloud early in the afternoon and on a drying, crumbling wicket the ball started to turn quickly. Nobody in the world could use these sort of conditions better than Laker and he ended Craig's brave resistance after he and McDonald had put on 59 runs together in four hours 20 minutes. Laker then sent back Ken Mackay, Keith Miller and Ron Archer at a cost of just three runs in nine overs. Richie Benaud joined McDonald with the score at 130 for six and they defied Laker and the less penetrative Lock for an hour and a quarter to the tea interval. There were just under two hours left to play and England needed to capture four more wickets for victory.

Jim Laker, the master of spin

Australia's chances of avoiding defeat disappeared with the second ball after tea when Laker had the courageous McDonald caught by Alan Oakman, one of five catches he held in the leg trap where he was deputising for the injured Tom Graveney. McDonald's rearguard action lasted five hours 37 minutes, and he scored 89 runs and kept his head while all about were losing theirs.

The tension was unbearable as Laker captured his eighth and ninth wickets. Now the question on everybody's lips, including those of the Aussies, was whether he could become the first bowler in Test history to take all ten wickets in an innings.

At 5.27pm there was a roar from the crowd greeting the historic tenth wicket as Laker trapped wicket-keeper Len Maddocks leg before with the second ball of his 52nd over.

Australia were all out for 205 and Laker had taken all ten wickets at a personal cost of 53 runs. He finished with astonishing match figures of 19 for 90.

His Surrey spin 'twin' Tony Lock bowled one more over than the 68 from Laker but managed to take only one wicket. The Aussies had been well and truly Lakered.

THE WITNESSES: Jim Laker: 'Of all the wickets, the one I particularly remember is Neil Harvey's second dismissal. He was on a pair when he came in the second time and I pushed Colin Cowdrey in really close to put pressure on him. I had bowled Neil with my best ball of the match in the first innings and I tried too hard to repeat it the second time. What was meant as a full length ball became a full toss. Neil, one of the finest batsman I ever bowled against, hit it straight down Colin's throat and I remember him chucking his bat up in the air in disgust. It was one of those games in which just everything went right. Obviously the conditions suited me, and I just concentrated on getting my line and length right. The mystery is that my mate Lockie took only one wicket. I think he was trying too hard and was pushing the ball through too quickly. I allowed the pitch to do a lot of the work for me.'

Cyril Washbrook, Lancashire skipper: 'It's absolute nonsense to say that the wicket was prepared to suit the England attack. It was not an unplayable sticky wicket, but one that was affected by rain. Nobody should be allowed to take away from Jim Laker the credit for a wonderful performance.'

Ian Johnson, Australian skipper: 'When the controversy and side issues of the match are forgotten, the memory of Laker's masterful bowling will remain. I doubt if we will ever see anything to match it.'

FOR THE RECORD: Laker's 19 wickets in a match is a record for any first-class game. He finished the series with a then record haul of 46 wickets, taking seven in the final Test that was hit by rain and finished as a draw. Playing for Surrey at The Oval in May that year Laker had taken ten for 88 in an innings. On the receiving end were the Australians. The tourists won the second Test by 185 runs after the rain-ruined first Test had ended in a draw. McDonald and Burke shared an opening stand in the first innings of 137, the highest by Australia against England since the partnerships of Woodfull and Ponsford on the run-drenched 1930 tour of England. Keith Miller took ten wickets in the match for 152, and wicket-keeper Gil Langley made a record nine dismissals. Laker took 11 wickets in the third Test when England won by an innings and 42 runs. Peter May was top scorer with 101. Batting highlight of the drawn final Test was a third-wicket first-innings stand of 156 between Denis Compton (94) and May (83 not out).

England v Australia, Fourth Test, 1956

ENGLAND

P.E. Richardson	c Maddocks b Benaud	104
M.C. Cowdrey	c Maddocks b Lindwall	80
Rev. D.S. Sheppard	b Archer	113
P.B.H. May*	c Archer b Benaud	43
T.E. Bailey	b Johnson	20
C. Washbrook	lbw b Johnson	6
A.S.M. Oakman	c Archer b Johnson	10
T.G. Evans†	st Maddocks b Johnson	47
J.C. Laker	run out	3
G.A.R. Lock	not out	25
J.B. Statham	c Maddocks b Lindwall	0
Extras	(B 2, LB 5, W 1)	8
Total		**459**

AUSTRALIA

C.C. McDonald	c Lock b Laker	32	— c Oakman b Laker	89
J.W. Burke	c Cowdrey b Lock	22	— c Lock b Laker	33
R.N. Harvey	b Laker	0	— c Cowdrey b Laker	0
I.D. Craig	lbw b Laker	8	— c Cowdrey b Laker	38
K.R. Miller	c Oakman b Laker	6	— b Laker	0
K.D. MacKay	c Oakman b Laker	0	— c Oakman b Laker	0
R.G. Archer	st Evans b Laker	6	— c Oakman b Laker	0
R. Benaud	c Statham b Laker	0	— b Laker	18
R.R. Lindwall	not out	6	— c Lock b Laker	8
L.V. Maddocks†	b Laker	4	— lbw b Laker	2
I.W. Johnson*	b Laker	0	— not out	1
Extras		0	(B 12, LB 4)	16
Total		**84**		**205**

AUSTRALIA	O	M	R	W
Lindwall	21.3	6	63	2
Miller	21	6	41	0
Archer	22	6	73	1
Johnson	47	10	151	4
Benaud	47	17	123	2

ENGLAND	O	M	R	W	O	M	R	W
Statham	6	3	6	0	16	10	15	0
Bailey	4	3	4	0	20	8	31	0
Laker	16.4	4	37	9	51.2	23	53	10
Lock	14	3	37	1	55	30	69	0
Oakman					8	3	21	0

FALL OF WICKETS

	E	A	A
Wkt	1st	1st	2nd
1st	174	48	28
2nd	195	48	55
3rd	288	62	114
4th	321	62	124
5th	327	62	130
6th	339	73	130
7th	401	73	181
8th	417	78	198
9th	458	84	203
10th	459	84	205

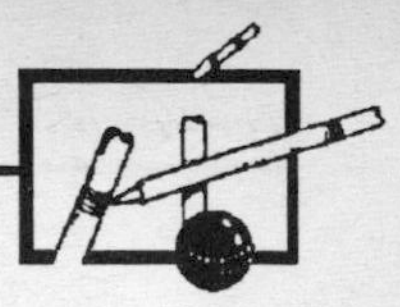

1957 May and Cowdrey share a record stand of 411

Match: England v West Indies, First Test
Venue: Edgbaston **Date:** May 30, 31, June 1, 3, 4

THE SETTING: The return of Test cricket to the Edgbaston stage after an absence of 28 years generated a Test match that had more twists and turns than an Alfred Hitchcock thriller, and it produced cricket of outstanding quality.

Spinners Sonny Ramadhin and Alf Valentine were back in England for the first time since they wreaked havoc on the 1950 tour. Valentine was out of form and was left on the sidelines, but there were still jitters among the England batsmen when skipper John Goddard tossed the ball to his little friend Ramadhin early on the first day after England had chosen to bat on what gave the appearance of being a perfect batting pitch.

THE MATCH: While Roy Gilchrist kept England pinned down with fiery pace from one end, Ramadhin baffled them with spin from the opposite end.

With his cap planted firmly on his head, sleeves buttoned down to the wrists and gliding in off a short run, Ramadhin kept the batsmen guessing as to whether he was going to bowl a leg-break or an off-break. They got themselves in such a muddle that they often allowed for spin that was not there and their tiny torturer took the majority of his wickets with balls that kept perfectly straight.

Ramadhin included 16 maidens in his 31-over spell and finished with a Test career best return of seven wickets for 49 runs. England were all out in four hours for 186 on a pitch that looked full of runs. Only opener Peter Richardson (47) could feel satisfied with his contribution.

Freddie Trueman yorked Bruce Pairaudeau for one in his second over, but Rohan Kanhai and Clyde Walcott played with flair and confidence as they steered West Indies to a commanding position of 83 for one at stumps on the first day.

Brian Statham trapped Kanhai leg before off the first ball of the second day, and then an excellent slip catch by Trevor Bailey removed Gary Sobers (53). Walcott (90)—handicapped by a pulled thigh muscle—was caught by Godfrey Evans off the bowling of Jim Laker who claimed four wickets for 119 runs in a 54-over stint. England were just feeling that they were back in the game when Collie Smith and Frank Worrell shared a fifth-wicket stand in which they put on 190 in five hours.

It was the last ball before lunch on the third day before Statham managed to break the stand by bowling Worrell (81). It brought to an end not only Worrell's innings but also a marathon spell in the middle by opener Pairaudeau. After scoring his one run he spent three and a quarter hours as the runner for Walcott and then ran for five hours for Worrell after he had injured his knee. Smith, who marked his debut against England with a century, was nearly seven hours at the wicket in scoring 161 in the West Indies total of 474.

West Indies, with substitutes fielding for injured Worrell and Walcott, had another blow when pace bowler Gilchrist limped off. England's openers put on 63 before Ramadhin struck by dismissing Richardson and Doug Insole in successive overs. Skipper Peter May and Brian Close steadied the ship and England had reached 102 for two at the close of the third day's play that was watched by a record Edgbaston crowd of 32,000.

Colin Cowdrey joined May after 20 minutes play on the fourth day to start one of the greatest partnerships in the history of Test cricket. They put on 411 together for the fourth wicket, the highest stand ever made for England and the third highest of all time. Only Don Bradman and Bill Ponsford (451 for Australia against England at The Oval in 1934) and Pankaj Roy and Vinoo Mankad (413 opening stand for India against New Zealand in 1956) had bettered the May-Cowdrey collection.

They were together for eight hours 20 minutes until Cowdrey was caught off the bowling of Collie Smith shortly after lunch on the final day. Cowdrey included 16 fours and 63 singles in his score of 154, his first Test century in England.

The imperious May batted on for another half hour, adding 59 runs in a whirlwind stand with Godfrey Evans before declaring at 583 for four.

England had been 65 for two and staring defeat in the face when May arrived at the wicket. His 285 not out lasted five minutes short of ten hours and he hit two sixes, 25 fours and 111 singles. His total was the highest score ever made by an England captain, surpassing the 240 made by Walter Hammond against Australia at The Oval in 1938. It was then also the highest individual score in post-war Test cricket, topping Denis Compton's 278 against Pakistan at Trent Bridge in 1954.

There was yet another record. Ramadhin sent down 588 balls in the England second innings, the most ever delivered in a single innings in first-class cricket. It lifted his match total to 774 balls which beat Hedley Verity's previous record of 766 for England against South Africa in Durban in 1939.

Ramadhin's final figures for the seconds innings were two wickets for 179 off 98 overs. Denis Atkinson also put in a marathon effort, bowling 72 overs in which he conceded 137 runs without the reward of a single wicket.

West Indies used only two balls throughout the long innnings, the first being changed after 96 overs. The second ball was delivered 996 times.

May's declaration left West Indies with a virtually out-of-reach victory target of 296 in two hours 20 minutes. A draw seemed a certainty until Trueman opened with a fierce burst during which he removed openers Pairaudeau and Kanhai for seven runs. Spinners Jim Laker and Tony Lock were called into action by May who surrounded the batsmen with

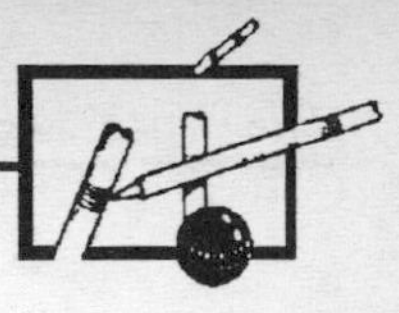

fielders.The West Indians were suddenly exposed to the perils of panic, and wickets fell at 25, 27, 43, 66 and 68. The injured players, Worrell and Walcott, were summoned to join the rearguard battle and skipper Goddard finally had to resort to desperate measures to save the match. He batted for the last 40 minutes without making a single scoring stroke, continually blocking the ball with his pads. At the close of an extraordinary match Goddard was undefeated on nought and West Indies were 72 for seven.

Lock took three wickets for 31 runs in 27 overs, including 19 maidens. Laker took two for 13 runs in 24 overs, including 20 maidens.

THE WITNESSES: Peter May: 'Colin and I decided to get our heads down and give some stability to our innings. Neither of us were aware of the records that were within range. We just concentrated on taking runs without risks. The important thing, particularly in the first half of our partnership, was that neither of us should lose our wicket. I did consider an earlier declaration, but West Indies had the sort of strokemakers who could have turned the match back in their favour if given any encouragement. I would have to class it as the most satisfying innings of my career.'

Colin Cowdrey: 'Peter was in such magnificent form that I was content to play a supporting role in the partnership. It was a perfect innings by Peter. His cover driving was exceptional, and he hardly made a false shot.'

Sonny Ramadhin: 'I had no idea that I had bowled so many overs until I was told after England's declaration. I was too busy trying to break the partnership between May and Cowdrey to count.'

FOR THE RECORD: England won the second Test at Lord's by an innings and 36 runs, thanks largely to the bowling of Trevor Bailey (match figures 11 for 98) and the batting of Colin Cowdrey (152) and Godfrey Evans (82). There was some magnificent batting in the drawn third Test at Trent Bridge. Tom Graveney (258) and Peter Richardson (126) shared a second wicket partnership of 266. Peter May (104) also scored a century in England's first innings total of 619 for six declared. Frank Worrell (191 not out) carried his bat in West Indies first innings total of 372. He opened the second innings when the tourists were asked to follow on and when he was bowled by Brian Statham for 16 runs had been on the pitch for all the 20 hours 28 minutes that the game had been in progress. A century by Collie Smith (168) saved West Indies from defeat. Freddie Trueman had match figures of nine for 143. England won the fourth Test at Headingley by an innings and five runs, with a hat-trick by Peter Loader (match figures: nine for 86) one of the highlights. Tony Lock (11 for 48) was the match winner when England beat West Indies by an innings and 237 runs in the final Test. Peter Richardson (107) and Tom Graveney (164) both scored centuries, and West Indies were twice dismissed for less than 100.

England v West Indies, First Test, 1957

ENGLAND

P.E. Richardson	c Walcott b Ramadhin	47	— c sub b Ramadhin	34
D.B. Close	c Kanhai b Gilchrist	15	— c Weekes b Gilchrist	42
D.J. Insole	b Ramadhin	20	— b Ramadhin	0
P.B.H. May*	c Weekes b Ramadhin	30	— not out	285
M.C. Cowdrey	c Gilchrist b Ramadhin	4	— c sub b Smith	154
T.E. Bailey	b Ramadhin	1		
G.A.R. Lock	b Ramadhin	0		
T.G. Evans†	b Gilchrist	14	— not out	29
J.C. Laker	b Ramadhin	7		
F.S. Trueman	not out	29		
J.B. Statham	b Atkinson	13		
Extras	(B 3, LB 3)	6	(B 23, LB 16)	39
Total		**186**	(4 wickets declared)	**583**

WEST INDIES

B.H. Pairaudeau	b Trueman	1	— b Trueman	7
R.B. Kanhai†	lbw b Statham	42	— c Close b Trueman	1
C.L. Walcott	c Evans b Laker	90	— c Lock b Laker	1
E. de C. Weekes	b Trueman	9	— c Trueman b Lock	33
G. St A. Sobers	c Bailey b Statham	53	— c Cowdrey b Lock	14
O.G. Smith	lbw b Laker	161	— lbw b Laker	5
F.M.M. Worrell	b Statham	81	— c May b Lock	0
J.D.C. Goddard*	c Lock b Laker	24	— not out	0
D. St E. Atkinson	c Statham b Laker	1	— not out	4
S. Ramadhin	not out	5		
R. Gilchrist	run out	0		
Extras	(B 1, LB 6)	7	(B 7)	7
Total		**474**	(7 wickets)	**72**

WEST INDIES	O	M	R	W	O	M	R	W
Worrell	9	1	27	0				
Gilchrist	27	4	74	2	26	2	67	1
Ramadhin	31	16	49	7	98	35	179	2
Atkinson	12.4	3	30	1	72	29	137	0
Sobers					30	4	77	0
Smith					26	4	72	1
Goddard					6	2	12	0

ENGLAND	O	M	R	W	O	M	R	W
Statham	39	4	114	3	2	0	6	0
Trueman	30	4	99	2	5	3	7	2
Bailey	34	11	80	0				
Laker	54	17	119	4	24	20	13	2
Lock	34.4	15	55	0	27	19	31	3
Close					2	1	8	0

FALL OF WICKETS

	E	WI	E	WI
Wkt	1st	1st	2nd	2nd
1st	32	4	63	1
2nd	61	83	65	9
3rd	104	120	113	25
4th	115	183	524	27
5th	116	197	—	43
6th	118	387	—	66
7th	121	466	—	68
8th	130	469	—	—
9th	150	474	—	—
10th	186	474	—	—

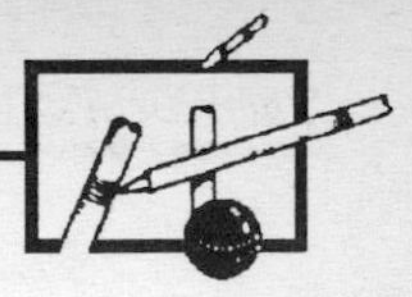

1957-58 Sobers plunders 365 runs against injury-hit Pakistan

Match: West Indies v Pakistan, Third Test
Venue: Sabina Park, Kingston **Date:** February 26, 27, 28, March 1, 3, 4

THE SETTING: Every English schoolboy knew that the highest individual innings in a Test match was the 364 scored by Yorkshire opener Len Hutton against Australia at The Oval in 1938. It was a proud performance written in the hearts and memories of England's cricket lovers.

But all record books were about to be rewritten when a tall, 21-year-old all-rounder from Barbados, who had never before scored a Test century, walked with a graceful stride to the wicket in the third Test against Pakistan at Sabina Park.

The batsman's name was Garfield St Aubrun Sobers.

THE MATCH: Abdul Kardar, Pakistan's vastly experienced skipper who had started his Test career with India, won the toss and elected to bat on a beautiful wicket. Kardar was defying medical advice by playing. He had broken a finger on his left hand, yet bowled 37 overs of his left-arm spinners and—a left-handed batsman—scored 74 runs in two visits to the wicket in, to say the least, an eventful six-day match.

Hanif Mohammad was an early victim for pace bowler Roy Gilchrist, caught behind by West Indies wicket-keeper and skipper Gerry Alexander for three. The reason the West Indian team and spectators celebrated Hanif's dismissal with such delight was that he had single-handedly saved the match in the first Test when Pakistan were forced to follow on. He scored 337 runs in the second innings and looked set to beat Hutton's long-standing record until caught behind by Alexander.

Hanif's opening partner Imtiaz Ahmed took over the role of anchor-man and it was his carefully accumulated score of 122 that enabled Pakistan to total a respectable 328. Wallis Mathias supported Imtiaz with a solid 77. Eric Atkinson was the most successful of the West Indian bowlers on a pitch enlivened by a shower on the second day, taking five wickets for 42 runs in 21 overs.

It might have been appropriate to have had a reporter from the medical publication *The Lancet* alongside the *Wisden* representative when Pakistan went into the field. Apart from the injury to skipper Kardar, Mahmood Hussain pulled a thigh muscle in his first over and16-year-old left-arm slow bowler Nasim-ul-Ghani fractured a thumb while fielding. So from early in the West Indies innings, Pakistan were reduced to just two fully fit specialist bowlers in Fazal Mahmood and Khan Mohammad.

Even a full battery of established bowlers would have had trouble containing Conrad Hunte and

Garfield Sobers when they came together to start a second-wicket partnership with the West Indies score at 87 for one. There were 533 runs on the scoreboard before they were parted. Together they put on 446 runs, which was then the second highest stand for any wicket in Test matches and they achieved the rare feat of sharing the wicket through a complete day of Test cricket.

Pakistan used nine bowlers in an attempt to break the partnership, and they all took terrible punishment. Fazal Mahmood put in one of the longest bowling stints of all time with his medium pacers and in 85.2 overs had two wickets to show for his concession of 247 runs. Khan suffered even greater indignity and in 54 overs was knocked all over the field, having 259 runs taken off him without the consolation of a single wicket.

For all their effort, neither Fazal nor Khan had the satisfaction of ending the marathon stand. The ending was self inflicted when Hunte was run out trying to add to his haul of 260 runs. This was only Hunte's third Test, and the score remained his highest Test innings throughout what was to become a long and distinguished career.

Sobers, supported first by Everton Weekes and then Clyde Walcott, took over the stage and proceeded to play majestic strokes all around the wicket. In all he scored 38 fours as he peppered the boundary with a range of improvised left-handed shots. He passed Len Hutton's near-20-year-old record of 364 after batting for 10 hours 14 minutes, which was three hours three minutes less than it took Hutton but against an appreciably weaker bowling attack. The crowd went wild with unbridled excitement when Sobers reached 365 at which point Gerry Alexander signalled the declaration at 790 for three, the third-highest total in Test cricket.

There was a stampede of spectators on to the pitch and Sobers was lifted up and carried around the ground as if he were a trophy. The pitch became so cut up during this joyous invasion that the umpires had to call for emergency ground repairs, and the last 55 minutes of the fourth day were abandoned while the work was carried out.

Pakistan, starting their second innings 462 runs in arrears, needed to bat through two full days to save the match. Their mountainous task was made even more difficult when both Mahmood Hussain and Nasim-ul-Ghani were ruled out of taking any further part in the match because of their injuries.

The Pakistanis got off to the worst possible start, losing their first innings century hero Imtiaz Ahmed for a duck when he was out leg before wicket to Tom Dewdney. All hopes now rested on the shoulders of Hanif Mohammad, but the master batsman who a year later was to harvest a world-record 499 runs in an innings for Karachi miscalculated against a deceptively quick ball from Gilchrist and was bowled for 13.

With both openers gone for 20 it was now a case of not whether the West Indies would win but when. They were held up by a stubborn fifth-wicket stand of 166 between skipper Kardar (57) and Wazir

Mohammad, the eldest of the famous Mohammad brothers. Wazir battled with enormous determination and scored 106 before becoming Eric Atkinson's eighth victim of the match.

The last three Pakistani wickets fell for three runs and the match was all over after just 40 minutes' play on the last day, with West Indies the winners by an innings and 174 runs.

THE WITNESSES:Garfield Sobers: 'I had given no thought to Len Hutton's record until I passed three hundred. You have to remember that I had never scored even a single Test century, so that great score of Hutton's never entered my mind. I got enormous encouragement from skipper Gerry Alexander and the rest of my team-mates once it became clear that the record was within sight, but I never let it worry me because, to be honest, I was never one for knowing one record from another. I just liked to go out and enjoy myself. I left the counting to others. I'll be the first to admit that I was lucky to play against a weakened Pakistan attack, but the runs still needed getting and I felt worn out at the end of my innings. I have to give full credit to Conrad Hunte. He played a great innings, and was unlucky to get run out, otherwise he might have got the record because he was going like an express train. The hardest job was getting off the pitch. The spectators just did not want to let me go.'

Gerry Alexander: 'We all knew that Gary had the ability to score centuries, but what he lacked in those young days was total concentration. But it all came together for him against Pakistan.'

Abdul Kardar: 'We just did not have the bowling strength to contain Sobers and Hunte. I thought Fazal and Khan deserved medals for the way they stuck at their job. But I don't wish to take anything away from Sobers. He batted splendidly.'

FOR THE RECORD: Sobers touched a new peak of perfection after his monumental innings in Kingston. He followed this with a century in each innings in the fourth Test and continued his Bradman-style consistency on the 1958-59 tour of India, scoring centuries in the first three Tests. His incredible sequence brought him 1,115 runs in six successive Tests. West Indies won the fourth Test against Pakistan by eight wickets to take a 3-1 lead in the series. They had won the second Test by 120 runs in the only match in the series not to include centuries by batsmen on either side. Pakistan completed the tour on a high note by winning the fifth and final Test, their first win against the West Indies. The West Indies never recovered from a nightmare start when openers Conrad Hunte and Rohan Kanhai were both dismissed for ducks, Hunte off the first ball of the match. The game was a triumph for one of the bowlers who took so much punishment in the third Test in Kingston. Fazal Mahmood claimed six for 83 in the first innings and Nasim-ul-Ghani six for 67 in the second. It was an innings of 189 by Wazir Mohammad that laid the foundation for Pakistan's victory by an innings and one run.

Sir Garfield St Aubrun Sobers, a king of cricketers with the bat and the ball

West Indies v Pakistan, Third Test, 1957-58

PAKISTAN

Hanif Mohammad	c Alexander b Gilchrist	3	— b Gilchrist	13
Imtiaz Ahmed†	c Alexander b Gilchrist	122	— lbw b Dewdney	0
Saeed Ahmed	c Weekes b Smith	52	— c Gilchrist b Gibbs	44
W. Mathias	b Dewdney	77	— c Alexander b Atkinson	19
Alimuddin	c Alexander b Atkinson	15	— b Gibbs	30
A.H. Kardar*	c Sobers b Atkinson	15	— lbw b Dewdney	57
Wazir Mohammad	c Walcott b Dewdney	3	— lbw b Atkinson	106
Fazal Mahmood	c Alexander b Atkinson	6	— c Alexander b Atkinson	0
Nasim-ul-Ghani	b Atkinson	5	— absent hurt	—
Mahmood Hussain	b Atkinson	20	— absent hurt	—
Khan Mohammad	not out	3	— not out	0
Extras	(LB 5, NB 3)	8	(B 16, LB 3)	19
Total		**328**		**288**

WEST INDIES

C.C. Hunte	run out	260
R.B. Kanhai	c Imtiaz b Fazal	25
G. St A. Sobers	not out	365
E. de C. Weekes	c Hanif b Fazal	39
C.L. Walcott	not out	88
O.G. Smith		
F.C.M. Alexander*†		
L.R. Gibbs		
E. St E. Atkinson		
R. Gilchrist		
D.T. Dewdney		
Extras	(B 2, LB 7, W 4)	13
Total	(3 wickets declared)	**790**

WEST INDIES	O	M	R	W	O	M	R	W
Gilchrist	25	3	106	2	12	3	65	1
Dewdney	26	4	88	2	19.3	2	51	2
Atkinson	21	7	42	5	18	6	36	3
Gibbs	7	0	32	0	21	6	46	2
Smith	18	3	39	1	8	2	20	0
Sobers	5	1	13	0	15	4	41	0
Weekes					3	1	10	0

PAKISTAN	O	M	R	W
Mahmood Hussain	0.5	0	2	0
Fazal	85.2	20	247	2
Khan	54	5	259	0
Nasim	15	3	39	0
Kardar	37	2	141	0
Mathias	4	0	20	0
Alimuddin	4	0	34	0
Hanif	2	0	11	0
Saeed	6	0	24	0

FALL OF WICKETS

	P	WI	P
Wkt	1st	1st	2nd
1st	4	87	8
2nd	122	533	20
3rd	223	602	57
4th	249	—	105
5th	287	—	120
6th	291	—	286
7th	299	—	286
8th	301	—	288
9th	317	—	—
10th	328	—	—

1959-60 Last-minute Patel pitches in with 14 Test wickets

Match: India v Australia, Second Test
Venue: Green Park, Kanpur **Date:** December 19, 20, 21, 23, 24

THE SETTING: Indian cricket followers were so disenchanted with their team's performance against Australia in the first Test at Delhi that they hurled bottles on to the pitch and pushed and shoved the umpires after the tourists had won by an innings and 127 runs.

The selectors deliberated as to what to do for the second Test at Kanpur and decided at the last minute to recall 35-year-old Jasubhai Patel, who had not played Test cricket for more than three years.

Patel was a right-arm off-break bowler who, because of a wrist injury when he was a boy, had a distinctive jerky bowling action. His previous Test appearance had been against Australia at Bombay in October, 1957, when he had been hit for 111 runs while taking two wickets.

A new, untested turf wicket had been laid at Kanpur and nobody knew how it would play. By the end of a thrilling Test Patel wished he could have rolled it up and taken it with him to wherever he was bowling.

THE MATCH: India had not beaten Australia in ten Tests since 1947 and another defeat looked likely when they collapsed in their first innings against the pace of Alan Davidson and the leg spin of skipper Richie Benaud. Bapu Nadkarni was the top scorer with 25 runs as India tumbled all out for 152. Davidson (five for 31) and Benaud (four for 63) were always in command on a pitch that had unpredictable pace and bounce.

Colin McDonald (53) and Neil Harvey (51) both moved smoothly to half-centuries when Australia replied, and with the score at 128 for two the tourists looked set for another innings victory. Then Patel started a remarkable sequence of success.

He made the ball turn with vicious spin and clean bowled five victims during a purple patch when he had the Australian batsmen totally baffled. He claimed nine wickets for 69 runs, and included 16 maidens in his stunning 35.5-over stint. Chandra Borde interrupted Patel's one-man show when he bowled Norm O'Neill.

Australia's last eight wickets fell for 91 runs. Alan Davidson (41) did his best to stop the decline with some powerful hitting until he was bowled by Patel, who at the peak of his performance took eight wickets for 24 runs.

Davidson then showed that the pitch was as suited to pace as to spin when he put Australia back in command by taking seven wickets for 93 in their second innings. He bowled a naggingly accurate line and length with his left-arm quickies and got just enough movement to deceive a pro-

cession of batsmen into making false strokes.

Davidson finished with match figures of 12 for 124, the best return by an Australian bowler against India. Thanks to solid knocks by Nariman Contractor (74) and Ramnath Kenny (51) India totalled 291 and left Australia needing 225 runs for victory.

Gordon Rorke was unwell and unable to bat, so Australia were reduced to ten batsmen. They lost their first wicket at 12 when Patel had Gavin Stevens caught by Kenny for seven. Then McDonald (34) and Harvey (25) put on 37 for the second wicket before Patel triggered another panic-propelled collapse.

Patel and Polly Umrigar (four for 27) bowled unchanged for 25 overs each and rushed Australia out on the final day for 105, leaving India winners by 119 runs.

The last seven Australian wickets fell for 56. Patel took five wickets for 55 to finish with match figures of 14 for 142. He had become the first Indian bowler to take 14 wickets in a Test and his first-innings return of nine for 69 bettered the previous Indian best set by Baloo Gupte, who had taken nine for 102 against the West Indies on the same ground the previous season.

THE WITNESSES: Jasubhai Patel: 'It was the greatest match of my life. I was beginning to think that I would not be playing Test cricket again when I got the late call to join the team at Kanpur. From the moment of my first ball I knew that the pitch was just made for me. It made me appreciate all the more what an extraordinary performance it was by Jim Laker when he took 19 wickets against the Australians three years earlier.'

Richie Benaud: 'It was an exceptional display of spin bowling by Patel on newly-laid turf. The pitch had not settled and its uneven bounce made life extremely difficult for the batsmen. I felt sorry for Alan Davidson. He bowled superbly and did not deserve to be on the losing side.'

FOR THE RECORD: Patel was selected for the third Test at Bombay but was taken ill on the morning of the match. His replacement, Salim Durani, injured his finger and was unable to bowl in a match that petered out into a draw. The highlights were a century by Contractor in India's first innings and a record 207 third-wicket partnership by Harvey (102) and O'Neill (163) in Australia's first innings during which Nadkarni took six wickets for 105. Les Favell (101) and Ken Mackay (89) laid the foundation for Australia's victory by an innings and 55 runs in the fourth Test at Madras. Richie Benaud, who had taken three wickets for no runs in the first Test, finished with match figures of eight for 86. Australia declined to chase a victory target of 203 runs in 150 minutes on the last day of the fifth and final Test at Calcutta. They elected to play for a draw that gave them the rubber by two matches to one. The match was memorable for a sparkling century by O'Neill and for the fact that it was Ray Lindwall's final Test. He took three wickets to finish with what was then an Australian record haul of 228. Benaud had a match return of seven for 162.

India v Australia, Second Test, 1959-60

INDIA

	1st innings		2nd innings	
P. Roy	c Harvey b Benaud	17	c Benaud b Davidson	8
N.J. Contractor	c Jarman b Benaud	24	c Harvey b Davidson	74
P.R. Umrigar	c Davidson b Kline	6	c Rorke b Davidson	14
A.A. Baig	b Davidson	19	c Harvey b Benaud	36
C.G. Borde	c Kline b Davidson	20	c O'Neill b Meckiff	44
G.S. Ramchand*	c Mackay b Benaud	24	b Harvey	5
R.B. Kenny	b Davidson	0	c Jarman b Davidson	51
R.G. Nadkarni	c Harvey b Davidson	25	lbw b Davidson	46
N.S. Tamhane†	b Benaud	1	c Harvey b Davidson	0
J.M. Patel	c Kline b Davidson	4	b Davidson	0
R. Surendranath	not out	8	not out	4
Extras	(B 2, NB 2)	4	(B 7, LB 2)	9
Total		**152**		**291**

AUSTRALIA

	1st innings		2nd innings	
C.C. McDonald	b Patel	53	st Tamhane b Patel	34
G.B. Stevens	c and b Patel	25	c Kenny b Patel	7
R.N. Harvey	b Patel	51	c Nadkarni b Umrigar	25
N.C. O'Neill	b Borde	16	c Nadkarni b Umrigar	5
K.D. Mackay	lbw b Patel	0	lbw b Umrigar	0
A.K. Davidson	b Patel	41	b Patel	8
R. Benaud*	b Patel	7	c Ramchand b Patel	0
B.N. Jarman†	lbw b Patel	1	b Umrigar	0
L.F. Kline	b Patel	9	b Patel	0
I. Meckiff	not out	1	not out	14
G.F. Rorke	c Baig b Patel	0	absent ill	—
Extras	(B 9, LB 2, NB 4)	15	(B 5, LB 7)	12
Total		**219**		**105**

AUSTRALIA	O	M	R	W	O	M	R	W
Davidson	20.1	7	31	5	57.3	23	93	7
Meckiff	8	2	15	0	18	4	37	1
Benaud	25	8	63	4	38	15	81	1
Rorke	2	1	3	0				
Kline	15	7	36	1	7	3	14	0
Mackay					10	5	14	0
Harvey					12	3	31	1
O'Neill					2	0	12	0

INDIA	O	M	R	W	O	M	R	W
Surendranath	4	0	13	0	4	2	4	0
Ramchand	6	3	14	0	3	0	7	0
Patel	35.5	16	69	9	25.4	7	55	5
Umrigar	15	1	40	0	25	11	27	4
Borde	15	1	61	1				
Nadkarni	2	0	7	0				

FALL OF WICKETS

	I	A	I	A
Wkt	1st	1st	2nd	2nd
1st	38	71	32	12
2nd	47	128	72	49
3rd	51	149	121	59
4th	77	159	147	61
5th	112	159	153	78
6th	112	174	214	78
7th	126	186	286	79
8th	128	216	286	84
9th	141	219	291	105
10th	152	219	291	—

1960-61 Dead-eye Solomon forces the first tie in Test history

Match: Australia v West Indies, First Test
Venue: Woolloongabba, Brisbane **Date:** December 9, 10, 12, 13, 14

THE SETTING: Of all the 'greatest' matches recalled in this dip into the treasure chest of cricket perhaps this is the Test that should wear the crown as *the* greatest of them all.

It is not only that it produced the first tie in the history of Test cricket that made it memorable, but the fact that it was played with an electrifying spirit of adventure by both sides who put the emphasis on attacking play from first ball to last—this in an era when the game was becoming hooked on the drug of defensive cricket.

Both Australia and West Indies showed the way the game could and should be played in a series that captured the attention and interest of record crowds in Australia and the imagination of cricket fans around the world.

It is the two captains, Richie Benaud and Frank Worrell, who were quite rightly given the credit for the series becoming one of the most unforgettable of all sporting occasions. They both pledged before a ball had been bowled that the game of cricket would be the winner and then proceeded to provide action to go with their words.

THE MATCH: It was a classic right from the first day when Garfield Sobers scored 132 runs in 174 minutes in a masterpiece of an innings. Supported by Frank Worrell (65) and Joe Solomon (65), Sobers reached his 50 in only 57 minutes and on his way to his century completed his 3,000th run in Test cricket. His lightning innings included 21 fours. Gerry Alexander (60) and Wes Hall (50) took part in a sparkling late-order stand that lifted the West Indies total to 453 which was scored at a rate of 4.5 runs per eight-ball over. Alan Davidson bowled his heart out and was rewarded with five wickets for 135 off 30 overs.

The Australian batsmen did their best to follow the West Indies lead and, while not getting their runs in quite the same majestic manner, managed to reach a mammoth total of 505 thanks to a sheet anchor innings by opener Bobby Simpson (92) and a patiently compiled 181 by Norm O'Neill, who was at the wicket for six and a half hours and scored 22 fours. There were fine supporting knocks by Colin McDonald (57), Les Favell (45) and the tireless Davidson (44).

Rohan Kanhai (54), Worrell (65) and Solomon (47) held the West Indies second innings together in the face of some fierce left-arm pace bowling from man-of-the-match Davidson, who took six for 87 to finish with match figures of 11 wickets for 222 runs. During the course of

Australia's second innings he became the first cricketer to complete the double of 100 runs and 10 wickets in a Test match but these impressive statistics were buried in the excitement generated by the extraordinary events of the final day.

West Indies were all out for 284, leaving Australia a victory target of 233 runs in 310 minutes.

Wes Hall unleashed a fearsome spell of pace bowling to skittle out half the Australian team for 57, and then a sixth wicket fell at 92. The Aussies looked doomed to defeat.

Then skipper Benaud joined Davidson in the middle and together they shared a marvellous seventh-wicket stand of 134 scored at a run a minute. They ran like greyhounds between the wickets, and bravely stood up to a bumper barrage by Hall, including a magnificent hook to the boundary by Davidson off a terrifying ball that was thundering towards his temple in what were the pre-helmet days.

With 12 minutes left on the clock, Benaud and Davidson were still together and only seven runs were required for victory. Then Davidson tried one stolen single too many and was brilliantly run out for 80 when Solomon scored a direct hit on the stumps with a perfect throw from 25 yards and square with the wicket on the leg side.

So Hall began the last eight-ball over of the match with Australia needing six to win with three wickets remaining. The first ball hit Wally Grout a painful blow on the thigh and he and Benaud scrambled a leg bye with the ball just five yards from the wicket. Five runs needed, seven balls left.

The second ball from Hall was a bouncer that Benaud, in the true spirit of the game, attemped to hook. He managed only to flick it on with his gloves and the West Indian fielders went into a dance of delight as wicket-keeper Gerry Alexander held a comfortable catch. Six balls left, two wickets to fall and five runs needed.

Ian Meckiff was next man in and he played his first ball back along the ground into the hands of Hall. Off the fourth ball of the over Meckiff and Grout scampered through for a bye. Four balls left, two wickets standing and four runs needed.

Grout skied the fifth ball high in the air and seemed doomed to be caught as he and Meckiff crossed for a single. Hall led a posse of fielders in the chase for the catch, got his huge hands under the ball and looked on in despair as it bounced out and on to the ground. Three balls left, two wickets still standing and three runs needed.

Meckiff swung his bat at the next ball and sent it over the heads of the close fielders towards leg, and as Hunte raced to collect it the two batsmen ran two and then made the decision to chase for a third run that would have won the match. Meantime Hunte had gathered the ball close to the square-leg boundary, and he sent it arrowing towards the stumps. Wicketkeeper Alexander whipped the bails off with Grout inches out of his ground despite a despairing dive for the line.

Two balls left and the scores were

level as last man Lindsay Kline came in to face Hall. Kline turned his first ball to mid-wicket and as Meckiff came charging in like a rugby wing three-quarter for what he thought would be the winning run sharp-eyed Solomon scored yet another direct hit on the stumps with an astonishingly accurate throw considering he had only a stump's width at which to aim.

This magnificent piece of fielding produced the first tie in the history of Test cricket. Meckiff left the pitch close to tears convinced that Australia had lost. It was some time before his team-mates were able to persuade him that he had just played a prominent part in the first-ever tied Test.

The see-sawing events of the last over caused such confusion that many people did not know whether the match had been won by the West Indians or whether the Australians had won. It took discussions between the scorers and the umpires before it was confirmed officially that the match had finished as a tie.

THE WITNESSES: Richie Benaud: 'Nobody who saw the final day of this match will ever forget it, and for all those of us lucky enough to have participated in it the memory of those last exciting moments will live with us for ever. The match was a wonderful advertisement for the game, which was played in a sporting but competitive spirit with both teams putting the accent on aggressive, attacking cricket.'

Frank Worrell: 'It would have been a pity for either team to have lost. It was the perfect result. I kept telling our players to try to keep cool. We had to maintain total concentration right until the end. The throwing by Conrad Hunte and Joe Solomon was magnificent, particularly considering the pressure on them.'

Sir Donald Bradman: 'This was without question the greatest Test match of all time.'

FOR THE RECORD: One of the most exciting Test rubbers ever played was decided on the penultimate day of the final Test when Australia's ninth-wicket pair dashed for a bye. It gave Australia a two-wicket win and victory in the series by 2-1 with one match drawn and the first tied.The second day's play of the final Test at Melbourne was watched by a world record 90,000 crowd. Alan Davidson took six wickets in the match to equal Clarrie Grimmett's record aggregate for Australia of 33 wickets, despite missing the fourth Test because of illness. Australia won the second Test by seven wickets. Conrad Hunte was the top scorer in the match, with 110 of the West Indies second innings total of 233. West Indies won the third Test at Sydney by 222 runs, thanks largely to centuries by Sobers (168) in the first innings and Alexander (108) in the second. Ken Mackay and Lindsay Kline earned Australia a draw in the fourth Test with an unbeaten tenth-wicket partnership that survived the final 100 minutes of the match. Kanhai scored a century in each innings and Lance Gibbs achieved a hat-trick. Benaud took seven wickets in the match including his 200th in Test cricket.

Australia v West Indies, First Test, 1960-61

WEST INDIES

C.C. Hunte	c Benaud b Davidson	24	— c Simpson b Mackay	39
C.W. Smith	c Grout b Davidson	7	— c O'Neill b Davidson	6
R.B. Kanhai	c Grout b Davidson	15	— c Grout b Davidson	54
G. St A. Sobers	c Kline b Meckiff	132	— b Davidson	14
F.M.M. Worrell*	c Grout b Davidson	65	— c Grout b Davidson	65
J.S. Solomon	hit wkt b Simpson	65	— lbw b Simpson	47
P.D. Lashley	c Grout b Kline	19	— b Davidson	0
F.C.M. Alexander†	c Davidson b Kline	60	— b Benaud	5
S. Ramadhin	c Harvey b Davidson	12	— c Harvey b Simpson	6
W.W. Hall	st Grout b Kline	50	— b Davidson	18
A.L. Valentine	not out	0	— not out	7
Extras	(LB 3, W 1)	4	(B 14, LB 7, W 2)	23
Total		**453**		**284**

AUSTRALIA

C.C. McDonald	c Hunte b Sobers	57	— b Worrell	16
R.B. Simpson	b Ramadhin	92	— c sub b Hall	0
R.N. Harvey	b Valentine	15	— c Sobers b Hall	5
N.C. O'Neill	c Valentine b Hall	181	— c Alexander b Hall	26
L.E. Favell	run out	45	— c Solomon b Hall	7
K.D. Mackay	b Sobers	35	— b Ramadhin	28
A.K. Davidson	c Alexander b Hall	44	— run out	80
R. Benaud*	lbw b Hall	10	— c Alexander b Hall	52
A.T.W. Grout†	lbw b Hall	4	— run out	2
I. Meckiff	run out	4	— run out	2
L.F. Kline	not out	3	— not out	0
Extras	(B 2, LB 8, W 1, NB 4)	15	(B 2, LB 9, NB 3)	12
Total		**505**		**232**

AUSTRALIA	O	M	R	W	O	M	R	W
Davidson	30	2	135	5	24.6	4	87	6
Meckiff	18	0	129	1	4	1	19	0
Mackay	3	0	15	0	21	7	52	1
Benaud	24	3	93	0	31	6	69	1
Simpson	8	0	25	1	7	2	18	2
Kline	17.6	6	52	3	4	0	14	0
O'Neill					1	0	2	0

WEST INDIES	O	M	R	W	O	M	R	W
Hall	29.3	1	140	4	17.7	3	63	5
Worrell	30	0	93	0	16	3	41	1
Sobers	32	0	115	2	8	0	30	0
Valentine	24	6	82	1	10	4	27	0
Ramadhin	15	1	60	1	17	3	57	1

FALL OF WICKETS

Wkt	WI 1st	A 1st	WI 2nd	A 2nd
1st	23	84	13	1
2nd	42	138	88	7
3rd	65	194	114	49
4th	239	278	127	49
5th	243	381	210	57
6th	283	469	210	92
7th	347	484	241	226
8th	366	489	250	228
9th	452	496	253	232
10th	453	505	284	232

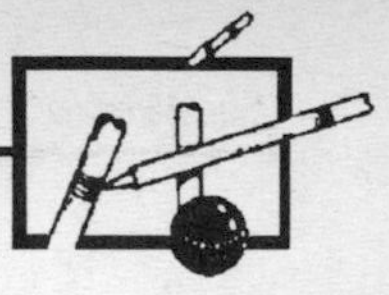

Richie bowls into the rough to put England in a spin

Match: England v Australia, Fourth Test
Venue: Old Trafford **Date:** July 27, 28, 29, 31, August 1

THE SETTING: It was with some trepidation that Australia returned to Old Trafford for this fourth Test against England exactly five years and a day since Jim Laker had skittled them to defeat with his historic 19-wicket performance.

The Aussies had three survivors from the team humiliated by Laker—Neil Harvey, Ken 'Slasher' Mackay and Richie Benaud, who was now the skipper. Brian Statham and captain Peter May were the only two 1956 players still in the England line-up.

The series was evenly balanced at one-all, Australia having won the second Test by five wickets and England the third by eight wickets after a draw in the first Test at Edgbaston.

Benaud won the toss for Australia and elected to bat on what looked a green pitch suited to pace. It was not the only spinning success that the Aussie skipper was to have during a dramatic match that went some way to wipe out the nightmare memories of when the tourists were Lakered.

THE MATCH: Benaud must have wondered about his decision to bat when Statham had Bobby Simpson caught behind by John Murray in his first over. At home on the Old Trafford pitch, Lancastrian Statham was looking more menacing than his Yorkshire pace partner Freddie Trueman and when he switched ends he dismissed Harvey with the Australian total at 51.

Norm O'Neill, who had been hit and hurt several times in a lively debut display by 32-year-old Worcestershire fast bowler Jack Flavell, was next out for 11 when he fell into his wicket while trying to hook Trueman.

With the familiar sight of rain clouds gathering over the Old Trafford ground, Flavell took his first wicket in Test cricket shortly after lunch when he bowled Peter Burge for 15. Australia were looking far from comfortable with the score at 106 for four when rain ended play for the day.

The pitch was even more lively the next morning and Australia's remaining six wickets crashed for the addition of just 66 runs. Statham, time and again beating the bat with his swing and late movement off the ground, finished with figures of five for 53 off 21 overs. Ted Dexter also got plenty of movement and took three wickets for 16 runs in 6.4 overs.

Australia were all out for 190, but it would have been more disastrous except for a resolute knock of 74 by opener Bill Lawry, who was at the wicket for three hours.

A third wicket stand of 111 by Geoff Pullar (63) and Peter May (95) put England in a commanding position at 154 for three after Ramon Subba Row and Ted Dexter had been dismissed cheaply.

At stumps on the second day England were only three runs behind and with seven wickets in hand. But thoughts of an easy victory evaporated on the third morning when May and Brian Close were sent back to the pavilion on the same score after only 25 runs had been added to the overnight total. The end of May's innings five runs short of a century was spectactular. Wicket-keeper Wally Grout dived full length to his right and scooped the ball up for Bobby Simpson to make a catch at first slip off the bowling of Davidson.

Ken Barrington (78) and Murray added 60 for the sixth wicket and then Barrington nursed David Allen (48) along in a seventh-wicket partnership that realised 87 runs. Just as England were were relishing the prospect of building an untouchable lead, Bobby Simpson rushed the innings to a conclusion by taking the last four wickets for two runs in 26 deliveries.

Lawry and Simpson reduced England's 177-run lead by 63 runs before the close. There was an unhappy sequence of spilled chances by the England close fielders before Simpson (51) was finally caught by Murray off the bowling of Flavell with the Australian total at 113. Lawry made the most of being dropped at 25 by scoring 102 before being brilliantly held at backward short leg by Trueman to give Allen the first of his four wickets for 58.

Australia cleared the backlog of runs for the loss of two wickets and Harvey (35) and O'Neill (67) both survived missed chances as they started to build a useful lead.

On the final morning the Aussies tumbled suddenly from 331 for six to 334 for nine, Gloucestershire off-spinner Allen taking all three wickets without conceding a run in a spell of 15 balls. While England's supporters celebrated this success, their batsmen pondered on what a leg-break bowler of Benaud's quality might achieve on a wicket that was now showing definite signs of taking spin.

What Benaud needed desperately was some runs to play with and these were provided by an exciting last-wicket stand between Alan Davidson (77 not out) and Garth McKenzie (32). The onslaught included Davidson smashing Allen for 20 off one over and they added 98 before Flavell at last ended the partnership by bowling McKenzie. It was Australia's highest last-wicket Test stand in England and gave them an outside chance of victory, although England were still the slight favourites as they set out to score 256 in 230 minutes. They would have had a much easier target if the rest of the fielders could have matched the catching ability of Murray, who held on to seven catches during the innings to equal the England record against Australia set by Godfrey Evans at Lord's in 1956.

England got off to a brisk start in their second innings, with openers Subba Row and Geoff Pullar putting on 40 before Pullar was caught by O'Neill off the bowling of Davidson for 26. Then came a marvellous innings by Dexter that looked to have put England on the way to victory.

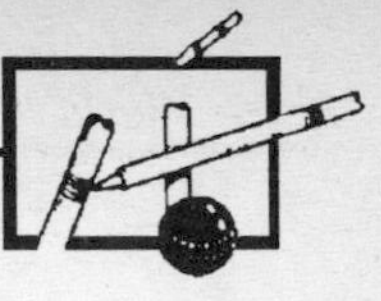

He gave a glorious exhibition of controlled aggression as he stroked his way to 76 runs in 84 minutes, including one six and 14 fours in his arsenal. He and Subba Row (49) added 110 for the second wicket and with 20 minutes to go to the tea interval it seemed only a question of time before England reached their victory target.

But this was not taking into account the skill and cunning of Benaud, who was still a formidable bowler despite a recurring shoulder problem. He started to bowl around the wicket, deliberately pitching his leg spinners into the rough ground kicked up by Trueman's follow-through footholds. He had the bold Dexter caught at the wicket, bowled May around his legs for a duck, punished Close for hitting a towering six by having him caught at backward short leg, and then clean bowled the stubborn Subba Row. In 20 minutes England had toppled from 150 for one to 163 for five.

Benaud could not wait to get back into action after a tea interval that left the England batsmen with indigestion. England needed 93 runs in 85 minutes with only Barrington of their established batsmen left. Benaud had Murray caught at first slip by Simpson to take his haul to five wickets for 12 runs in the space of 25 balls. Mackay then trapped Barrington lbw and England were now 171 for seven. The only question was whether Australia could snatch the three remaining wickets in the time left.

They won the match—and so retained the Ashes—with 20 minutes to spare, Benaud claiming David Allen's wicket to take his figures to six for 70, his best performance against England who were all out for 201—54 runs short of what had at one time seemed an easy target.

THE WITNESSES: Richie Benaud: 'I made the most of the footholds left by Freddie Trueman, and allowed the pitch to do much of the work. It was just a case of pitching the ball in the rough and then waiting to see the result. We owed a lot to that enterprising last-wicket stand between Davidson and McKenzie. I must say I feel better than I did after Jim Laker had gone through us on our last visit to Old Trafford.'

Peter May: 'We were punished for not holding our catches. But all credit to Richie Benaud. He made the most of the conditions and produced a fine spell just when it looked as if Ted Dexter had put us into a match-winning position.'

FOR THE RECORD: England had to battle desperately to get a draw in the fifth Test at The Oval. Only May (71), playing in his final Test, and Barrington (53) saved a total rout in England's first innings when they were all out for 256. Australia lost opener Bill Lawry without a run being scored but centuries by Norm O'Neill (117) and Peter Burge (181) put them on the way to a total of 494. Subba Row (137), Barrington (83), Murray (40) and Allen (42 not out) led England's resistance movement as they clung on for a draw at 370 for eight in a rain-interrupted match. Wally Grout held six catches to take his total for the series to a record 21.

England v Australia, Fourth Test, 1961

AUSTRALIA

W.M. Lawry	lbw b Statham	74	— c Trueman b Allen	102
R.B. Simpson	c Murray b Statham	4	— c Murray b Flavell	51
R.N. Harvey	c Subba Row b Statham	19	— c Murray b Dexter	35
N.C. O'Neill	hit wkt b Trueman	11	— c Murray b Statham	67
P.J.P. Burge	b Flavell	15	— c Murray b Dexter	23
B.C. Booth	c Close b Statham	46	— lbw b Dexter	9
K.D. Mackay	c Murray b Statham	11	— c Close b Allen	18
A.K. Davidson	c Barrington b Dexter	0	— not out	77
R. Benaud*	b Dexter	2	— lbw b Allen	1
A.T.W. Grout†	c Murray b Dexter	2	— c Statham b Allen	0
G.D. McKenzie	not out	1	— b Flavell	32
Extras	(B 4, LB 1)	5	(B 6, LB 9, W 2)	17
Total		**190**		**432**

ENGLAND

G. Pullar	b Davidson	63	— c O'Neill b Davidson	26
R. Subba Row	c Simpson b Davidson	2	— b Benaud	49
E.R. Dexter	c Davidson b McKenzie	16	— c Grout b Benaud	76
P.B.H. May*	c Simpson b Davidson	95	— b Benaud	0
D.B. Close	lbw b McKenzie	33	— c O'Neill b Benaud	8
K.F. Barrington	c O'Neill b Simpson	78	— lbw b Mackay	5
J.T. Murray†	c Grout b Mackay	24	— c Simpson b Benaud	4
D.A. Allen	c Booth b Simpson	42	— c Simpson b Benaud	10
F.S. Trueman	c Harvey b Simpson	3	— c Benaud b Simpson	8
J.B. Statham	c Mackay b Simpson	4	— b Davidson	8
J.A. Flavell	not out	0	— not out	0
Extras	(B 2, LB 4, W 1)	7	(B 5, W 2)	7
Total		**367**		**201**

ENGLAND	O	M	R	W	O	M	R	W
Trueman	14	1	55	1	32	6	92	0
Statham	21	3	53	5	44	9	106	1
Flavell	22	8	61	1	29.4	4	65	2
Dexter	6.4	2	16	3	20	4	61	3
Allen					38	25	58	4
Close					8	1	33	0

AUSTRALIA	O	M	R	W	O	M	R	W
Davidson	39	11	70	3	14.4	1	50	2
McKenzie	38	11	106	2	4	1	20	0
Mackay	40	9	81	1	13	7	33	1
Benaud	35	15	80	0	32	11	70	6
Simpson	11.4	4	23	4	8	4	21	1

FALL OF WICKETS

	A	E	A	E
Wkt	1st	1st	2nd	2nd
1st	8	3	113	40
2nd	51	43	175	150
3rd	89	154	210	150
4th	106	212	274	158
5th	150	212	290	163
6th	174	272	296	171
7th	185	358	332	171
8th	185	362	334	189
9th	189	367	334	193
10th	190	367	432	201

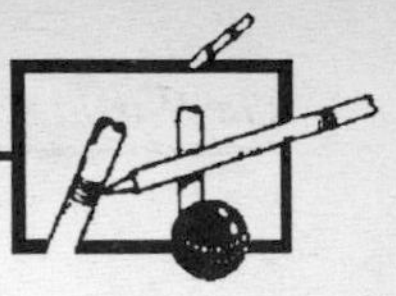

1961-62 Gibbs has Indians playing into the fielders' hands

Match: West Indies v India, Third Test
Venue: Kensington Oval, Bridgetown **Date:** March 23, 24, 26, 27, 28

THE SETTING: India came into this match under a cloud of gloom after a match against Barbados during which their skipper Nari Contractor had come perilously close to death. He was struck on the head as he ducked to try to avoid a rising ball from the thunder-paced Charlie Griffith.

Contractor's skull was fractured and he underwent an emergency brain operation. The incident ended his Test career, although he recovered sufficiently to return to first-class cricket.

The Nawab of Pataudi, son of India's first post-war captain, was appointed emergency skipper in place of Contractor for the third Test. 'Tiger' Pataudi, who celebrated his 21st birthday on January 5, thus became the youngest captain in the history of Test cricket. He himself was making an astonishing comeback after losing the sight of his right eye in a car crash the previous year.

West Indies skipper Frank Worrell won the toss and invited India to bat.

THE MATCH: Openers Motganhalli Jaisimha (41) and Dilip Sardesai (31) gave India their soundest start of the series, but a middle-order collapse left them struggling at 112 for five. Only defiant batting by Pataudi (48) and a last-wicket dash by Salim Durani (48 not out) boosted the total to 258 on a wicket that had looked made for runs.

West Indies had few problems keeping the scorer busy on the second day and a sparkling innings of 89 in two hours by Rohan Kanhai put them firmly in command. Garfield Sobers was just getting into his matchless rhythm when he was caught behind by Farokh Engineer for 42 off the left-arm slow bowling of Bapu Nadkarni, who took two wickets for 92 runs during a marathon chore of 67 overs, 28 of which were maidens.

Joe Solomon (96), Conrad Hunte (59) and Worrell (77) boosted the West Indies reply, but a laborious third day in which they scored just 164 runs off 131 overs displeased their vociferous supporters who were accustomed to seeing their team score in double-quick time. Wicket-keeper David Allan marked his Test debut by scoring an undefeated 40 to lift the total to 475.

The reason the West Indies were unable to increase their run rate was some deadly accurate medium pace bowling by Polly Umrigar, who despite an attack of fibrositis and his 35 years bowled 27 maidens in his 49-over stint which was rewarded with just two wickets for 48 runs.

India, needing to score 275 runs to make West Indies bat again, got off to the worst possible start when Jaisimha was out leg before wicket to Charlie Stayers without a run being scored.

Rusi Surti also went lbw to Stayers with the total at 60, but then Sardesai (60) and Manjrekar (51) steered India patiently to 158 for two by lunch on the final day, and it was looking increasingly likely that they would manage to salvage a draw. Then Lance Gibbs, he of the extraordinarily long fingers and prodigious spinning skills, stepped on to the stage to weave one of the most phenomenal bowling spells in Test match history.

The Indian batsmen seemed to become almost hypnotised by his flight and spin, and he literally had them playing into the hands of the West Indian fielders. There was a long procession to the pavilion as they took it in turns to spoon and edge catches to the fielders surrounding the bat like a spider's web around a fly.

India were spun out for 187, and lost the match by an innings and 30 runs. It all happened with such stunning and dramatic suddeness that it was some time before the full impact of what Gibbs had achieved was fully appreciated. In a spell of 15.3 overs —14 of which were maidens—he took eight wickets for just six runs.

Before he decimated the Indian innings immediately after lunch, Gibbs had bowled 38 overs and taken no wickets for 32 runs.

THE WITNESSES: Lance Gibbs: 'I think it was as much panic by the Indian batsmen as anything else that caused them to collapse so dramatically. I just concentrated on accuracy and giving the ball plenty of air. I'd been bowling the same way all the match but without any luck, but once I had started the breakthrough I was able to set a really attacking field and some of the catching was out of this world.'

Nawab of Pataudi: 'There is no sensible explanation for what happened. We just suddenly became mesmerised by Gibbs. It was a quite astonishing spell of bowling.'

FOR THE RECORD: Gibbs finished the series with 24 wickets on his way to what was then a world record haul of 309 Test wickets. West Indies won the series 5-0, the first time they had achieved a whitewash. The highlights were, first Test: Wes Hall taking three wickets in four balls to put West Indies on the way to victory by ten wickets; second Test: Easton McMorris (125) and Rohan Kanhai (138) sharing a second-wicket stand of 255 and Sobers (153) boosting the total to 631 for eight declared, before Hall (six for 49) destroyed India in their second innings to leave West Indies winners by an innings and 18 runs; fourth Test: Kanhai (139) top scoring for West Indies, and Hall forcing the follow-on with five for 20 and then gallant batting by Polly Umrigar (172 not out) and Durani (104) holding up the West Indies on their way to a seven-wickets victory; fifth Test: Sobers scoring 104 in a total of 253 and then Lester King capturing India's first five wickets in his first four overs in Test cricket, and Worrell top scoring with an undefeated 98 in the second innings to steer West Indies to victory by 123 runs.

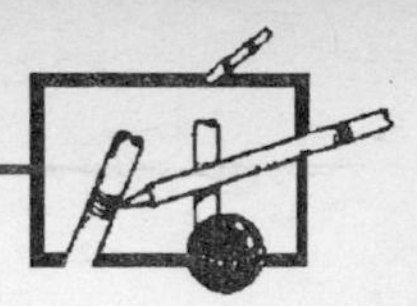

Lance Gibbs mesmerised the Indian batsmen and had them under his spell

West Indies v India, Third Test, 1961-62

INDIA

M.L. Jaisimha	c Allan b Hall	41	— lbw b Stayers	0
D.N. Sardesai	c McMorris b Gibbs	31	— c Sobers b Gibbs	60
R.F. Surti	lbw b Worrell	7	— lbw b Stayers	36
V.L. Manjrekar	c Worrell b Hall	8	— c Worrell b Gibbs	51
P.R. Umrigar	c Allan b Hall	8	— c Allan b Gibbs	10
Nawab of Pataudi, jr*	c and b Valentine	48	— c Sobers b Gibbs	0
C.G. Borde	c Allan b Sobers	19	— c Worrell b Gibbs	8
R.G. Nadkarni	b Stayers	22	— not out	2
F.M. Engineer†	c Worrell b Sobers	12	— st Allan b Gibbs	0
S.A. Durani	not out	48	— c Hunte b Gibbs	5
R.B. Desai	b Worrell	12	— c Sobers b Gibbs	1
Extras	(NB 2)	2	(B 8, LB 3, W 2, NB 1)	14
Total		**258**		**187**

WEST INDIES

C.C. Hunte	c Engineer b Surti	59
E.D.A. St J. McMorris	c Engineer b Durani	39
R.B. Kanhai	run out	89
G. St A. Sobers	c Engineer b Nadkarni	42
J.S. Solomon	c Desai b Durani	96
L.R. Gibbs	b Borde	7
F.M.M. Worrell*	b Unrigar	77
S.C. Stayers	c Umrigar b Nadkarni	7
W.W. Hall	lbw b Umrigar	3
D.W. Allan†	not out	40
A.L. Valentine	b Borde	4
Extras	(LB 5, NB 7)	12
Total		**475**

WEST INDIES	O	M	R	W	O	M	R	W
Hall	22	4	64	3	10	3	17	0
Stayers	11	0	81	1	18	8	24	2
Worrell	7.1	3	12	2	27	18	16	0
Gibbs	16	7	25	1	53.3	37	38	8
Valentine	17	7	28	1	29	19	26	0
Sobers	16	2	46	2	17	10	14	0
Solomon					29	17	33	0
Kanhai					2	1	5	0

INDIA	O	M	R	W
Desai	19	7	25	0
Surti	29	6	80	1
Durani	45	13	123	2
Nadkarni	67	28	92	2
Borde	31.3	4	89	2
Jaisimha	1	0	6	0
Umrigar	49	27	48	2

FALL OF WICKETS

	I	WI	I
Wkt	1st	1st	2nd
1st	56	67	0
2nd	76	152	60
3rd	82	226	158
4th	89	255	159
5th	112	282	159
6th	153	378	174
7th	171	394	177
8th	188	399	177
9th	229	454	183
10th	258	475	187

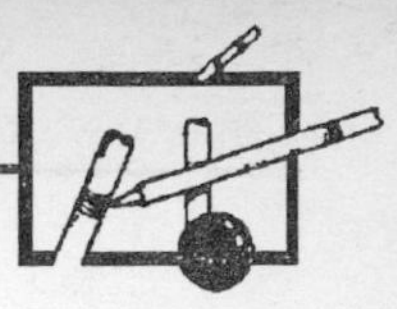

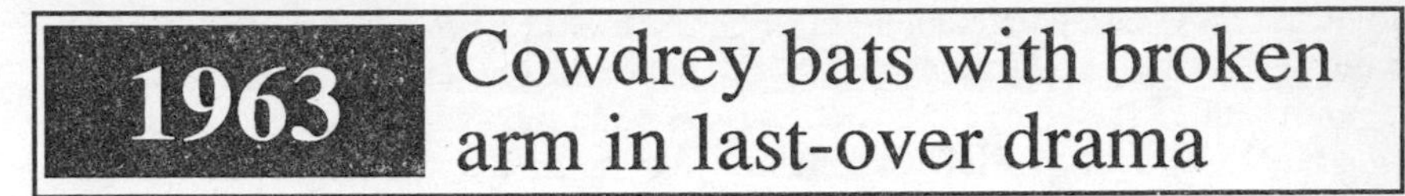

1963 Cowdrey bats with broken arm in last-over drama

Match: England v West Indies, Second Test
Venue: Lord's **Date:** June 20, 21, 22, 24, 25

THE SETTING: From first ball to last, this was a classic contest. As Wes Hall prepared to bowl the final over any one of four results was possible—a win for either side, a draw or a tie.

England had gone into the match with something less than total confidence after being outplayed in the first Test on the way to a defeat by ten wickets. They had struggled against the pace of Hall and Charlie Griffith and then tumbled to the spin of Lance Gibbs whose match figures of 11 wickets for 157 were the best of his 79-Test career.

The selectors made the surprising decision of recalling 38-year-old Hampshire seamer Derek Shackleton after 11 years in the Test wilderness. His incredibly accurate but relatively sedate bowling was preferred to the pace of Brian Statham.

THE MATCH: West Indies opener Conrad Hunte gave the match a sensational send-off when he imperiously struck Freddie Trueman's first three balls for four. But, typically, fiery Fred refused to have his extraordinary enthusiasm doused and he took six wickets for 100 in the first innings and finished the match with figures of 11 for 152.

It was Shackleton who brought the West Indies first innings to a close at 301 by taking the final three wickets in four balls. Rohan Kanhai (73) and Joe Solomon (56) were the top scorers for the tourists.

England lost openers Mickey Stewart and John Edrich to the fearsome Griffith for two runs before skipper Ted Dexter unleashed a rush hour of awesome strokes as he dashed to 70 off 73 balls before Garfield Sobers brought one back to trap him lbw. Ken Barrington battled to 80 and Freddie Titmus was not out on 52 in England's fighting reply of 297.

Trueman (five for 52) and Shackleton (four for 72) threatened to run through the West Indies batting in their second innings until Basil Butcher applied the brake and thrashed 133 out of a total of 229, including two sixes and 17 fours in his battery of runs.

England staggered to 31 for three and lost Colin Cowdrey with a broken wrist after he had been hit by a wickedly rising ball from Hall when he was on 19. Barrington (70) and then the unbelievably brave Brian Close (60) pulled England back into the game with a fighting chance of victory. Close walked down the wicket to meet Hall and Griffth, almost challenging them to try to hit him with the ball. Several times he allowed lightning-quick short balls to hit him on the chest and shoulders rather than risk a shot which might get him out. Bruised but unbowed, he was finally caught by wicket-keeper Deryk Murray after hitting England to within sight of the victory target of 234 runs.

So to the final over and a nail-biting finish almost on a par with the tied Test between Australia and West Indies in 1960-61. England started the over with eight wickets down and needing eight runs to win. Tail-enders Derek Shackleton and David Allen were at the wicket while Colin Cowdrey, his left arm in plaster, sat padded up in the pavilion ready to resume his innings in dire emergency. England scored singles off the second and third balls. Three balls left, six runs needed.

Shackleton missed the fourth ball but set off down the pitch in a wild charge for a bye. Wicket-keeper Murray fielded the ball and shied at the stumps...and missed. Frank Worrell coolly collected the ball and dashed to the far end of the pitch in a race between two cricketing veterans. The West Indies skipper won by a short head as he knocked the bails off to run out Shackleton. Two balls left, six runs needed...and coming to the non-striker's end was the plastered Cowdrey.

He planned if necessary to bat left-handed and had been practising his improvised stance in front of the mirror in the Lord's dressing-room. But David Allen played the last two balls with a defensive straight bat to clinch just about the most exciting drawn result ever witnessed in a Test match.

THE WITNESSES: Colin Cowdrey: 'David Allen and I had a brief conference in mid-wicket when I went out for the final act. He said that he had not given up hope of winning and that if he could he would swipe the next ball for four. "Then," David said, with the light of battle in his eyes, "we shall run no matter what off the last ball." It wasn't to be, but I shall never forget that climax. I was almost looking forward to batting left-handed and was going to show John Edrich how it should be done! It was one of the most memorable matches I ever played in.'

Wes Hall: 'Skipper Frank Worrell was shouting something to me just before I started my run-up for the final delivery, but the noise of the crowd was so great that I couldn't hear a thing. Afterwards he told me that he was shouting, "Make sure you don't bowl a no-ball."'

FOR THE RECORD: Freddie Trueman took 12 wickets for 119 in the third Test to steer England to victory by 217 runs. A century by Sobers that included his 4,000th run in Test cricket was the highlight of the West Indies victory by 221 runs in the fourth Test. Conrad Hunte was the batting star of the fifth and final Test at The Oval. He scored 80 in the first innings and an unbeaten 108 in the second to lift West Indies to victory by eight wickets and so make them the first holders of the newly introduced Wisden Trophy. Phil Sharpe (63 and 83) was top scorer in both England innings. Freddie Trueman's three wickets brought his haul in the rubber to 34, a record for the series.

England v West Indies, Second Test, 1963

WEST INDIES

C.C. Hunte	c Close b Trueman	44	— c Cowdrey b Shackleton	7
E.D.A. St J. McMorris	lbw b Trueman	16	— c Cowdrey b Trueman	8
G. St A. Sobers	c Cowdrey b Allen	42	— c Parks b Trueman	8
R.B. Kanhai	c Edrich b Trueman	73	— c Cowdrey b Shackleton	21
B.F. Butcher	c Barrington b Trueman	14	— lbw b Shackleton	133
J.S. Solomon	lbw b Shackleton	56	— c Stewart b Allen	5
F.M.M. Worrell*	b Trueman	0	— c Stewart b Trueman	33
D.L. Murray†	c Cowdrey b Trueman	20	— c Parks b Trueman	2
W.W. Hall	not out	25	— c Parks b Trueman	2
C.C. Griffith	c Cowdrey b Shackleton	0	— b Shackleton	1
L.R. Gibbs	c Stewart b Shackleton	0	— not out	1
Extras	(B 10, LB 1)	11	(B 5, LB 2, NB 1)	8
Total		**301**		**229**

ENGLAND

M.J. Stewart	c Kanhai b Griffith	2	— c Solomon b Hall	17
J.H. Edrich	c Murray b Griffith	0	— c Murray b Hall	8
E.R. Dexter*	lbw b Sobers	70	— b Gibbs	2
K.F. Barrington	c Sobers b Worrell	80	— c Murray b Griffith	60
M.C. Cowdrey	b Gibbs	4	— not out	19
D.B. Close	c Murray b Griffith	9	— c Murray b Griffith	70
J.M. Parks†	b Worrell	35	— lbw b Griffith	17
F.J. Titmus	not out	52	— c McMorris b Hall	11
F.S. Trueman	b Hall	10	— c Murray b Hall	0
D.A. Allen	lbw b Griffith	2	— not out	4
D. Shackleton	b Griffith	8	— run out	4
Extras	(B 8, LB 8, NB 9)	25	(B 5, LB 8, NB 3)	16
Total		**297**	(9 wickets)	**228**

ENGLAND	O	M	R	W	O	M	R	W
Trueman	44	16	100	6	26	9	52	5
Shackleton	50.2	22	93	3	34	14	72	4
Dexter	20	6	41	0				
Close	9	3	21	0				
Allen	10	3	35	1	21	7	50	1
Titmus					17	3	47	0

WEST INDIES	O	M	R	W	O	M	R	W
Hall	18	2	65	1	40	9	93	4
Griffith	26	6	91	5	30	7	59	3
Sobers	18	4	45	1	4	1	4	0
Gibbs	27	9	59	1	17	7	56	1
Worrell	13	6	12	2				

FALL OF WICKETS

	WI	E	WI	E
Wkt	1st	1st	2nd	2nd
1st	51	2	15	15
2nd	64	20	15	27
3rd	127	102	64	31
4th	145	115	84	130
5th	219	151	104	158
6th	219	206	214	203
7th	263	235	224	203
8th	297	271	226	219
9th	297	274	228	228
10th	301	297	229	—

1964-65 Venkat takes a turn to break the deadlock in Delhi

Match: India v New Zealand, Fourth Test
Venue: Feroz Shah Kotla, New Delhi **Date:** March 19, 20, 21, 22

THE SETTING: India and New Zealand were at an impasse as they went into the fourth and final Test at New Delhi. The first three Tests had been drawn, with the pendulum of play so evenly balanced that there was nothing to choose between the two teams.

It was obviously going to take an inspirational individual performance to break the deadlock, and this was provided by a player who was popular with everybody except commentators. His name: Srinivasaraghavan Ventkataraghavan.

He was known affectionately as 'Venkat' throughout an international career that started in the first Test of this series and stretched across two decades to 1985. Of all his 57 Tests, this was the one in which he touched a peak of perfection with his biting off-spinners.

THE MATCH: New Zealand were in trouble from the moment Venkat joined the attack after medium pacers Ramakant Desai and Motganhalli Jaisimha had made little impact against openers Graham Dowling and Terry Jarvis. A dry, powdery wicket was showing signs of wear on the first morning, and Venkat exploited the conditions to the full to make the New Zealanders regret their decision to leave their left-arm specialist spinner Bryan Yuile on the sidelines.

With leg spinner Bhagwat Chandrasekhar playing a supporting role, Venkat put in a marathon session during which he tied the Kiwi batsmen down with spin bowling that was both accurate and penetrative.

It was slow torture for the New Zealanders, who were punished every time they tried to knock Venkat off his nagging line and length. He bowled 51.1 overs—26 of them maidens—and he took eight wickets for 72.

Chandrasekhar interrupted Venkat's domination with two wickets for 96 in 37 overs. Only Ross Morgan (82) and Bev Congdon (48) put up spirited resistance but once Venkat had broken their second wicket stand of 54, New Zealand slowly came apart and were dismissed for 262.

The tourists were just not armed for this turning wicket, and their battery of medium and fast-medium bowlers took heavy punishment as India replied with 465 runs before declaring with eight wickets down. Opener Dilip Sardesai followed up his double century of the third Test with 106, and skipper, the Nawab of Pataudi, produced an array of glorious strokes on his way to 113 before he became one of Richard Collinge's four victims. Chandra Borde (87)

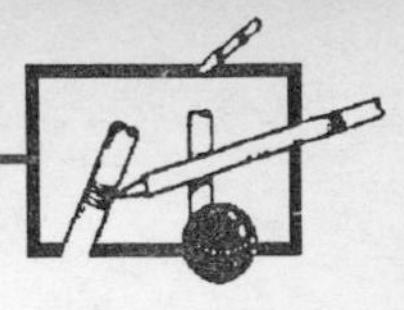

and Hanumant Singh (82) gleefully joined in the run riot. Singh was caught behind by Congdon who took over as emergency wicket-keeper after John Ward had gone off injured.

The Kiwis went into the second innings 203 runs behind, and looking certain to be beaten after they had lost their first four wickets for 68 runs. But they battled desperately to save the match, and Jarvis (77), Bert Sutcliffe (54) and Collinge (54) held up India, who suddenly found themselves running out of time.

Venkat bowled throughout most of the innings and in 61.2 overs took four for 80 to lift his match figures to 12 for 152. New Zealand's last three wickets added 93, with Frank Cameron unbeaten on 27. More worrying for India was the fact that the tail-enders ate up valuable time and they were left with a target of 70 runs in the last hour to win.

India promoted the hard-hitting wicket-keeper Farokh Engineer to open the innings with Sardesai but he was quickly sent back to the pavilion when bowled for two by Bruce Taylor. Jaisimha was then run out for one, but once the Nawab of Pataudi joined Sardesai at the wicket India raised the run rate and started to hit the New Zealand bowlers to all points of the compass. The Nawab (29) powered his team to within sight of their target before being bowled by his rival captain John Reid.

India clinched victory by seven wickets with 13 minutes to spare, with Sardesai not out on 28 and three wickets down for 73.

THE WITNESSES: Venkat: 'It was only my fourth Test, and so I was quite nervous. But I realised very quickly that the wicket suited me and I knew that provided I concentrated on accuracy I would get the better of the batsmen. New Zealand gave us problems in the second innings with their stout defensive batting, but we did not panic. Cricket is a game in which patience pays, particularly on the pitches that we have in India where you have to work at outwitting the batsmen.'

John Reid: 'We knew within an hour or so of the match starting that the parched wicket was going to suit the spin of the Indian attack. In Venkat they had the ideal bowler to exploit the conditions and we just could not force him off his line. But we had the satisfaction of making them fight every inch of the way.'

Nawab of Pataudi: 'Venkat announced his arrival as a spinner of the highest quality in this match. He showed that mixture of perserverance and patience that is so crucial for slow bowlers.'

FOR THE RECORD: Venkat's 12 wickets in the fourth Test lifted his haul for the series to 21 wickets. Bruce Taylor marked his debut in the second Test in Calcutta by scoring 105 in 158 minutes and then took five wickets for 86 in India's first innings. It was his first century in first-class cricket and he achieved the record of being the only player to score 100 and to take five wickets in his Test debut. Bert Sutcliffe scored 151 not out in the second Test in which the Nawab of Pataudi was the top scorer with 153.

India v New Zealand, Fourth Test, 1964-65

NEW ZEALAND

G.T. Dowling	lbw b Venkataraghavan	7	— lbw b Subramanya	0
T.W. Jarvis	b Venkataraghavan	34	— b Venkataraghavan	77
R.W. Morgan	lbw b Venkataraghavan	82	— c Venkataraghavan b Desai	4
B.E. Congdon	c Chandrasekhar b Venkat.	48	— b Chandrasekhar	7
J.R. Reid*	b Chandrasekhar	9	— b Venkataraghavan	22
B. Sutcliffe	b Venkataraghavan	2	— c Engineer b Chandrasekhar	54
B.R. Taylor	c Borde b Chandrasekhar	21	— c Sardesai b Venkataraghavan	3
V. Pollard	b Venkataraghavan	27	— c Engineer b Subramanya	6
J.T. Ward†	lbw b Venkataraghavan	11	— run out	0
R.O. Collinge	not out	4	— c Engineer b Venkat.	54
F.J. Cameron	b Venkataraghavan	0	— not out	27
Extras	(B 8, LB 6, NB 3)	17	(B 15, LB 1, NB 2)	18
Total		**262**		**272**

INDIA

D.N. Sardesai	c Jarvis b Morgan	106	— not out	28
M.L. Jaisimha	c Dowling b Reid	10	— hit wkt b Cameron	1
Hanumant Singh	c Congdon b Collinge	82	— not out	7
C.G. Borde	c Jarvis b Cameron	87		
Nawab of Pataudi, jr*	b Collinge	113	— b Reid	29
V. Subramanya	b Taylor	9		
F.M. Engineer†	b Collinge	5	— b Taylor	2
R.G. Nadkarni	not out	14		
R.B. Desai	b Collinge	7		
S. Venkataraghavan				
B.S. Chandrasekhar				
Extras	(B 23, LB 4, W 1, NB 4)	32	(LB 4, NB 2)	6
Total	(8 wickets declared)	**465**	(3 wickets)	**73**

INDIA	O	M	R	W	O	M	R	W
Desai	9	2	36	0	18	3	35	1
Jaisimha	5	2	12	0	1	0	2	0
Subramanya	5	2	3	0	16	5	32	2
Venkataraghavan	51.1	26	72	8	61.2	30	80	4
Chandrasekhar	37	14	96	2	34	14	95	2
Nadkarni	16	8	21	0	19	13	10	0
Hanumant Singh	2	0	5	0				

NEW ZEALAND	O	M	R	W	O	M	R	W
Taylor	18	4	57	1	4	0	31	0
Collinge	20.4	4	89	4				
Reid	24	4	89	1	1	0	3	1
Cameron	26	5	86	1	4	0	29	1
Morgan	15	1	68	1				
Pollard	10	1	44	0				
Sutcliffe					0.1	0	4	0

FALL OF WICKETS

Wkt	NZ 1st	I 1st	NZ 2nd	I 2nd
1st	27	56	1	9
2nd	54	179	10	13
3rd	108	240	22	66
4th	117	378	68	—
5th	130	414	172	—
6th	157	421	178	—
7th	194	457	179	—
8th	256	465	213	—
9th	260	—	264	—
10th	262	—	272	—

1965 The Pollock brothers give England relative problems

Match: England v South Africa, Second Test
Venue: Trent Bridge **Date:** August 5, 6, 7, 9

THE SETTING: Cricket history is adorned with exceptional performances by brothers in the Test arena. Going back as far as the Grace brothers and all the way through to the likes of the Mohammads, the Chappells and the Hadlees, there has been a procession of relatively outstanding players.

This second Test between England and South Africa at Trent Bridge unveiled what was arguably the greatest of all the brotherly acts. It came from the Pollock brothers, Graeme and Peter, who between them lifted the Springboks to their first victory over England for ten years.

England had not lost a match in 14 successive Tests under the thoughtful captaincy of Mike Smith and he was confident of continuing his success as he eyed the heavy cloud formation on the first morning of the match. He was quite happy when Springboks skipper Peter van der Merwe won the toss and decided to bat. Smith knew that in Tom Cartwright he had a medium-pace bowler who would relish the overcast conditions.

THE MATCH: Cartwright, who could trouble even the greatest of batsmen on any wicket that offered him encouragement, had the South Africans in all sorts of trouble as they edged nervously at deliveries that often swung like boomerangs. Half the side was whipped out for just 80 runs, but the tall, elegant left-handed Graeme Pollock managed to play as easily and fluently as if he was practising in the nets.

There were 160 runs scored while Pollock was at the wicket—and 125 of them came off his bat as he pounded the boundary with 21 fours. His early runs came at a leisurely pace, but then he went into overdrive and collected 91 runs in only 70 scorching minutes while his partner, skipper Van der Merwe, scored just ten. It was an incredibly assured performance from a player who was only 21 years old.

Cartwright finally ended the Pollock blitz when he had him caught at slip by Colin Cowdrey, but his stunning innings had brought respectibility to what had been the wreckage of the South African scoreboard and they were all out for 269. Tragically for England, Cartwright broke a thumb after taking six wickets for 94. He was unable to play any further part in a match that he at one stage looked capable of winning on his own.

England finished the day talking in wonder of Graeme Pollock's innings and worrying about the threat of Peter Pollock, who in a brief spell just before stumps dismissed Geoff Boycott for a duck and Ken Barrington for one.

Peter was just as much of a handful on the second day and finished with five wickets for 53 as England were rushed out for 240. Only a disciplined innings by Colin Cowdrey (105) gave any backbone to the England reply.

Missing the swing of injured Cartwright, Mike Smith called Geoff Boycott into the attack and he gave a tight performance in which he conceded only 25 runs in 19 overs, but he was then given the old heave-ho by the late-order South African batsmen and in his remaining seven overs was hammered for another 35.

Eddie Barlow (76), Ali Bacher (67) and the graceful Graeme Pollock (59) were the chief runmakers between spells of fierce pace bowling by David Larter (five for 68) and John Snow (three for 83).

South Africa were all out for 289, leaving England needing 319 runs to win. It looked a mountain of a target when they lost their first four wickets for 14 runs, two of the players to depart being nightwatchmen. Boycott got himself stuck in one of his ruts and took two hours 20 minutes compiling just 16 runs before being clean bowled by Atholl McKinnon. Peter Parfitt (86) and Jim Parks (44 not out) tried to hit England out of trouble, but the Springboks eased to a comfortable 94-runs victory with a day to spare once Parfitt had been bowled by Peter Pollock.

Peter, the elder of the Pollock brothers, finished with a match analysis of 10 wickets for 87 runs. Graeme scored a total of 184 runs, held a fine slip catch and took the vital wicket of Mike Smith during a five-over spell in England's second innings. This family double act has few parallels in Test cricket history.

THE WITNESSES: Graeme Pollock: 'I saw the carnage being caused by Tom Cartwright, and I decided the best thing was to just try to play my normal game. It would have been suicide to try to play defensively because of the movement that Cartwright was getting in the air and off the ground.'

Peter Pollock: 'I was really proud of Graeme's knock in the first innings, and it inspired not only me but the entire team.'

David Gower: 'I was a schoolboy in the crowd at Trent Bridge, and I watched in wonder as Graeme Pollock unwrapped his marvellous innings. It made a tremendous impression on everybody, and he became an idol of mine. A few years later when I was on a tour of South Africa with an England schools side I saw him play an even greater innings. He was a real master.'

FOR THE RECORD: South Africa won the three-match series 1-0, with the first and second Tests drawn. Ken Barrington (91) was top scorer in the first Test, and Colin Bland (127) compiled the only century of the third Test in which Lancashire pace bowler Brian Statham made his final appearance for England. He marked his farewell to Test cricket with match figures of seven for 145 to take his final tally to 252 wickets in 70 Tests.

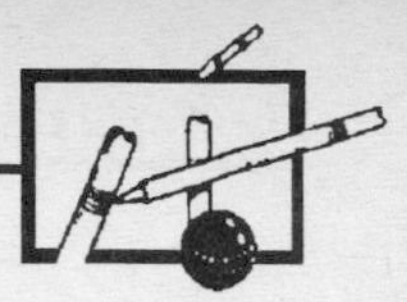

Graeme Pollock blitzed the Trent Bridge boundary with 21 fours

England v South Africa, Second Test, 1965

SOUTH AFRICA

E.J. Barlow	c Cowdrey b Cartwright	19	— b Titmus	76
H.R. Lance	lbw b Cartwright	7	— c Barber b Snow	0
D.T. Lindsay†	c Parks b Cartwright	0	— c Cowdrey b Larter	9
R.G. Pollock	c Cowdrey b Cartwright	125	— c Titmus b Larter	59
K.C. Bland	st Parks b Titmus	1	— b Snow	10
A. Bacher	b Snow	1	— lbw b Larter	67
P.L. van der Merwe*	run out	38	— c Parfitt b Larter	4
R. Dumbrill	c Parfitt b Cartwright	30	— b Snow	13
J.T. Botten	c Parks b Larter	10	— b Larter	18
P.M. Pollock	c Larter b Cartwright	15	— not out	12
A.H. McKinnon	not out	8	— b Titmus	9
Extras	(LB 4)	4	(B 4, LB 5, NB 3)	12
Total		**269**		**289**

ENGLAND

G. Boycott	c Lance b P.M. Pollock	0	— b McKinnon	16
R.W. Barber	c Bacher b Dumbrill	41	— c Lindsay b P.M. Pollock	1
K.F. Barrington	b P.M. Pollock	1	— c Lindsay b P.M. Pollock	1
F.J. Titmus	c R.G. Pollock b McKinnon	20	— c Lindsay b McKinnon	4
M.C. Cowdrey	c Lindsay b Botten	105	— st Lindsay b McKinnon	20
P.H. Parfitt	c Dumbrill b P.M. Pollock	18	— b P.M. Pollock	86
M.J.K. Smith*	b P.M. Pollock	32	— lbw b R.G. Pollock	24
J.M. Parks†	c and b Botten	6	— not out	44
J.A. Snow	run out	3	— b Botten	0
J.D.F. Larter	b P.M. Pollock	2	— c van der Merwe b P.M. Poll.	10
T.W. Cartwright	not out	1	— lbw b P.M. Pollock	0
Extras	(B 1, LB 3, W 1, NB 6)	11	(LB 5, W 2, NB 11)	18
Total		**240**		**224**

ENGLAND	O	M	R	W	O	M	R	W
Larter	17	6	25	1	29	7	68	5
Snow	22	6	63	1	33	6	83	3
Cartwright	31.3	9	94	6				
Titmus	22	8	44	1	19.4	5	46	2
Barber	9	3	39	0	3	0	20	0
Boycott					26	10	60	0

SOUTH AFRICA	O	M	R	W	O	M	R	W
P.M. Pollock	23.5	8	53	5	24	15	34	5
Botten	23	5	60	2	19	5	58	1
McKinnon	28	11	54	1	27	12	50	3
Dumbrill	18	3	60	1	16	4	40	0
R.G. Pollock	1	0	2	0	5	2	4	1
Barlow					7	1	20	0

FALL OF WICKETS

Wkt	SA 1st	E 1st	SA 2nd	E 2nd
1st	16	0	2	1
2nd	16	8	35	10
3rd	42	63	134	10
4th	43	67	193	13
5th	80	133	228	41
6th	178	225	232	59
7th	221	229	243	114
8th	242	236	265	207
9th	252	238	269	207
10th	269	240	289	224

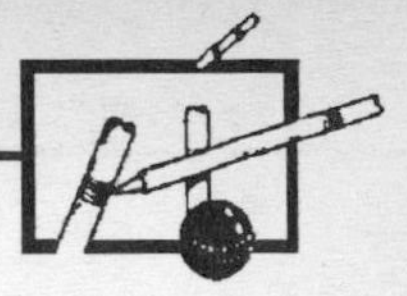

1966 Basil steers jeers to cheers as he butchers England

Match: England v West Indies, Third Test
Venue: Trent Bridge **Date:** June 30, July 1, 2, 4, 5

THE SETTING: When West Indies skipper Garfield Sobers won the toss he eyed the Trent Bridge pitch that he knew so well with some suspicion.

It looked fast and true, and Sobers wondered whether he might not be best off putting England in to bat against his dynamic duo of Wes Hall and Charlie Griffiths, who had the pace to make even slow wickets seem fast.

But after deliberating, Sobers elected to bat and must have wondered about the wisdom of his decision when half the team were back in the pavilion with only 144 runs on the board. These were just the first shocks in a match that was packed with thrilling twists and turns.

THE MATCH: Thirteen wickets went down on the first day for just 268 runs. Three of the fallen wickets belonged to England after the West Indies had been hurried out for what was by their standards a mediocre total of 235.

John Snow (four for 82) and Ken Higgs (four for 71) caused the early collapse, and it was only a sparkling innings by Seymour Nurse (93), supported by studious batting from Peter Lashley (49), that saved a complete rout. But England were feeling less than happy when in the final 50 minutes they lost Geoff Boycott, Colin Milburn and Eric Russell for just 33 runs.

There was enormous responsibility on the shoulders of Tom Graveney and skipper Colin Cowdrey, and they answered the call to duty with a defiant fourth-wicket partnership in the face of some intimidating bowling from the West Indies pace men.

The imperious Graveney was the senior partner, leading the way with his third consecutive century in a Trent Bridge Test before falling to a marvellous left-handed catch in the gully by David Holford. Graveney scored a six and 11 fours in contributing 109 runs to a stand of 172.

Cowdrey departed four runs short of his century but a last-wicket stand of 65 between Basil D'Oliveira (76) and debutant Derek Underwood (12 not out) pushed the score up to 325, and England went into the field holding a useful lead of 90 runs.

D'Oliveira then struck with the ball and sent back openers Conrad Hunte and Lashley with West Indies still 25 runs behind England's first innings total. Basil Butcher joined Rohan Kanhai at the wicket and they were slow handclapped for their stonewall batting while adding just 73 runs in the last two and a half hours of the third day.

But all the jeers for Butcher turned to cheers on the fourth day when he shared in three consecutive century partnerships on his way to an undefeated 209. Butcher's stand with Sobers (94) added 173 runs for the fourth wicket in just 120 minutes. Thanks largely to some slipshod fielding by England, Sobers was able to declare at 482 for five—leaving England a sporting victory target of 393 at exactly a run a minute.

When Colin Milburn hooked Wes Hall for six early in the second innings it looked as if England meant business. But the pace and aggression of Hall and Griffith, supported by the swing of Sobers and the spin of Lance Gibbs proved too much and they were all out for 253 despite a sound foundation innings from Boycott (71) that included a pulled six off Sobers and six fours.

D'Oliveira hit the boundary ten times in a rush to 54, but could not find the partners to match his spirit of adventure. Underwood was again not out, this time for ten runs. He had to show courage to stay at the wicket after an unnecessary bouncer from Griffith had struck him in the mouth.

It was a commendable victory by West Indies considering they started their second innings 90 runs behind and lost their first two wickets when replying for 65 runs. Not many captains would have dared declare leaving England with such a tempting target, but Sobers had total confidence in his bowling strength which was fully justified on the last day.

Sobers had an outstanding captain's match. Apart from his vital innings of 94, he took five wickets (including Boycott for a duck in England's first innings), held five catches, and set attacking fields that always made life difficult for the England batsmen.

THE WITNESSES: Garfield Sobers: 'It was Basil Butcher's innings that swung the match for us. He was criticised for his slow batting on the third day, but it was the right thing to do in the circumstances and his patience paid off. Once he had bedded himself in he produced all the strokes to show what a fine attacking batsman he is.'

Colin Cowdrey: 'We paid the price for not holding our catches. It was Butcher's excellent innings that won the match for them, but there were several occasions when we should have had him out.'

FOR THE RECORD: England lost the series 3-1, with the second Test drawn. Their only victory came in the fifth and final Test when Tom Graveney (165) and John Murray (112) shared an eighth-wicket partnership of 217 in 235 minutes to hoist England's total to 527 and put them on the way to victory by an innings and 34 runs. Graveney celebrated his recall to the England team at Lord's in the second Test with a superbly compiled 96 on what was his 39th birthday. Cousins Sobers (163 not out) and Holford (105 not out) shared an unbroken stand of 274 in the West Indies second innings. Milburn (126 not out) and Graveney (30 not out) had put on 130 when the match finished drawn with England at 197 for four when chasing a victory target of 284 in 240 minutes.

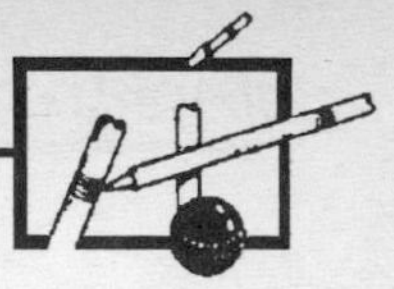

England v West Indies, Third Test, 1966

WEST INDIES

	1st innings		2nd innings	
C.C. Hunte	lbw b Higgs	9	— c Graveney b D'Oliveira	12
P.D. Lashley	c Parks b Snow	49	— lbw b D'Oliveira	23
R.B. Kanhai	c Underwood b Higgs	32	— c Cowdrey b Higgs	63
B.F. Butcher	b Snow	5	— not out	209
S.M. Nurse	c Illingworth b Snow	93	— lbw b Higgs	53
G. St A. Sobers*	c Parks b Snow	3	— c Underwood b Higgs	94
D.A.J. Holford	lbw b D'Oliveira	11	— not out	17
J.L. Hendriks†	b D'Oliveira	2		
C.C. Griffith	c Cowdrey b Higgs	14		
W.W. Hall	b Higgs	12		
L.R. Gibbs	not out	0		
Extras	(B 3, LB 2)	5	(LB 6, W 5)	11
Total		**235**	(5 wickets declared)	**482**

ENGLAND

	1st innings		2nd innings	
G. Boycott	lbw b Sobers	0	— c Sobers b Griffith	71
C. Milburn	c Sobers b Hall	7	— c Griffith b Hall	12
W.E. Russell	b Hall	4	— c Sobers b Gibbs	11
T.W. Graveney	c Holford b Sobers	109	— c Hendriks b Griffith	32
M.C. Cowdrey*	c Hendriks b Griffith	96	— c Sobers b Gibbs	32
J.M. Parks†	c Butcher b Sobers	11	— c Lashley b Hall	7
B.L. D'Oliveira	b Hall	76	— lbw b Griffith	54
R. Illingworth	c Lashley b Griffith	0	— c Lashley b Sobers	4
K. Higgs	c Lashley b Sobers	5	— c Sobers b Gibbs	4
J.A. Snow	b Hall	0	— b Griffith	3
D.L. Underwood	not out	12	— not out	10
Extras	(LB 2, NB 3)	5	(B 8, LB 2, NB 3)	13
Total		**325**		**253**

ENGLAND	O	M	R	W	O	M	R	W
Snow	25	7	82	4	38	10	117	0
Higgs	25.4	3	71	4	38	6	109	3
D'Oliveira	30	14	51	2	34	8	77	2
Underwood	2	1	5	0	43	15	86	0
Illingworth	8	1	21	0	25	7	82	0

WEST INDIES	O	M	R	W	O	M	R	W
Sobers	49	12	90	4	31	6	71	1
Hall	34.3	8	105	4	16	3	52	2
Griffith	20	5	62	2	13.3	3	34	4
Gibbs	23	9	40	0	48	16	83	3
Holford	8	2	23	0				

FALL OF WICKETS

	WI	E	WI	E
Wkt	1st	1st	2nd	2nd
1st	19	0	29	32
2nd	68	10	65	71
3rd	80	13	175	125
4th	140	182	282	132
5th	144	221	455	142
6th	180	238	—	176
7th	190	247	—	181
8th	215	255	—	222
9th	228	260	—	240
10th	235	325	—	253

1967 Barrington completes a full house of Test centuries

Match: England v Pakistan, Third Test
Venue: The Oval **Date:** August 24, 25, 26, 28

THE SETTING: Ken Barrington had scored 18 Test centuries around the world during a distinguished career, but the one arena at which he had never reached a century was on his own special stage at The Oval.

He was a master batsman with Surrey and had dominated many county matches on his home ground, yet a Test century had always eluded him in front of his adoring supporters.

Barrington had just battled through a rough passage in his career. He had been rested by England the previous year during the series against West Indies because he was suffering from the strain of too much front-line cricket.

But against the 1967 Pakistanis he had begun to show all his old command and enthusiasm. He scored centuries in the first two Test matches, and now all eyes were on him as he set out to make it a hat-trick on his favourite Oval pitch.

THE MATCH: England skipper Brian Close won the toss and put Pakistan in to bat on a misty morning. The heavy atmosphere suited the bowling of Geoff Arnold (five for 58) and Ken Higgs (three for 61), who both got movement in the air and off the pitch. Only an inventive innings by the gifted Mushtaq Mohammad (66) prevented a total capitulation and Pakistan were all out for 216.

Brian Close promoted himself to open the England innings after Geoff Boycott had pulled out with a throat infection, but the gamble did not pay off for the England captain who was caught behind by Wasim Bari off the bowling of Intikhab Alam for six. Ken Barrington got a hero's welcome from his home supporters as he walked to the wicket and when he was joined by Tom Graveney with the score at 35 for two the two England veterans put on a show of batting at its best.

Graveney was all elegance and style as he stroked his way to 77 runs, including ten fours. Barrington was more powerful and pugnacious than his partner, and got a lot of his runs with off drives and heavy hooks. They put on 141 runs together before Graveney's glorious innings was ended by a Majid Khan catch off the bowling of Intikhab Alam.

Barrington continued to punish the Pakistan attack and at the end of the day he was not out on 129, and England were in a commanding position at 257 for three. The Surrey bulldog (it was of Barrington that Aussie wicket-keeper Wally Grout once said, 'When Ken walks to the wicket you can see the Union Jack trailing behind him') had thus become the first England batsman to

score a century at each of the six main home Test grounds. It was his 52nd score of 50 or more in his 74 Tests, and this equalled the world record set by Len Hutton.

The sparkle went out of the England batting on the third day, but after Barrington had departed for 142 Freddie Titmus (65) and Geoff Arnold (59) brought about a revival and they were all out for 414 and left Pakistan needing 224 to avoid an innings defeat.

Asif Iqbal produced an exceptional innings just as it looked as if Pakistan were going to be rushed out by Ken Higgs (5-58) who took the first three wickets without conceding a run. Pakistan were 26 for four at the close on the Saturday, and when Asif arrived at the wicket on Bank Holiday Monday morning the score was 53 for seven. It was then odds-on an innings defeat for the tourists. But Asif thrilled the large crowd with a breath-taking innings of 146 off 244 balls in 200 minutes. He slammed two sixes and 21 fours, and he shared a Test record ninth-wicket stand of 190 in 170 minutes with Intikhab (51). When Asif completed his first century in Test cricket the wicket was invaded by hundreds of cheering Pakistani supporters, who chaired their hero shoulder-high around the ground.

Asif finally had to be rescued by police, and he got such a battering from the fans that he needed five minutes to recover.

Due almost entirely to Asif, England were forced to bat again and he then turned hero with the ball, dismissing both Cowdrey and Close before Barrington and Dennis Amiss steered England to victory by eight wickets in the last hour of the fourth day.

THE WITNESSES: Asif Iqbal: 'I had nothing to lose when I went to the wicket, and so I just decided to play my shots. The supporters who came on the pitch meant well, but they gave me a severe battering. It was quite frightening for a moment because I was absolutely swamped by them. It is certainly an innings that I will never forget.'

Ken Barrington: 'Tom Graveney and I had a quick chin-wag and agreed to play it steadily, and to hit any loose balls that came our way. It had always been an ambition of mine to score a Test century at The Oval, and at last I've achieved it. I've got a lot to thank Tom for, because I could not have had a better partner.'

FOR THE RECORD: England won the three-Test series 2-0 after the first Test had ended in a draw. Barrington (148) and Graveney (81) had put on 201 in 223 minutes for the third wicket in the first Test, a partnership that they repeated at The Oval. Hanif Mohammad (187 not out) and Asif Iqbal (76) put on 141 in 191 minutes in an eighth-wicket stand. Alan Knott made his debut in the rain-interrupted second Test at Trent Bridge and claimed seven victims as England romped to a ten wickets victory. His Kent team-mate Derek Underwood took six wickets in the match for 69 runs. Barrington scored 109 not out, but this time at a snail's pace. He was at the wicket for nearly seven hours.

England v Pakistan, Third Test, 1967

PAKISTAN

Hanif Mohammad*	b Higgs	3	— c Knott b Higgs	18
Mohammad Ilyas	b Arnold	2	— c Cowdrey b Higgs	1
Saeed Ahmed	b Arnold	38	— c Knott b Higgs	0
Majid Khan	c Knott b Arnold	6	— b Higgs	0
Mushtaq Mohammad	lbw b Higgs	66	— c D'Oliveira b Underwood	17
Javed Burki	c D'Oliveira b Titmus	27	— b Underwood	7
Ghulam Abbas	c Underwood b Titmus	12	— c Knott b Higgs	0
Asif Iqbal	c Close b Arnold	26	— st Knott b Close	146
Intikhab Alam	b Higgs	20	— b Titmus	51
Wasim Bari†	c Knott b Arnold	1	— b Titmus	12
Salim Altaf	not out	7	— not out	0
Extras	(B 5, LB 2, NB 1)	8	(B 1, LB 1, NB 1)	3
Total		**216**		**255**

ENGLAND

M.C. Cowdrey	c Mushtaq b Majid	16	— c Intikhab b Asif	9
D.B. Close*	c Wasim b Asif	6	— b Asif	8
K.F. Barrington	c Wasim b Salim	142	— not out	13
T.W. Graveney	c Majid b Intikhab	77		
D.L. Amiss	c Saeed b Asif	26	— not out	3
B.L. D'Oliveira	c Mushtaq b Asif	3		
F.J. Titmus	c sub b Mushtaq	65		
A.P.E. Knott†	c Ilyas b Mushtaq	28		
G.G. Arnold	c Majid b Mushtaq	59		
K. Higgs	b Mushtaq	7		
D.L. Underwood	not out	2		
Extras	(LB 4, NB 5)	9	(NB 1)	1
Total		**440**	(2 wickets)	**34**

ENGLAND	O	M	R	W	O	M	R	W
Arnold	29	9	58	5	17	5	49	0
Higgs	29	10	61	3	20	7	58	5
D'Oliveira	17	6	41	0				
Close	5	1	15	0	1	0	4	1
Titmus	13	6	21	2	29.1	8	64	2
Underwood	9	5	12	0	26	12	48	2
Barrington					8	2	29	0

PAKISTAN	O	M	R	W	O	M	R	W
Salim	40	14	94	1	2	1	8	0
Asif	42	19	66	3	4	1	14	2
Majid	10	0	29	1				
Mushtaq	26.4	7	80	4				
Saeed	21	5	69	0	2	0	7	0
Intikhab	28	3	93	1				
Hanif					0.2	0	4	0

FALL OF WICKETS

	P	E	P	E
Wkt	1st	1st	2nd	2nd
1st	3	16	1	17
2nd	5	35	5	20
3rd	17	176	5	—
4th	74	270	26	—
5th	138	276	26	—
6th	155	276	41	—
7th	182	323	53	—
8th	188	416	65	—
9th	194	437	255	—
10th	216	440	255	—

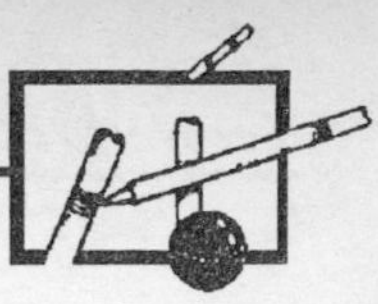

Underwood mops up seven in an Oval water miracle

Match: England v Australia, Fifth Test
Venue: The Oval **Date:** August 22, 23, 24, 26, 27

THE SETTING: What the scoreboard for this astounding match fails to show is that England had the support of hundreds of hidden heroes who made what seemed an impossible victory possible.

Australia looked a beaten side at 85 for five at lunch on the final day, but just as the players entered the pavilion the heavens suddenly opened and rain came bucketing down. In no time at all the Oval ground was hidden under a giant lake, and an abandonment seemed the only decision left to the umpires. Then, just as suddenly as it had started, the freak storm passed over and the sun beat down on what was now a shimmering lagoon covering the entire pitch. Hundreds of spectators became volunteer groundsmen and began prodding the waterlogged ground with wooden staves.

After two hours of mopping-up and baling-out duty, the army of helpers and the expert groundstaff had the satisfaction of seeing the water almost miraculously drain away. Forty-five minutes after the tea interval play resumed on a sodden, sawdust-covered ground that was drying rapidly under the sun. There was no better bowler in the world suited to such conditions than Kent's deadly left-arm spinner Derek Underwood.

THE MATCH: John Edrich (164), Basil D'Oliveira (158) and Tom Graveney (63) were the chief run compilers in an England total of 494 after Colin Cowdrey had won the toss. Bill Lawry (135), Ian Redpath (67) and Ashley Mallett (43 not out) were the only batsmen to make substantial scores in Australia's reply of 324.

England surrendered wickets in a mad run chase in their second innings, and were all out for 181 to leave Australia requiring 352 runs to win in seven hours.

The tourists never got within sight of their target of 54 runs an hour, and lost their first four wickets for 29 and only opener John Inverarity was left of their recognised batsmen when the rains came down.

For 40 minutes after tea on the final day, Inverarity—surrounded by England fielders—led a rearguard action that looked likely to save the match and win the series for the Australians. But when with just a little over half an hour of play left D'Oliveira bowled Barry Jarman with a leg-cutter Cowdrey called Underwood back to bowl from the pavilion end.

Ashley Mallett and Graham McKenzie fell to the first and sixth balls of his first over. Australia had lost three wickets without scoring and were 110 for 8. John Gleeson survived until 12 minutes from the end before Underwood bowled him with a vicious spinner. With just five minutes left, the defiant Inverarity padded up to one of the few balls from Underwood that did not turn and was given out lbw as the ball rapped him on the pads. He was first man in and last man out with Australia 226 runs short of their target but just minutes away from an amazing draw.

Underwood's final figures were seven for 50 off 31.3 overs.

THE WITNESSES: Derek Underwood: 'We all thought the thunderstorm had robbed us of victory, and we were quite miserable during the lunch interval. It was incredible the way the spectators joined the groundstaff in clearing the water and even more incredible that they managed to get it fit for play.'

John Inverarity: 'It was heartbreaking to get so close to saving the match. I couldn't believe it when the Underwood delivery that got me leg before kept straight. Just about every other ball he bowled that afternoon had turned. The crowd worked miracles to get the ground cleared of the water, but in all honesty it wasn't really fit for play.'

FOR THE RECORD: Australia won the first Test by 159 runs, thanks to solid batting performances by Bill Lawry (81), Paul Sheahan (88), Ian Chappell (73) and Doug Walters (81 and 86). Pat Pocock took six for 79 in Australia's second innings. Rain wrecked the second and third Tests, both of which ended in draws. The fourth Test was also drawn, with England on 230 for four at the close on the final day when chasing a victory target of 326 in 295 minutes.

Derek Underwood mopped up seven Australian wickets at The Oval

England v Australia, Fifth Test, 1968

ENGLAND

J.H. Edrich	b Chappell	164	— c Lawry b Mallett	17
C. Milburn	b Connolly	8	— c Lawry b Connolly	18
E.R. Dexter	b Gleeson	21	— b Connolly	28
M.C. Cowdrey*	lbw b Mallett	16	— b Mallett	35
T.W. Graveney	c Redpath b McKenzie	63	— run out	12
B.L. D'Oliveira	c Inverarity b Mallett	158	— c Gleeson b Connolly	9
A.P.E. Knott†	c Jarman b Mallett	28	— run out	34
R. Illingworth	lbw b Connolly	8	— b Gleeson	10
J.A. Snow	run out	4	— c Sheahan b Gleeson	13
D.L. Underwood	not out	9	— not out	1
D.J. Brown	c Sheahan b Gleeson	2	— b Connolly	1
Extras	(B 1, LB 11, W 1)	13	(LB 3)	3
Total		**494**		**181**

AUSTRALIA

W.M. Lawry*	c Knott b Snow	135	— c Milburn b Brown	4
R.J. Inverarity	c Milburn b Snow	1	— lbw b Underwood	56
I.R. Redpath	c Cowdrey b Snow	67	— lbw b Underwood	8
I.M. Chappell	c Knott b Brown	10	— lbw b Underwood	2
K.D. Walters	c Knott b Brown	5	— c Knott b Underwood	1
A.P. Sheahan	b Illingworth	14	— c Snow b Illingworth	24
B.N. Jarman†	st Knott b Illingworth	0	— b D'Oliveira	21
G.D. McKenzie	b Brown	12	— c Brown b Underwood	0
A.A. Mallett	not out	43	— c Brown b Underwood	0
J.W. Gleeson	c Dexter b Underwood	19	— b Underwood	5
A.N. Connolly	b Underwood	3	— not out	0
Extras	(B 4, LB 7, NB 4)	15	(LB 4)	4
Total		**324**		**125**

AUSTRALIA	O	M	R	W	O	M	R	W
McKenzie	40	8	87	1	4	0	14	0
Connolly	57	12	127	2	22.4	2	65	4
Walters	6	2	17	0				
Gleeson	41.2	8	109	2	7	2	22	2
Mallett	36	11	87	3	25	4	77	2
Chappell	21	5	54	1				

ENGLAND	O	M	R	W	O	M	R	W
Snow	35	12	67	3	11	5	22	0
Brown	22	5	63	3	8	3	19	1
Illingworth	48	15	87	2	28	18	29	1
Underwood	54.3	21	89	2	31.3	19	50	7
D'Oliveira	4	2	3	0	5	4	1	1

FALL OF WICKETS

Wkt	E 1st	A 1st	E 2nd	A 2nd
1st	28	7	23	4
2nd	84	136	53	13
3rd	113	151	67	19
4th	238	161	90	29
5th	359	185	114	65
6th	421	188	126	110
7th	458	237	149	110
8th	468	269	179	110
9th	489	302	179	120
10th	494	324	181	125

1968-69 Last-wicket pair force draw in an Adelaide run feast

Match: Australia v West Indies, Fourth Test
Venue: Adelaide Oval **Date:** January 24, 25, 27, 28, 29

THE SETTING: It has to be something special for a drawn match to warrant a billing as one of the greatest of all Tests, and this game in Adelaide had all the ingredients that go to make a match memorable long after the final ball has been bowled.

The game went into cricket's hall of fame not only because it was the highest-scoring Test ever played in Australia, but also because at the end of the feast of scoring only 20 runs and one wicket separated the two sides.

In a tense and exciting finish, Australia's tenth wicket pair were together with three eight-ball overs and a new ball to face.

THE MATCH: The West Indies batsmen seemed intent on throwing away their wickets with a catalogue of careless shots during a first innings in which only a storming century from Garfield Sobers (110) and a useful 52 from Basil Butcher signalled the runs that were available on an easy-paced pitch.

The tourists were all out for 276, more because of their lackadaisical attitude than any devilment in the bowling. Australia occupied the wicket for the next two days, with Doug Walters giving a repeat of the Sobers innings with a score of 110. He was the only player to reach three figures, but skipper Bill Lawry (62), Keith Stackpole (62), Ian Chappell (76), Paul Sheahan (51) and Graham McKenzie (59) all topped the half-century and collectively they pushed the Aussie reply to a total of 533 and a commanding lead of 257.

West Indies applied themselves much better in their second innings, but their star batsmen were still tending to lose their wickets through loose shots after getting set for big scores. Despite a century from Basil Butcher (118) and healthy contributions from Joey Carew (90), Rohan Kanhai (80), Sobers (52), Clive Lloyd (42) and a lightning strike of 40 from Seymour Nurse, the tourists were only 235 runs ahead at tea on the fourth day at 492 for eight.

Then an outstanding ninth-wicket partnership between David Holford (80) and Jackie Hendricks (37 not out) added 122 in two hours 20 minutes and suddenly Australia saw the likelihood of victory slipping away towards the possibility of defeat.

West Indies were all out for 616, their highest total in Australia. Alan Connolly bowled his heart out for a return of five wickets for 122. Spinner John Gleeson had his heart broken after getting hammered for 176 for the reward of one wicket.

The Australians were left a last-day goal of 360 runs in five and

three-quarter hours, and Lawry (89), Keith Stackpole (50), Ian Chappell (96) and Doug Walters (50) hoisted them to within reach of the target with some aggressive batting. There was some ill feeling threaded into the action when non-striker Ian Redpath was run out by bowler Charlie Griffith while backing-up before the ball had been delivered.

Australia were 298 for three and requiring 62 runs from 120 balls when the last hour started.

Ian Chappell was leg before to Griffith four short of his century and in the next 15 minutes the Aussies committed a cricketing form of hara-kiri as Walters, Eric Freeman and Barry Jarman were all run out. Paul Sheahan was the batsman at the opposite end during each dismissal.

Graham McKenzie was caught trying to swing Lance Gibbs to square leg and then Gleeson was out leg before to Griffith. The Aussies had slumped from 304 for four to 333 for nine.

Sheahan and Connolly were thrown together as last-wicket partners to face 26 balls—16 of them with the new ball in the hands of the West Indies pacemen.

Sobers was off target with his deliveries, sending the ball swinging wildly down the leg side. Sheahan played two maidens and the game finished drawn with just 20 separating the two teams after 1,764 runs had been scored.

As they came off at the end, Sheahan (11 not out) and Connolly (6 not out) got the kind of reception from the crowd usually reserved for century-makers.

THE WITNESSES: Garfield Sobers: 'It was almost as exciting and dramatic as our tied Test with Australia eight years earlier. It was frustrating for us that we couldn't break the last partnership, but the result was a good one for cricket.'

Bill Lawry: 'The turning point was the three run outs. Suddenly from trying to win the match we were having to fight like mad to save it. The last ten minutes of the match seemed more like ten hours.'

FOR THE RECORD: Australia won the six-day fifth Test by 382 runs to win the series 3-1. It was a memorable Test for Doug Walters who became the first player to score a century and a double century in the same Test. He scored 242 in the first innings and shared a fourth wicket partnership of 336 with Lawry (151). In the second innings Walters (103) put on 210 runs for the fourth wicket with Ian Redpath (132). Sobers (113) and Nurse (137) scored centuries for West Indies in their second innings but they were nowhere near their victory target of 735. Lawry (105) and Ian Chappell (117) scored centuries in the first Test but could not stop West Indies winning by 125 runs thanks to a century by Lloyd (129) and some fine swing bowling in the second innings by Sobers (six for 73). Lawry (205) and Chappell (165), plus match figures of ten for 159 by Graham McKenzie, set up Australia's victory by an innings and 30 runs in the second Test. Walters (118) and Butcher (101) both scored centuries in the third Test won by Australia by ten wickets.

Australia v West Indies, Fourth Test, 1968-69

WEST INDIES

R.C. Fredricks	lbw b Connolly	17	— c Chappell b Connolly	23
M.C. Carew	c Chappell b Gleeson	36	— c Chappell b Connolly	90
R.B. Kanhai	lbw b Connolly	11	— b Connolly	80
B.F. Butcher	c Chappell b Gleeson	52	— c Sheahan b McKenzie	118
S.M. Nurse	c and b McKenzie	5	— lbw b Gleeson	40
G. St A. Sobers*	b Freeman	110	— c Walters b Connolly	52
C.H. Lloyd	c Lawry b Gleeson	10	— c Redpath b Connolly	42
D.A.J. Holford	c McKenzie b Freeman	6	— c Stackpole b McKenzie	80
C.C. Griffith	b Freeman	7	— run out	24
J.L. Hendriks†	not out	10	— not out	37
L.R. Gibbs	c Connolly b Freeman	4	— b McKenzie	1
Extras	(B 5, LB 2, NB 1)	8	(B 5, LB 12, NB 12)	29
Total		**276**		**616**

AUSTRALIA

W.M. Lawry*	c Butcher b Sobers	62	— c sub b Sobers	89
K.R. Stackpole	c Hendriks b Holford	62	— c Hendriks b Gibbs	50
I.M. Chappell	c Sobers b Gibbs	76	— lbw b Griffith	96
I.R. Redpath	lbw b Carew	45	— run out	9
K.D. Walters	c and b Griffith	110	— run out	50
A.P. Sheahan	b Gibbs	51	— not out	11
E.W. Freeman	lbw b Griffith	33	— run out	1
B.N. Jarman†	c Hendriks b Gibbs	3	— run out	4
G.D. McKenzie	c Nurse b Holford	59	— c sub b Gibbs	4
J.W. Gleeson	b Gibbs	17	— lbw b Griffith	0
A.N. Connolly	not out	1	— not out	6
Extras	(B 3, LB 6, NB 5)	14	(B 8, LB 10, NB 1)	19
Total		**533**	(9 wickets)	**339**

AUSTRALIA	O	M	R	W	O	M	R	W
McKenzie	14	1	51	1	22.2	4	90	3
Connolly	13	3	61	2	34	7	122	5
Freeman	10.3	0	52	4	18	3	96	0
Gleeson	25	5	91	3	35	2	176	1
Stackpole	3	1	13	0	12	3	44	0
Chappell					14	0	50	0
Walters					1	0	6	0
Redpath					1	0	3	0

WEST INDIES	O	M	R	W	O	M	R	W
Sobers	28	4	106	1	22	1	107	1
Griffith	22	4	94	2	19	2	73	2
Holford	18.5	0	118	2	15	1	53	2
Gibbs	43	8	145	4	26	7	79	2
Carew	9	3	30	1	2	0	8	0
Lloyd	6	0	26	0				

FALL OF WICKETS

Wkt	WI 1st	A 1st	WI 2nd	A 2nd
1st	21	89	35	86
2nd	39	170	167	185
3rd	89	248	240	215
4th	107	254	304	304
5th	199	345	376	315
6th	215	424	404	318
7th	228	429	476	322
8th	261	465	492	333
9th	264	529	614	333
10th	276	533	616	—

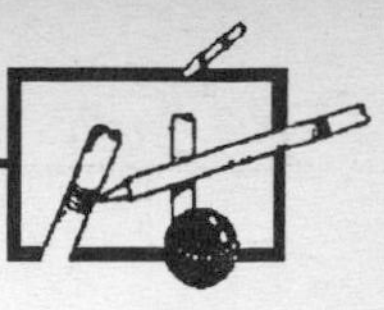

1969-70 Pollock and Richards touch a rare peak of perfection

Match: South Africa v Australia, Second Test
Venue: Kingsmead, Durban **Date:** February 5, 6, 7, 9

THE SETTING: Bill Lawry led an Australian team to South Africa that was brimming with confidence after successful tours of England, the West Indies and India.

Their team was packed with talented players. Supporting Lawry with the bat were prolific scorers of the quality of Ian Chappell, Doug Walters, Ian Redpath and Keith Stackpole. Graham McKenzie was the main strike bowler, and he had support from the giant-hearted Alan Connolly. In Johnny Gleeson they had an unorthodox spinner who had been baffling some of the finest batsmen in the world.

The Australian confidence was dented in the first Test in Cape Town where they came up against South Africa's new discoveries Barry Richards and Mike Procter, who had joined forces with established stars like Graeme and Peter Pollock, Eddie Barlow, Lee Irvine, Denis Lindsay and the veteran all-rounder Trevor Goddard.

South Africa won the first Test by 170 runs, but it proved just a dress rehearsal for a full production of their power in the electrifying second Test in Durban.

THE MATCH: Bill Lawry lodged an official protest before a ball had been bowled because South African skipper Ali Bacher had ordered an extra cut of the wicket after winning the toss and deciding to bat. Barry Richards and Graeme Pollock did not allow the grass to grow under their feet and pushed the argument between the captains out of their minds as they concentrated on gathering runs at a phenomenal pace.

The rampant Richards was just six runs short of a century before lunch on the first morning, and he reached his first 100 in Test cricket off only 116 balls. The 24-year-old Natal and Hampshire opener scored 140 of the 229 runs on the board before he was finally bowled by Eric Freeman. Richards had Graeme Pollock as his partner for his last hour at the wicket and together they gave an exhibition of attacking cricket that was considered by onlookers to have rivalled the finest ever witnessed in a Test match. They added 103 for the third wicket with a series of copybook strokes.

Pollock dominated the stage once Richards had departed. Gliding and glancing the ball to all parts of the field with consummate ease, he stroked 43 fours and ran a five on his merry way to the highest score by any Test batsman in South Africa. He was eventually caught and bowled by Stackpole for 274 after a record sixth-wicket partnership of

200 with Herbert 'Tiger' Lance (61), who played a supporting role while Pollock took the Australian attack apart .

His onslaught against an Australian team demoralised by a procession of dropped catches lasted 417 minutes, and it allowed Ali Bacher to declare with a colossal 622 for nine on the scoreboard

The tourists managed to make batting seem difficult on a pitch on which the South Africans always looked comfortable. Lawry and Stackpolc put on 44 for the first wicket in even time, but then in the space of ten deliveries Eddie Barlow sent back key batsmen Lawry, Chappell and Walters. From 44 for 0, the Aussies were struggling at 44 for three and then 48 for four. Half the team were out for 56 before Paul Sheahan (62) staged a one-man fight back, but he could not find a partner to stay with him as Procter and Peter Pollock polished off the tail.

All out for 157 and still 465 runs behind, the Australians were invited to follow on and the second time around they showed more backbone after an opening stand of 65 between Stackpole (71) and Lawry (14). Walters and Redpath started to raise Australian hopes of saving the game as they dug in, but once Walters had departed for 74 Redpath ran out of established partners. It was Barlow who again caused the major problems, whipping out Freeman, Taber and McKenzie in quick succession for just four runs.

The valiant Redpath was unbeaten on 74 when the innings closed at 336 with a full day's play still remaining.

THE WITNESSES: Barry Richards: 'It was near perfection when Graeme and I were together at the wicket. We inspired each other, and both of us were really middling the ball. The sort of form Graeme was in, I would have hated to have been bowling to him. He broke a lot of Australian hearts.'

Ali Bacher: 'There could not have been many better batting performances in the history of Test cricket than those given by Graeme and Barry. Both were in command from the first ball they received. It was a pleasure to watch from the pavilion.'

Bill Lawry: 'I am not one for making excuses, but it has to be said that I have never skippered a side with so many players out of form at the same time. Perhaps we came here too soon after our tour of India. Richards and Pollock both played exceptionally well, and are now established as world-class batsmen.'

FOR THE RECORD: South Africa won one of the most unequal Test series in history 4-0. They outplayed the Australians in every department, scoring six centuries and building five century partnerships to none by the tourists. The Springboks averaged 40 runs per wicket throughout the series to just 22 by the Aussies. Most worrying of all for Bill Lawry's team was the breakdown of the bowling attack. Main strike bowler Graham McKenzie had a miserable tour and finished the series with one wicket for 333 runs. Barry Richards averaged 72.57 for the four Tests, the last played by South Africa before their isolation from world cricket.

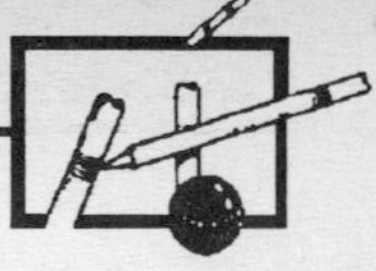

S. Africa v Australia, Second Test, 1969-70

SOUTH AFRICA

B.A. Richards	b Freeman	140
T.L. Goddard	c Lawry b Gleeson	17
A. Bacher*	b Connolly	9
R.G. Pollock	c and b Stackpole	274
E.J. Barlow	lbw b Freeman	1
B.L. Irvine	b Gleeson	13
H.R. Lance	st Taber b Gleeson	61
M.J. Procter	c Connolly b Stackpole	32
D. Gamsy†	lbw b Connolly	7
P.M. Pollock	not out	36
A.J. Traicos	not out	5
Extras	(B 1, LB 3, NB 23)	27
Total	(9 wickets declared)	**622**

AUSTRALIA

K.R. Stackpole	c Gamsy b Goddard	27	— lbw b Traicos	71
W.M. Lawry*	lbw b Barlow	15	— c Gamsy b Goddard	14
I.M. Chappell	c Gamsy b Barlow	0	— c Gamsy b P.M. Pollock	14
K.D. Walters	c Traicos b Barlow	4	— c R.G. Pollock b Traicos	74
I.R. Redpath	c Richards b Procter	4	— not out	74
A.P. Sheahan	c Traicos b Goddard	62	— c Barlow b Procter	4
E.W. Freeman	c Traicos b P.M. Pollock	5	— b Barlow	18
H.B. Taber†	c and b P.M. Pollock	6	— c Lance b Barlow	0
G.D. McKenzie	c Traicos b Procter	1	— lbw b Barlow	4
J.W. Gleeson	not out	4	— c Gamsy b Procter	24
A.N. Connolly	c Bacher b Traicos	14	— lbw b Procter	0
Extras	(LB 5, NB 10)	15	(B 9, LB 8, NB 22)	39
Total		**157**		**336**

AUSTRALIA	O	M	R	W
McKenzie	25.5	3	92	0
Connolly	33	7	104	2
Freeman	28	4	120	2
Gleeson	51	9	160	3
Walters	9	0	44	0
Stackpole	21	2	75	2

SOUTH AFRICA	O	M	R	W	O	M	R	W
Procter	11	2	39	2	18.5	5	62	3
P.M. Pollock	10	3	31	2	21.3	4	45	1
Goddard	7	4	10	2	17	7	30	1
Barlow	10	3	24	3	31	10	63	3
Traicos	8.2	3	27	1	30	8	70	2
Lance	2	0	11	0	7	4	11	0
Richards					3	1	8	0
R.G. Pollock					3	1	8	0

FALL OF WICKETS

Wkt	SA 1st	A 1st	A 2nd
1st	88	44	65
2nd	126	44	83
3rd	229	44	151
4th	231	48	208
5th	281	56	222
6th	481	79	264
7th	558	100	264
8th	575	114	268
9th	580	139	336
10th	—	157	336

1970-71 Snow drops in Sydney and Lawry's men are buried

Match: Australia v England, Fourth Test
Venue: Sydney **Date:** January 9, 10, 11, 13, 14

THE SETTING: Australia and England went into the fourth Test at Sydney deadlocked at 0-0 in the series. The first two Tests had ended drawn and the third had been washed out without a ball being bowled after the two captains, Bill Lawry and Ray Illingworth, had tossed under a leaden sky in Melbourne.

Illingworth, a demanding perfectionist of a captain, had moulded England into one of the most formidable teams to tour Down Under. There had been more individually talented sides, but few to match the will to win and total determination that Illingworth had instilled into the team.

He had gone to Australia with the one target in mind of regaining the Ashes, and with fellow-Yorkshireman Geoff Boycott and Sussex fast bowler John Snow at the peak of their powers, he knew he had two aces who could give him a winning hand. They both came up trumps in Sydney.

THE MATCH: Boycott and Brian Luckhurst gave England a flying send-off with an opening stand of 116 off the first 31 overs. So often criticised for his negative attitude, Boycott was in free-flowing form and struck 11 fours before being caught on the boundary while trying to add to the 77 runs he had contributed to the partnership. England looked set for a mammoth score at 201 for two, but then four wickets tumbled for the addition of only 18 runs. Ashley Mallett, cagey South Australian off-spinner, caused the collapse when he took three wickets for six runs immediately after the tea interval.

John Snow (37), Peter Lever (36) and Bob Willis (15 not out) wielded the bat so effectively that the last four wickets put on 119 to boost the England total to 332.

Only Ian Redpath (64) and Doug Walters (55) played with any confidence when Australia replied against a varied England attack, and Derek Underwood claimed four of the last six Aussie wickets that went down for 47 on the third morning.

England, trying to build on a lead of 96, lost their first three wickets for 48 including the untidy run-out of John Edrich by Boycott. He made up for his lapse by sharing stands of 133 with Basil D'Oliveira and 95 with skipper Illingworth. Boycott was so dominant that his unbeaten 142 enabled Illingworth to declare at 319 for five, leaving Australia over nine hours to try to get 416 runs.

Enter John Snow. On a wicket more suited to spin than pace, he produced the best bowling performance of his career. His leg cutter in particular caused consternation

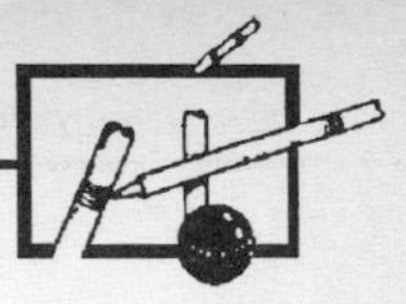

among the Australian batsmen, several of whom took painful knocks. They were hesitant about playing forward to any full length ball as Snow smacked his venomous deliveries continually into the rough patches left by the other bowlers. Bill Lawry, patiently building a fighting captain's innings, could only watch in dismay from the other end as Snow sent a procession of victims back to the pavilion.

Snow finished with figures of seven for 40 off 17.5 overs and rushed the Aussies to defeat by 299 runs. Lawry had the consolation of carrying his bat through the wreckage of the innings and being 60 not out.

THE WITNESSES: John Snow: 'It was my most memorable day in Test cricket. Geoff Boycott made it all possible with a magnificent knock that gave us the runs with which to play. It meant we could set a really attacking field, and I was supported by some first-class fielding.'

Ray Illingworth: 'John bowled as well as any fast bowler I've ever seen. Few batsmen in the world could have played him. He got chest-high bounce from only just short of a length, got movement off the pitch and he always bowled a perfect line.'

FOR THE RECORD: A seventh Test was added at Sydney to make up for the washed-out Third Test. England won it by 62 runs to regain the Ashes by a 2-0 margin, with the rest of the Tests drawn. It was a bad-tempered match during which Illingworth led the England team off the field following crowd disturbances after a Snow bouncer had struck Terry Jenner on the head.

John Snow rushed the Australians to defeat with a fiery spell at Sydney

Australia v England, Fourth Test, 1970-71

ENGLAND

G. Boycott	c Gleeson b Connolly	77	— not out	142
B.W. Luckhurst	lbw b Gleeson	38	— c I. Chappell b McKenzie	5
J.H. Edrich	c Gleeson b G. Chappell	55	— run out	12
K.W.R. Fletcher	c Walters b Mallett	23	— c Stackpole b Mallett	8
B.L. D'Oliveira	c Connolly b Mallett	0	— c I. Chappell b G. Chappell	56
R. Illingworth*	b Gleeson	25	— st Marsh b Mallett	53
A.P.E. Knott†	st Marsh b Mallett	6	— not out	21
J.A. Snow	c Lawry b Gleeson	37		
P. Lever	c Connolly b Mallett	36		
D.L. Underwood	c G. Chappell b Gleeson	0		
R.G.D. Willis	not out	15		
Extras	(B 5, LB 2, W 1, NB 12)	20	— (B 9, LB 4, NB 9)	22
Total		332	(5 wickets declared)	**319**

AUSTRALIA

W.M. Lawry*	c Edrich b Lever	9	— not out	60
I.M. Chappell	c Underwood b Snow	12	— c D'Oliveira b Snow	0
I.R. Redpath	c Fletcher b D'Oliveira	64	— c Edrich b Snow	6
K.D. Walters	c Luckhurst b Illingworth	55	— c Knott b Lever	3
G.S. Chappell	c and b Underwood	15	— b Snow	2
K.R. Stackpole	c Boycott b Underwood	33	— c Lever b Snow	30
R.W. Marsh†	c D'Oliveira b Underwood	8	— c Willis b Snow	0
A.A. Mallett	b Underwood	4	— c Knott b Willis	6
G.D. McKenzie	not out	11	— retired hurt	6
J.W. Gleeson	c Fletcher b D'Oliveira	0	— b Snow	0
A.N. Connolly	b Lever	14	— c Knott b Snow	0
Extras	(NB 11)	11	— (B 2, NB 1)	3
Total		**236**		**116**

AUSTRALIA	O	M	R	W	O	M	R	W
McKenzie	15	3	74	0	15	0	65	1
Connolly	13	2	43	1	14	1	38	0
Gleeson	29	7	83	4	23	4	54	0
G.S. Chappell	11	4	30	1	15	5	24	1
Mallett	16.7	5	40	4	19	1	85	2
Walters	3	1	11	0	2	0	14	0
Stackpole	7	2	31	0	6	1	17	0

ENGLAND	O	M	R	W	O	M	R	W
Snow	14	6	23	1	17.5	5	40	7
Willis	9	2	26	0	3	2	1	1
Lever	8.6	1	31	2	11	1	24	1
Underwood	22	7	66	4	8	2	17	0
Illingworth	14	3	59	1	9	5	9	0
D'Oliveira	9	2	20	2	7	3	16	0
Fletcher					1	0	6	0

FALL OF WICKETS

	E	A	E	A
Wkt	1st	1st	2nd	2nd
1st	116	14	7	1
2nd	130	38	35	11
3rd	201	137	48	14
4th	205	160	181	21
5th	208	189	276	66
6th	219	199	—	66
7th	262	208	—	86
8th	291	208	—	116
9th	291	219	—	116
10th	332	236	—	—

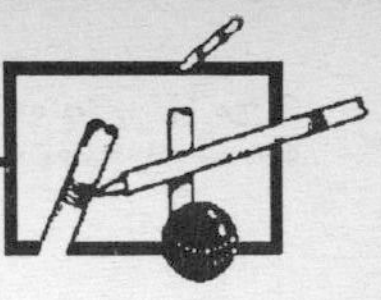

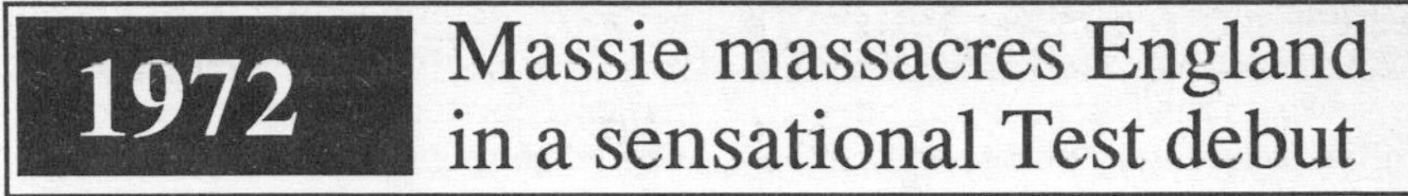

1972 Massie massacres England in a sensational Test debut

Match: England v Australia, Second Test
Venue: Lord's **Date:** June 22, 23, 24, 26

THE SETTING: We need to go back two years to 1970 to put into perspective the mind-boggling performance of Australian medium-fast bowler Bob Massie in his Test debut against England.

Massie had been playing in the Scottish League and was offered a trial by Northamptonshire. He was picked for Northants Second Eleven and in two matches returned the uninspiring figures of three wickets for 166 runs. Northants decided not to offer him a contract, and nobody expected to hear of him again in the context of first-class cricket.

Two years later the 25-year-old Western Australian from Perth earned a trip back to England as a member of the 1972 touring party after taking six for 27 in 11 overs for Australia against the Rest of the World.

England beat the Australians by 89 runs in the first Test at Old Trafford, and the tourists called up Massie for the second Test as partner to Dennis Lillee who had taken eight wickets at Old Trafford without any real support. The selectors wondered whether Massie could be the man to play second fiddle to the formidable Lillee.

THE MATCH: England were first to bat after a light drizzle had delayed the start for 25 minutes. Lillee, bowling flat out, quickly sent back John Edrich (10) and Brian Luckhurst (1), and Massie emitted early danger signals to the England batsmen by clean bowling Geoff Boycott for 11.

Determined batting by Mike Smith (34), Basil D'Oliveira (32), Tony Grieg (54) and Alan Knott (43) raised the England score to 249 for seven at the close on the first day. They all had something in common—the four of them were dismissed by Massie.

The new ball was due early the next morning and Massie quickly snatched the remaining three wickets to finish with eight wickets for 84 runs off 32.5 overs. It was an astonishing debut performance...and there was much more still to come.

Australia made a nightmare start in reply. Bruce Francis was bowled for a duck by John Snow and then with just seven runs on the scoreboard Keith Stackpole was caught by Norman Gifford off the bowling of John Price.

It then became the Chappell brothers versus England—and it was, relatively speaking, a triumph for the family cricketers. While skipper Ian attacked with aggression and fire, his younger brother Greg was content to play a sound and sensible supporting role. Once Ian had departed for 56, Greg took over as the main run compiler and he purred to a century that he completed in the last over of the day with Australia 71 runs behind but with half their wickets still intact. Snow (five for 57) was always a handful for the Australian batsmen but he could not prevent Greg Chappell (131) and Rodney Marsh (50) pushing the tourists into a 36-run lead.

Lillee started the fall of England in their second innings and Massie completed it. Boycott was first to go, unluckily playing the ball on to his bails after allowing a rising ball from Lillee to hit him in the ribs. Luckhurst soon followed, caught behind by Rodney Marsh off the bowling of Lillee.

It then became the Bob Massie show. He swung the ball around as if he had it on a piece of elastic, and England stumbled from one crisis to another as their batsmen became almost hypnotised by the incredible movement of the ball.

Half the side were out for 31, and at the close of play on the third day England were just 50 runs ahead with nine wickets down. Massie had claimed seven of the wickets and made it eight for 53 on Monday morning when he ended a bright stand of 35 between Gifford and Price.

Massie finished with a match analysis of 16 for 137, a record for any bowler making his Test debut and then the third best Test return of all time.

Australia needed only 81 runs to win, and Stackpole saw them comfortably home with an unbeaten 57.

THE WITNESSES: Bob Massie: 'It was the sort of thing you only dream about. It could not have happened in a better setting for me because Lord's is the ground on which every cricketer in the world wants to perform well. I got all the credit, but Dennis Lillee was marvellous to play with. I capitalised on his hostility. He was really rocketing the ball down.'

John Snow: 'I have never seen swing bowling like that produced by Bob Massie. It was like facing a boomerang, and you felt that the ball would have returned to him if everybody had left it alone down at the batsman's end. No wonder everybody in cricket just refers to this as "Massie's match."'

FOR THE RECORD: Massie never again touched the heights that he reached at Lord's. He took only seven wickets in the three remaining Tests and just 31 in all in six Test appearances. Highlights of the drawn third Test were a century by Keith Stackpole (114), an unbeaten 170 by Ross Edwards and a battling 96 by Brian Luckhurst. Derek Underwood (ten for 82) spun England to a nine-wickets victory in the fourth Test at Headingley on a grassless pitch that had been flooded by a cloudburst five days before the first ball was bowled. Australia squared the rubber by winning by five wickets on the sixth day of the final Test at The Oval. The Chappells provided the first instance of brothers each scoring a century in the same innings, and Dennis Lillee took ten wickets for 181 to lift his haul for the series to a record 31 wickets.

England v Australia, Second Test, 1972

ENGLAND

	1st innings		2nd innings	
G. Boycott	b Massie	11	b Lillee	6
J.H. Edrich	lbw b Lillee	10	c Marsh b Massie	6
B.W. Luckhurst	b Lillee	1	c Marsh b Lillee	4
M.J.K. Smith	b Massie	34	c Edwards b Massie	30
B.L. D'Oliveira	lbw b Massie	32	c G.S. Chappell b Massie	3
A.W. Greig	c Marsh b Massie	54	c I.M. Chappell b Massie	3
A.P.E. Knott†	c Colley b Massie	43	c G.S. Chappell b Massie	12
R. Illingworth*	lbw b Massie	30	c Stackpole b Massie	12
J.A. Snow	b Massie	37	c Marsh b Massie	0
N. Gifford	c Marsh b Massie	3	not out	16
J.S.E. Price	not out	4	c G.S. Chappell b Massie	19
Extras	(LB 6, W 1, NB 6)	13	(W 1, NB 4)	5
Total		**272**		**116**

AUSTRALIA

	1st innings		2nd innings	
K.R. Stackpole	c Gifford b Price	5	not out	57
B.C. Francis	b Snow	0	c Knott b Price	9
I.M. Chappell*	c Smith b Snow	56	c Luckhurst b D'Oliveira	6
G.S. Chappell	b D'Oliveira	131	not out	7
K.D. Walters	c Illingworth b Snow	1		
R. Edwards	c Smith b Illingworth	28		
J.W. Gleeson	c Knott b Greig	1		
R.W. Marsh†	c Greig b Snow	50		
D.J. Colley	c Greig b Price	25		
R.A.L. Massie	c Knott b Snow	0		
D.K. Lillee	not out	2		
Extras	(LB 7, NB 2)	9	(LB 2)	2
Total		**308**	(2 wickets)	**81**

AUSTRALIA	O	M	R	W	O	M	R	W
Lillee	28	3	90	2	21	6	50	2
Massie	32.5	7	84	8	27.2	9	53	8
Colley	16	2	42	0	7	1	8	0
G.S. Chappell	6	1	18	0				
Gleeson	9	1	25	0				

ENGLAND	O	M	R	W	O	M	R	W
Snow	32	13	57	5	8	2	15	0
Price	26.1	5	87	2	7	0	28	1
Greig	29	6	74	1	3	0	17	0
D'Oliveira	17	5	48	1	8	3	14	1
Gifford	11	4	20	0				
Illingworth	7	2	13	1				
Luckhurst					0.5	0	5	0

FALL OF WICKETS

	E	A	E	A
Wkt	1st	1st	2nd	2nd
1st	22	1	12	20
2nd	23	7	16	51
3rd	28	82	18	—
4th	84	84	25	—
5th	97	190	31	—
6th	193	212	52	—
7th	200	250	74	—
8th	260	290	74	—
9th	265	290	81	—
10th	272	308	116	—

1972-73 Walters plunders a century between lunch and tea

Match: West Indies v Australia, Third Test
Venue: Queen's Park Oval, Trinidad **Date:** March 23, 24, 25, 27, 28

THE SETTING: Doug Walters was hailed as 'the new Bradman' when he exploded on to the international cricket scene in the mid-1960s. There are a queue of West Indian bowlers who would concede that he lived up to the billing.

In the home Test series against the West Indies in 1968-69, he plundered 699 runs in four Tests including 242 and 103 at Sydney. He punished them severely again in the 1972-73 series in the West Indies, averaging 71 for the five Tests.

It was in this third Test at the Queen's Park Oval in Trinidad that he unleashed the most spectacular of all his innings, producing a rarity in international cricket—a century between lunch and tea.

THE MATCH: Australia got off to a shaky start when Keith Stackpole was removed by Keith Boyce off the third ball of the match for a duck, but Greg Chappell and Ian Redpath then shared a rapid stand of 107 before Chappell (56) was caught by Alvin Kallicharran off the bowling of Lance Gibbs in the last over before lunch.

This brought Walters to the wicket, and he set about the West Indian bowlers from the moment he took strike. He drove, cut and pulled with an ease and a certainty that made batting look the simplest thing in the world. West Indies skipper Rohan Kanhai was forced into setting a defensive field as Walters let loose with a volley of shots that brought roars of appreciation from the West Indian fans who knew better than anybody that they were seeing attacking play of the highest calibre.

It was batsmanship Caribbean style, and included flashing hooks and extravagant drives off the front and back foot. He was exactly 100 at the tea interval, and added another 12 runs before being caught by Roy Fredericks off the bowling of left-arm spinner Inshan Ali.

The Walters extravaganza lasted two hours 28 minutes and his battery of runs included one six and 16 fours. His century was compiled out of 130 runs scored in the afternoon session.

Lance Gibbs was the most impressive of the West Indies bowlers on a wicket that was taking spin from the early stages, but he like all his colleagues was on the receiving end of some rough treatment from Walters and he finished with figures of three for 79. Ian Redpath (66) was the second most successful of the Australian batsmen in a substantial total of 332.

There was a sad blow for the West Indies late on the first day when batsman Lance Rowe fell while fielding and damaged ankle ligaments

which prevented him taking any further part in the match.

Solid half-centuries by Alvin Kallicharran and Rohan Kanhai and a a well-judged 40 by wicket-keeper Deryck Murray brought stability to an otherwise shaky reply by the ten-man West Indies team who were all out 52 runs short of the Australian total. Leg break bowler Terry Jenner had success in fits and starts and finished with figures of four for 98.

Highlight of Australia's second innings was a sparkling 97 by skipper Ian Chappell. Redpath (44) and Walters (32) also made useful contributions to the total of 281. Gibbs (five for 102) pinned down the early batsmen, but he became uncharacteristically loose late in the innings and took a tanking from the tail-enders that weighed heavily against the West Indies in the final count. Australia's last two wickets put on 50 runs, with big-hitting Max Walker not out 23.

The ten men of West Indies were left 334 runs to win on a wicket that was taking considerable turn. Roy Fredericks (76) gave them a flying send-off and then Kallicharran unwrapped an innings in the Walters class. By lunch on the final day he and Maurice Foster had taken the score to 268 for four and, with only 66 more runs needed to win, it looked odds-on a West Indies victory.

But there was a dramatic transformation immediately after lunch when off the first ball of the afternoon session Kallicharran played a casual shot back to Max Walker and was caught behind by Rodney Marsh nine short of his century. Soon after Foster (34) was snapped up by Greg Chappell at forward short leg off the bowling of Kerry O'Keeffe.

West Indies crashed from 268 for four to 289 all out, 44 runs short of their target. O'Keeffe (four for 57) and Walker (three for 43) were the main wicket takers.

THE WITNESSES: Doug Walters: 'It was one of the most satisfying knocks of my career. I did not deliberately set out to score a century before the tea interval. It was just one of those days when everything clicked.'

Ian Chappell: 'It's not often you get a match-winning innings on the first day of a Test match, but I think that's how you could describe Doug's knock. It put us in the driving seat and West Indies were always having to chase to catch up. The other major turning point was when Max Walker got Kallicharran out with the first ball after lunch. It was just beginning to look as if they were going to pull the game out of the fire.'

Rohan Kanhai: 'Walters played some glorious strokes, and we are just about sick to death of the sight of him. I think the result might have been different if we had not lost Lawrence Rowe on the first day. He was one of our key batsmen.'

FOR THE RECORD: Australia won the series 2-0, with three Tests drawn. Clive Lloyd (178) and Ian Chappell (109) scored centuries in the fourth Test that Australia won by ten wickets after the West Indies had been tumbled out for 109 in their second innings. Doug Walters punished them with the ball in their first innings, taking five for 66.

West Indies v Australia, Third Test, 1972-73

AUSTRALIA

K.R. Stackpole	c Foster b Boyce	0	— c Fredericks b Boyce	18
I.R. Redpath	run out	66	— c Kanhai b Willett	44
G.S. Chappell	c Kallicharran b Gibbs	56	— c and b Gibbs	1
K.D. Walters	c Fredericks b Ali	112	— c Gibbs b Willett	32
R. Edwards	lbw b Boyce	12	— b Gibbs	14
I.M. Chappell*	c and b Ali	8	— c Fredericks b Willett	97
R.W. Marsh†	b Ali	14	— b Ali	8
K.J. O'Keeffe	run out	37	— c Kallicharran b Gibbs	7
T.J. Jenner	lbw b Gibbs	2	— b Gibbs	6
M.H.N. Walker	b Gibbs	0	— not out	23
J.R. Hammond	not out	2	— c Kanhai b Gibbs	19
Extras	(B 10, LB 7, NB 6)	23	(B 5, LB 7)	12
Total		**332**		**281**

WEST INDIES

R.C. Fredericks	c I.M. Chappell b Jenner	16	— c Redpath b Stackpole	76
M.L.C. Foster	lbw b Jenner	25	— c G.S. Chappell b O'Keeffe	34
A.I. Kallicharran	c G.S. Chappell b Jenner	53	— c Marsh b Walker	91
C.H. Lloyd	c and b G.S. Chappell	20	— c Stackpole b O'Keeffe	15
R.B. Kanhai*	c Redpath b O'Keeffe	56	— b G.S. Chappell	14
D.L. Murray†	lbw b Hammond	40	— c Redpath b Walker	7
K.D. Boyce	c Marsh b O'Keeffe	12	— c I.M. Chappell b O'Keeffe	11
Inshan Ali	c Marsh b Walker	15	— b Walker	2
E.T. Willett	not out	4	— b O'Keeffe	0
L.R. Gibbs	c O'Keeffe b Jenner	6	— not out	0
L.G. Rowe	absent hurt	—	— absent hurt	—
Extras	(B 17, LB 11, W 1, NB 4)	33	(B 19, LB 13, NB 7)	39
Total		**280**		**289**

WEST INDIES	O	M	R	W	O	M	R	W
Boyce	18	4	54	2	10	1	41	1
Lloyd	7	3	13	0	3	1	11	0
Gibbs	38	11	79	3	45	14	102	5
Willett	19	3	62	0	28	15	33	3
Ali	41.1	11	89	3	21	2	82	1
Foster	6	2	12	0				

AUSTRALIA	O	M	R	W	O	M	R	W
Walker	30	8	55	1	25	6	43	3
Hammond	7	3	7	1	6	3	12	0
Jenner	38.3	7	98	4	15	2	46	0
O'Keeffe	28	10	62	2	24.1	5	57	4
G.S. Chappell	14	8	16	1	32	10	65	1
Stackpole	2	0	8	0	11	4	27	1
I.M. Chappell	2	1	1	0				

FALL OF WICKETS

	A	WI	A	WI
Wkt	1st	1st	2nd	2nd
1st	1	33	31	39
2nd	108	44	96	141
3rd	181	100	99	177
4th	240	149	156	219
5th	257	206	185	268
6th	262	230	208	274
7th	312	265	231	281
8th	321	267	231	288
9th	321	280	248	289
10th	332	—	281	—

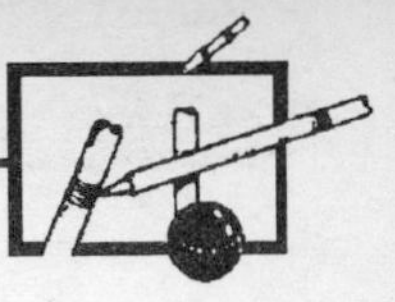

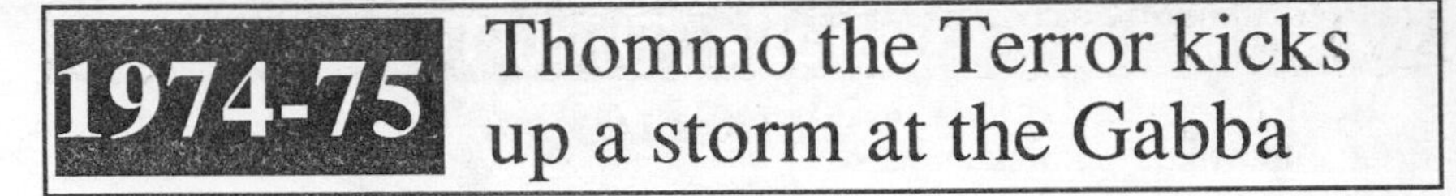

1974-75 Thommo the Terror kicks up a storm at the Gabba

Match: Australia v England, First Test
Venue: 'The Gabba', Brisbane **Date:** November 29, 30, December 1, 3, 4

THE SETTING: Jeff Thomson finished his Test debut against Pakistan in 1973 with the miserable figures of nought for 100 and nought for 10. Many people thought he was just making excuses for his sterile performance when he claimed that he had kept secret the fact that he was bowling with a broken bone in his foot. It was 1974-75 before the selectors almost reluctantly gave him a second chance against Mike Denness's England team.

The sensational impact he made in that series will never be forgotten, particularly by the England batsmen who were on the receiving end of some of the most ferocious bowling since the 'bodyline' tour 40 years earlier when it had been the Aussies dodging the thunderbolts from Larwood and Voce.

England had no idea what they were in for when they faced Thommo for the first time on a Gabba pitch that was not properly prepared because of an outbreak of tropical thunderstorms. Thomson came into the match like a clap of thunder.

THE MATCH: The Chappell brothers, Ian (90) and Greg (58), put some beef into the Australian first innings in which they totalled 309 against some spirited fast bowling by Bob Willis (four for 56). England then got their first taste of Thomson, and it gave them indigestion. He removed openers Dennis Amiss and Brian Luckhurst with just ten runs on the board and in his second spell had John Edrich caught by skipper Ian Chappell. Only a defiant century by all-rounder Tony Greig held the England innings together and they were all out for 265. The talk in the England dressing-room was not so much of the express speed of Dennis Lillee—that they expected. It was of the sheer pace and hostility of Thomson, who was getting the ball to buck and rear off the length after delivering it at speeds of close to 100 mph.

An adventurous race for runs by Greg Chappell (71), Ross Edwards (53), Doug Walters (62 not out) and Rodney Marsh (46 not out) enabled Ian Chappell to declare at 288 for five, leaving England the formidable target of 333 runs for victory.

At the close of play on the fourth day England were ten for no wicket. It was on the final day that they discovered 'Thommo the Terror' waiting to greet them with an awesome display of some of the quickest bowling ever witnessed.

Batsmen ducked for their lives in these pre-helmet days as Thomson rocketed the ball down with a competitive urge that convinced the England players that he was happy to knock them out if he couldn't bowl them out.

He clean bowled Edrich, Greig, Knott and Mike Hendrick and also claimed the wickets of Amiss and Denness while returning figures of six for 46 off 17.5 overs. England were hustled out for 166, with Derek Underwood the top scorer on 30.

In truth, England had suffered a nervous breakdown and Thomson had sown seeds of doubt in the minds of several batsmen about their ability to cope with him.

THE WITNESSES: Dennis Amiss: 'I don't think any of us could quite believe the speed that Thomson produced. It was to say the least demoralising to see the ball lifting so violently off a length. We had all known what to expect from Dennis Lillee. But Thomson was a surprise package.'

Mike Denness: 'Thomson was in exceptional form in Sydney, but I rated Lillee the superior bowler. He was not only tremendously quick but could also move the ball either way. There have not been many better combinations than Lillee and Thomson at their peak.'

Ian Chappell: 'I saw the stunned look on the faces of the England batsmen when they faced Thommo in the first innings, and decided to go flat out for runs in our second knock. Some of the England players were looking almost shell shocked and I was confident they wouldn't be able to get a big score when batting last against Thommo and Lillee.'

Jeff Thomson stunned England

FOR THE RECORD: The psychological advantage Thomson had given Australia in the first Test lasted virtually throughout the tour. The Aussies won the second, fourth and fifth Tests, with the third drawn. England had the consolation of winning the sixth Test, but Australia were without the injured Thomson and Lillee broke down after just six overs. Thomson finished the series with 33 wickets and Lillee was just as menacing with 25 wickets.

Australia v England, First Test, 1974-75

AUSTRALIA

	1st innings		2nd innings	
I.R. Redpath	b Willis	5	b Willis	25
W.J. Edwards	c Amiss b Hendrick	4	c Knott b Willis	5
I.M. Chappell*	c Greig b Willis	90	c Fletcher b Underwood	11
G.S. Chappell	c Fletcher b Underwood	58	b Underwood	71
R. Edwards	c Knott b Underwood	32	c Knott b Willis	53
K.D. Walters	c Lever b Willis	3	not out	62
R.W. Marsh†	c Denness b Hendrick	14	not out	46
T.J. Jenner	c Lever b Willis	12		
D.K. Lillee	c Knott b Greig	15		
M.H.N. Walker	not out	41		
J.R. Thomson	run out	23		
Extras	(LB 4, NB 8)	12	(B 1, LB 7, W 1, NB 6)	15
Total		**309**	(5 wickets declared)	**288**

ENGLAND

	1st innings		2nd innings	
D.L. Amiss	c Jenner b Thomson	7	c Walters b Thomson	25
B.W. Luckhurst	c Marsh b Thomson	1	c I.M. Chappell b Lillee	3
J.H. Edrich	c I.M. Chappell b Thomson	48	b Thomson	6
M.H. Denness*	lbw b Walker	6	c Walters b Thomson	27
K.W.R. Fletcher	b Lillee	17	c G.S. Chappell b Jenner	19
A.W. Greig	c Marsh b Lillee	110	b Thomson	2
A.P.E. Knott†	c Jenner b Walker	12	b Thomson	19
P. Lever	c I.M. Chappell b Walker	4	c Redpath b Lillee	14
D.L. Underwood	c Redpath b Walters	25	c Walker b Jenner	30
R.G.D. Willis	not out	13	not out	3
M. Hendrick	c Redpath b Walker	4	b Thomson	0
Extras	(B 5, LB 2, W 3, NB 8)	18	(B 8, LB 3, W 2, NB 5)	18
Total		**265**		**166**

ENGLAND	O	M	R	W	O	M	R	W
Willis	21.5	3	56	4	15	3	45	3
Lever	16	1	53	0	18	4	58	0
Hendrick	19	3	64	2	13	2	47	0
Greig	16	2	70	1	13	2	60	0
Underwood	20	6	54	2	26	6	63	2

AUSTRALIA	O	M	R	W	O	M	R	W
Lillee	23	6	73	2	12	2	25	2
Thomson	21	5	59	3	17.5	3	46	6
Walker	24.5	2	73	4	9	4	32	0
Walters	6	1	18	1	2	2	0	0
Jenner	6	1	24	0	16	5	45	2

FALL OF WICKETS

	A	E	A	E
Wkt	1st	1st	2nd	2nd
1st	7	9	15	18
2nd	10	10	39	40
3rd	110	33	59	44
4th	197	57	173	92
5th	202	130	190	94
6th	205	162	—	94
7th	228	168	—	115
8th	229	226	—	162
9th	257	248	—	163
10th	309	265	—	166

1975-76 Handy Andy interrupts an Australian run harvest

Match: Australia v West Indies, Second Test
Venue: WACA, Perth **Date:** December 12, 13, 14, 16

THE SETTING: In 1974 Andy Roberts became the first cricketer from Antigua to play in a Test match and until the emergence soon after of Vivian Richards he was that tiny island's favourite and most famous sporting son. He was still something of an unknown force when he went to Australia as the main strike bowler for the West Indies during the 1975-76 tour, but by the time this second Test was over he was being mentioned in the same respectful breath as Lillee and Thomson.

The Aussies had won the first Test comfortably by eight wickets, and Roberts had hardly distinguished himself with returns of three for 85 and one for 47. But the Perth Test stood out like an oasis in the desert for the West Indies, who had a thoroughly miserable tour that was brightened by this one match and the sensational bowling of Roberts.

THE MATCH: Roberts gave a hint of what was to come when he trapped Rick McCosker lbw for a duck in his first over, and he then had left-handed opener Alan Turner caught by Lance Gibbs with the Australian total at 37.

Ian Chappell, free from the cares and pressures of captaincy, came in during the first over and proceeded to play an innings of controlled aggression. Thanks almost entirely to him and a lusty knock from Gary Gilmour (45), Australia managed to total 329 to which Chappell contributed 156 runs.

Young Michael Holding, playing in his second Test match, finished off the innings with three wickets in an over when he clean bowled Chappell, Jeff Thomson and Ashley Mallett. Holding would be making his own mark in future matches, but this Test belonged to Andy Roberts and aggressive opening batsman Roy Fredericks, who opened the West Indies innings with a ferocious display of power batting.

He hooked Dennis Lillee for six off his second ball and put on 91 at hurricane pace with makeshift opening partner Bernard Julien (25). Fredericks reached his 50 off 33 balls, his 100 off 71 balls and was finally caught by Greg Chappell off the bowling of Lillee for 169. Alvin Kallicharran joined in the run harvest until he was taken to hospital with a broken nose after mishooking a bouncer from Lillee. He resumed his innings the next day and reached 57. Clive Lloyd emerged as Australia's main tormentor after the departure of Fredericks and scored 149 in his own inimitable style. Deryck Murray (63) and Keith Boyce (49 not out) finished off the destruction

of the Australian attack to raise the West Indies total to 585.

Then Roberts took over. He had Turner caught behind by Murray for a duck in his first over and had four Australian batsmen back in the pavilion with just 45 runs on the board in the final session of the third day.

Only Greg Chappell (43) and Marsh (39) put up any real resistance until both were dismissed by Roberts who finished a memorable match with figures of seven for 54. Australia were whipped out for 169 and were beaten by an innings for the first time in a Test against the West Indies.

THE WITNESSES: Andy Roberts: 'I just gave it all I'd got and felt very proud when I was told that my figures in the second innings were the best ever for West Indies against Australia.'

Clive Lloyd: 'Andy's deceptive because he does not have that long a run-up, but he gets a lot of pace and power into his deliveries. He is going to give a lot of batsmen problems in the years to come.'

FOR THE RECORD: Roberts finished the series with 22 wickets, but could not stop the West Indies being completely outplayed for the rest of the rubber. They lost five of the six Tests. Greg Chappell set a captain's example with a century in each innings in the first Test, and hammered 182 in the fourth. Ian Redpath scored a hat-trick of hundreds, and Gary Cosier, Alan Turner and Rick McCosker were also centurians. Lance Gibbs was on the end of some heavy hidings from the Australian batsmen, but he had the consolation of passing Fred Trueman as the top Test wicket taker, reaching 309 in what was his last series.

Andy Roberts gives Rodney Marsh a torrid time in Perth

Australia v W. Indies, Second Test, 1975-76

AUSTRALIA

	1st innings		2nd innings	
R.B. McCosker	lbw b Roberts	0	— c Rowe b Roberts	13
A. Turner	c Gibbs b Roberts	23	— c Murray b Roberts	0
I.M. Chappell*	b Holding	156	— c sub b Roberts	20
G.S. Chappell	c Murray b Julien	13	— c Rowe b Roberts	43
I.R. Redpath	c Murray b Julien	33	— lbw b Roberts	0
R.W. Marsh†	c Julien b Boyce	23	— c Murray b Roberts	39
G.J. Gilmour	c Julien b Gibs	45	— c Fredericks b Roberts	3
M.H.N. Walker	c Richards b Holding	1	— c sub b Julien	3
D.K. Lillee	not out	12	— c Lloyd b Julien	4
J.R. Thomson	b Holding	0	— b Julien	9
A.A. Mallett	b Holding	0	— not out	18
Extras	(B 12, LB 5, NB 6)	23	(B 13, LB 2, NB 2)	17
Total		**329**		**169**

WEST INDIES

R.C. Fredericks	c G.S. Chappell b Lillee	169
B.D. Julien	c Mallett b Gilmour	25
L.G. Rowe	c Marsh b Thomson	19
A.I. Kallicharan	c I.M. Chappell b Walker	57
I.V.A. Richards	c Gilmour b Thomson	12
C.H. Lloyd*	b Gilmour	149
D.L. Murray†	c Marsh b Lillee	63
M.A. Holding	c Marsh b Thomson	0
K.D. Boyce	not out	49
A.M.E. Roberts	b Walker	0
L.R. Gibbs	run out	13
Extras	(B 2, LB 16, NB 11)	29
Total		**585**

WEST INDIES	O	M	R	W	O	M	R	W
Roberts	13	1	65	2	14	3	54	7
Boyce	12	2	53	1	2	0	8	0
Holding	18.7	1	88	4	10.6	1	53	0
Julien	12	0	51	2	10.1	1	32	3
Gibbs	14	4	49	1	3	1	3	0
Fredericks					1	0	2	0

AUSTRALIA	O	M	R	W
Lillee	20	0	123	2
Thomson	17	0	128	3
Gilmour	14	0	103	2
Walker	17	1	99	2
Mallett	26	4	103	0
I.M. Chappell	1.4	1	0	0

FALL OF WICKETS

Wkt	A 1st	WI 1st	A 2nd
1st	0	91	0
2nd	37	134	25
3rd	70	258	45
4th	149	297	45
5th	189	461	124
6th	277	461	128
7th	285	522	132
8th	329	548	142
9th	329	548	146
10th	329	585	169

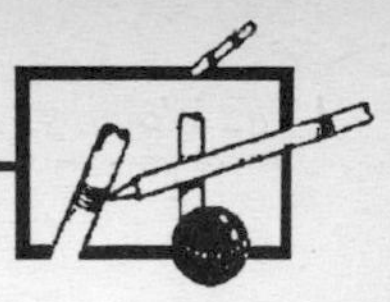

1976 Holding capitalises on a master blast from Richards

Match: England v West Indies, Fifth Test
Venue: The Oval **Date:** August 12, 13, 14, 16, 17

THE SETTING: There have been few more stunning sights in modern cricket than that of Vivian Richards in full flow with the bat…or more beautiful sights than that of Michael Holding running in to bowl with his graceful, rhythmic action. It came almost as a shock to the system that Holding's smooth, artistic approach to the wicket could produce such violent deliveries that for a decade left some of the greatest batsmen in the world playing and missing and often listening to the unwelcome sound of falling timber.

To see both Richards and Holding at the peak of their powers in the same match was, for cricket lovers of any nationality, like being transported to paradise. Lucky spectators at this fifth Test between England and the West Indies at The Oval witnessed the double event.

But it was not heavenly for the England batsmen and bowlers. They must have felt they had found a hell on earth as they came face to face with the dynamic duo.

THE MATCH: Richards was first to take the stage after skipper Clive Lloyd had won the toss and decided to bat on a featherbed wicket that looked full of runs. There was a false dawn of hopes that England would run through the West Indies team when Bob Willis dismissed the formidable Gordon Greenidge for a duck with the last ball of his second over. The sight of Greenidge departing was the good news…the bad news was that Viv Richards was strolling to the wicket with that almost-casual stride of his. There was nothing casual in the way that Richards set about the England bowlers as he produced an innings that even by his sky-scraping standards was something quite special.

He occupied the crease for eight minutes short of eight hours and during his stay treated the spectators to every shot in his vast repertoire. With sensible support from Roy Fredericks (71) and Lawrence Rowe (70), Richards raced to exactly 200 by the close of play on the first day with the West Indies powerfully poised on 373 for three.

There was cause for brief celebration by the England players when Alan Knott stumped Rowe off the bowling of Derek Underwood in the final session. Playing in his 78th Test, Knott had overtaken the world Test record of 219 dismissals by his predecessor at Kent, Godfrey Evans, who had set the record over a span of 91 Tests.

Richards continued to pound the England attack on the second morning, and harassed skipper Tony

Greig—who had unwisely claimed before the series started that England would make the West Indies grovel—tried a battery of nine bowlers in a bid to end the Richards monopoly.

He and Clive Lloyd (84) put on 141 in the 32 overs sent down before lunch. Lloyd was content to play second fiddle, although it was more like a rocket-launcher than a violin that Richards was using. With his 300 in sight, everybody was beginning to think that the 'Master Blaster' was going to threaten the world record 365 set by Garfield Sobers. He drove Greig imperiously high towards the Vauxhall Road boundary, and as he attempted to give a carbon copy of the shot off the next ball his timing at last failed him and he touched it onto his stumps.

His awesome innings included 38 fours and his 291 runs came off 386 balls. It lifted his record haul of Test runs for the calendar year to 1,710.

There were 524 runs on the board for the loss of four wickets when he finally departed, leaving a trail of broken English hearts behind him. And still the misery was not over as the West Indies set out to make Greig and his men grovel. They went on to their highest ever score in a Test against England, Lloyd at last putting an end to the punishment when he declared with the total at 687 for eight.

Now it was Holding's turn to torture England. Many experts were criticial of the West Indies decision to rely on pace on a pitch that was slow and dusty and looking tailor-made for spin. But Holding had not read that script. With so many runs to play with, Lloyd was able to encourage his ace bowler with an attacking field throughout the innings and Holding responded with some of the quickest bowling ever seen at this famous old ground.

Dennis Amiss and Bob Woolmer safely negotiated the 12 overs they had to face at the end of the second day, and the classical way that Amiss struck the ball for 22 runs suggested he was back to his old form after a miserable loss of confidence that had cost him his place in the England team.

He proved he was back with a vengeance the next day as he shepherded England through a trying day when he was the only batsman who looked comfortable against the rocketing deliveries fom Holding. Amiss produced an innings that would have been considered a classic in any other match had it not followed so soon after the magical performance from Richards. Even so it was a memorable effort, particularly as so many of his colleagues had difficulty getting settled.

With gritty assistance from David Steele (44), Peter Willey (33) and Alan Knott (50), Amiss battled through until the fourth day. Skipper Greig threatened to produce the sort of rousing support Amiss needed when he cracked two glorious cover drives off Holding, but he got too ambitious and as he tried for a third boundary he was bowled off his pads. This triggered a crowd invasion of West Indian supporters mocking the England captain, who was paying the price for his over-the-top statement before a ball had been bowled in the

Master Blaster Vivian Richards pulls Peter Willey for four on his way to 291

series. The umpires suspended play for nine minutes and then Amiss and Underwood survived the last seven minutes. At the close England were 304 for five, with the defiant Warwickshire opener unbeaten and unbowed on 178. He was at the wicket for five hours 20 minutes before becoming England's seventh man out when bowled around his legs by Holding, who was managing to make the ball rise and zip off what all other bowlers considered a lifeless pitch.

Amiss compiled a hero's innings of 203 that included 28 fours, but despite his magnificent effort England were still struggling to save the follow-on at 342 for seven. Thanks to a spirited stand between Knott and Miller (36) and a contribution of 40 extras, they managed to get the score up to 435. It was still 252 runs short and Lloyd could have asked them to bat again, but he thought that Holding deserved a rest particularly as his support pace bowler Wayne Daniel was injured. Holding had sent down 33 overs and was rewarded with the best ever return by a West Indies bowler against England of eight wickets for 92 runs.

Openers Fredericks and Greenidge took great pleasure in continuing where the West Indies had left off in the first innings, and for two hours 20 minutes they hoisted the England bowlers all over the vast Oval ground. Lloyd declared for a second time with Fredericks (86) and Greenidge (85) both unbeaten and the scoreboard showing 182 without loss.

This meant England had six hours 20 minutes in which to get the 435 runs for victory or, more realistically, to save the match. England's fast bowlers had made no impact on the unhelpful wicket, so there was hope in the dressing-room that perhaps Holding would not be able to repeat his fiery deliveries of the first innings.

These hopes were given a boost in the closing moments of the fourth day when Amiss and Woolmer hit out freely to put on 43 runs. But within the first hour of the final day England had crashed to 78 for five and the match was virtually all over.

Holding was again the man who caused most of the damage, with support from Vanburn Holder and Andy Roberts. He unleashed a deadly spell of sustained fast bowling that had all the established England batsmen in trouble and he took six wickets for 57 off 20.4 overs. Only another brave display from Steele (42) and a late resistance movement by Knott (57) and Miller (24) saved England from an embarrasing rout and they were finally all out for 203, leaving West Indies winners by 231 runs and with 80 minutes to spare.

Holding was the first West Indian bowler to take more than 12 wickets in a Test and his match return of 14 for 149 was hailed as one of the finest performances of all time on a wicket that offered no assistance.

THE WITNESSES: Bob Willis: 'Michael Holding gave the finest display of fast bowling I have ever seen. Having bowled on the pitch I know what I'm speaking about when I say there was nothing there to help the pace bowlers. But Michael managed to make it seem perfect for speed.'

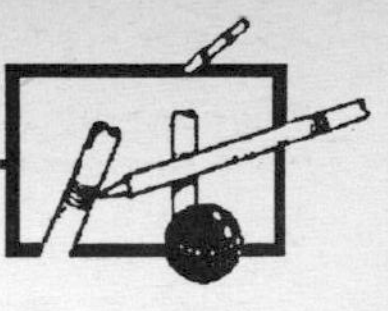

Dennis Amiss: 'I was under pressure to do well because I had only just been recalled. It took tremendous concentration out in the middle because Michael Holding was bowling as well as I've ever seen anybody bowl. He got my wicket twice in the match but thank goodness I had the consolation of my second double century against the West Indies to follow the one I scored in Jamaica in 1974.'

Michael Holding: 'This was the most memorable match of my Test career. I remember it not only for my success with the ball but because Viv Richards produced the sort of marvellous knock that only he could play.'

FOR THE RECORD: West Indies won the 1976 series 3-0, with the first two Tests drawn. Holding claimed five for 17 when England were rushed out for 71 in the third Test. Roberts took six for 37 in the second innings. Fredericks (109) and Greenidge (115) shared an opening stand of 192 in the fourth Test as West Indies helped themselves to 437 runs on the first day. Greig and Knott each scored 116. Bob Willis took five for 42 in West Indies' second innings.

Michael Holding wrecks Tony Greig's stumps for a second time at The Oval

England v West Indies, Fifth Test, 1976

WEST INDIES

R.C. Fredericks	c Balderstone b Miller	71	— not out	86
C.G. Greenidge	lbw b Willis	0	— not out	85
I.V.A. Richards	b Greig	291		
L.G. Rowe	st Knott b Underwood	70		
C.H. Lloyd*	c Knott b Greig	84		
C.L. King	c Selvey b Balderstone	63		
D.L. Murray†	c and b Underwood	36		
V.A. Holder	not out	13		
M.A. Holding	b Underwood	32		
A.M.E. Roberts				
W.W. Daniel				
Extras	(B 1, LB 17, NB 9)	27	(B 4, LB 1, W 1, NB 5)	11
Total	(8 wickets declared)	**687**	(0 wickets declared)	**182**

ENGLAND

R.A. Woolmer	lbw b Holding	8	— c Murray b Holding	30
D.L. Amiss	b Holding	203	— c Greenidge b Holding	16
D.S. Steele	lbw b Holding	44	— c Murray b Holder	42
J.C. Balderstone	lbw b Holding	0	— b Holding	0
P. Willey	c Fredericks b King	33	— c Greenidge b Holder	1
A.W. Greig*	b Holding	12	— b Holding	1
D.L. Underwood	b Holding	4	— c Lloyd b Roberts	2
A.P.E. Knott†	b Holding	50	— b Holding	57
G. Miller	c sub b Holder	36	— b Richards	24
M.W.W. Selvey	b Holding	0	— not out	4
R.G.D. Willis	not out	5	— lbw b Holding	0
Extras	(B 8, LB 11, NB 21)	40	(B 15, LB 3, W 8)	26
Total		**435**		**203**

ENGLAND	O	M	R	W	O	M	R	W
Willis	15	3	73	1	7	0	48	0
Selvey	15	0	67	0	9	1	44	0
Underwood	60.5	15	165	3	9	2	38	0
Woolmer	9	0	44	0	5	0	30	0
Miller	27	4	106	1				
Balderstone	16	0	80	1				
Greig	34	5	96	2	2	0	11	0
Willey	3	0	11	0				
Steele	3	0	18	0				

WEST INDIES	O	M	R	W	O	M	R	W
Roberts	27	4	102	0	13	4	37	1
Holding	33	9	92	8	20.4	6	57	6
Holder	27.5	7	75	1	14	5	29	2
Daniel	10	1	30	0				
Fredericks	11	2	36	0	12	5	33	0
Richards	14	4	30	0	11	6	11	1
King	7	3	30	1	6	2	9	0
Lloyd					2	1	1	0

FALL OF WICKETS

Wkt	WI 1st	E 1st	WI 2nd	E 2nd
1st	5	47	—	49
2nd	159	147	—	54
3rd	350	151	—	64
4th	524	279	—	77
5th	547	303	—	78
6th	640	323	—	148
7th	642	342	—	196
8th	687	411	—	196
9th	—	411	—	202
10th	—	435	—	203

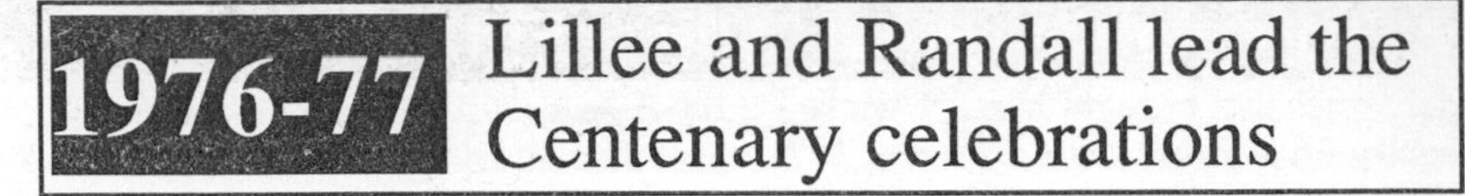

1976-77 Lillee and Randall lead the Centenary celebrations

Match: Australia v England, Centenary Test
Venue: Melbourne **Date:** March 12, 13, 14, 16, 17

THE SETTING: It was Hans Ebeling, a vice-president of Melbourne Cricket Club, who had the brainwave of marking the centenary of the first Test between Australia and England with a special match on the same ground where the inaugural game had been staged in 1877.

Ebeling, a former Australian Test bowler, provided action to go with his thoughts and turned a dream into reality with the help of an army of sponsors and cricket lovers.

The background to the Centenary Test was an unashamed wallow in the waters of nostalgia, with the largest gathering of international cricketers in history descending on Melbourne to swap memories about their moments in cricket.

Meantime, out on the field the 1977 cricketers were conjuring up magical memories for their own old age as they put together a game worthy of the occasion. David Gregory's Australians had beaten James Lillywhite's England tourists by 45 runs in the first ever Test. In a thrilling finish that could have come out of the pages of *Boys' Own* the two teams managed to produce a carbon copy of that result.

THE MATCH: England skipper Tony Greig won the toss with a specially minted gold coin and decided to put Australia in on a moistened pitch that looked suited to pace. The 61,000 crowd, including many overseas visitors, were witnesses to the fact that Greig had taken the right course of action as the trio of England fast-medium bowlers, Bob Willis, John Lever and Chris Old, combined with Derek Underwood to bowl Australia out for just 138 runs.

It was an unhappy innings for the Aussies who never recovered from the early blow of losing opener Rick McCosker with a fractured jaw after a whiplash delivery from Willis had flown into his face off his glove.

Skipper Greg Chappell (40) and wicket-keeper Rodney Marsh (28) were the top scorers on an extremely lively pitch that had Aussie's thoroughbred fast bowler Dennis Lillee licking his lips in anticipation of what he might achieve on it.

The feeling was that if England's quickies could make the pitch work for them, then the considerably faster Lillee should be able to get lift and life out of it. And so it proved. With big Max Walker (four for 54) swinging in from one end, Lillee dominated from the other and the England batsmen caved in like a condemned building with no foundation.

There was a sad procession of England players making the long, lonely trip back to the pavilion as Lillee unleashed blindingly fast deliveries that brought him six wickets for 26 runs off just 13.3 overs. It was one of the most impressive bowling displays in a century of cricket between the two countries as England were bulldozed out for just 95, with Tony Greig the top scorer with 18 runs.

From being a spiteful pitch, the wicket suddenly became docile and Australia batted with comfort and flair as they built a substantial second innings total of 419 before Chappell declared with nine wickets down and leaving England 463 to win at a rate of 40 runs an hour.

Rodney Marsh, that competitive and totally committed wicket-keeper, chose this glittering occasion to put himself in the record books. In England's first innings he overtook his boyhood hero Wally Grout's record of 187 Test victims. Then when batting for a second time he became the first Australian wicket-keeper to score a century against England with a typically breezy and unbeaten 110. There were also powerful knocks from Ian Davis (68), Doug Walters (66) and 21-year-old David Hookes, a ferocious hitter who in one over struck Tony Greig for five fours on his way to a jet-paced 56.

Chris Old worked like a trojan for his four wickets for 104 off 27.6 overs.

With the Queen and the Duke of Edinburgh looking on, England set about their task of trying to win the match with a spirit of adventure that would have been admired by all their ancestors who had helped make the Ashes the greatest cricketing competition in history.

It was the effervescent, fidgety Derek Randall who set the pace in his

Dennis Lillee and Rodney Marsh celebrate the dismissal of Derek Randall

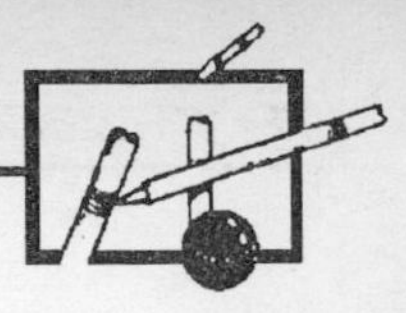

debut against Australia with a brilliantly composed innings of 174 that brought about a distinct possiblity of an England victory. He clowned around at the wicket but was serious when it came to gathering runs, and he despatched to the boundary 21 of the 353 balls that were bowled to him. Lillee worked up to full steam in his bid to remove him, and was far from amused when the extrovert entertainer from Nottingham struck one four with an improvised tennis-smash type of shot, and then—after stumbling when avoiding a Lillee bouncer—scrambled up and doffed his hat in a Chaplinesque gesture. Another bouncer knocked him to the floor and as the crowd wondered whether he was injured he playfully rolled over like a circus tumbler before getting up and resuming as if nothing had happened.

It was great entertainment, but the Aussies were struggling to see the funny side as the England runs began to pile up. There was a moment of sportsmanship that captured the spirit of the game when Randall was given out caught behind on 161. He was on his way back to the pavilion when Marsh informed the umpire that he had not taken the ball cleanly and Randall was recalled. Thirteen runs later there was no doubt that his sparkling innings was over when Gary Cosier caught him off the bowling of Kerry O'Keeffe.

Spirited knocks by Mike Brearley (43), Dennis Amiss (64), Tony Greig (41) and Alan Knott (42) gave England the chance to reach their target, but then Lillee dug down into his vast reserves and came up with a burst of bowling that swept aside the England tail and gave the Australians victory by 45 runs—the identical victory margin of 100 years before.

Lillee finished with five wickets for 139 and match figures of 11 for 165. He was chaired off at the end of a memorable match by his celebrating colleagues.

THE WITNESSES: Rodney Marsh: 'I was lucky enough to keep wicket to Dennis in many State and Test matches, and I never saw him bowl better than in the Centenary Test. His line and his length were excellent throughout the game, and he kept digging in even though the conditions were against him in England's second innings. There is no doubt that he was the man of the match.'

Derek Randall: 'I enjoyed every second of it out there. It was a terrific sporting gesture of Rodney Marsh to get me recalled. That's the way the game should always be played. I got a bit confused when I came off. I went through the wrong gate and found myself walking towards the royal box!'

Sir Donald Bradman: 'All the players deserve congratulations for giving us a game worthy of the occasion. There is not a soul who did not enjoy every moment of the match. The game of cricket was the big winner.'

FOR THE RECORD: Derek Randall was voted the Man of the Match, although most Australians thought the award should have gone to Lillee. England's total of 417 was the highest for any fourth innings in the 226 matches between the two countries.

Australia v England, Centenary Test, 1977

AUSTRALIA

I.C. Davis	lbw b Lever	5	— c Knott b Greig	68
R.B. McCosker	b Willis	4	— c Greig b Old	25
G.J. Cosier	c Fletcher b Lever	10	— c Knott b Lever	4
G.S. Chappell*	b Underwood	40	— b Old	2
D.W. Hookes	c Greig b Old	17	— c Fletcher b Underwood	56
K.D. Walters	c Greig b Willis	4	— c Knott b Greig	66
R.W. Marsh†	c Knott b Old	28	— not out	110
G.J. Gilmour	c Greig b Old	4	— b Lever	16
K.J. O'Keeffe	c Brearley b Underwood	0	— c Willis b Old	14
D.K. Lillee	not out	10	— c Amiss b Old	25
M.H.N. Walker	b Underwood	2	— not out	8
Extras	(B 4, LB 2, NB 8)	14	(LB 10, NB 15)	25
Total		**138**	(9 wickets declared)	**419**

ENGLAND

R.A. Woolmer	c Chappell b Lillee	9	— lbw b Walker	12
J.M. Brearley	c Hookes b Lillee	12	— lbw b Lillee	43
D.L. Underwood	c Chappell b Walker	7	— b Lillee	7
D.W. Randall	c Marsh b Lillee	4	— c Cosier b O'Keeffe	174
D.L. Amiss	c O'Keeffe b Walker	4	— b Chappell	64
K.W.R. Fletcher	c Marsh b Walker	4	— c Marsh b Lillee	1
A.W. Greig*	b Walker	18	— c Cosier b O'Keeffe	41
A.P.E. Knott†	lbw b Lillee	15	— lbw b Lillee	42
C.M. Old	c Marsh b Lillee	3	— c Chappell b Lillee	2
J.K. Lever	c Marsh b Lillee	11	— lbw b O'Keeffe	4
R.G.D. Willis	not out	1	— not out	5
Extras	(B 2, LB 2, W 1, NB 2)	7	(B 8, LB 4, W 3, NB 7)	22
Total		**95**		**417**

ENGLAND	O	M	R	W	O	M	R	W
Lever	12	1	36	2	21	1	95	2
Willis	8	0	33	2	22	0	91	0
Old	12	4	39	3	27.6	2	104	4
Underwood	11.6	2	16	3	12	2	38	1
Greig					14	3	66	2

AUSTRALIA	O	M	R	W	O	M	R	W
Lillee	13.3	2	26	6	34.4	7	139	5
Walker	15	3	54	4	22	4	83	1
O'Keeffe	1	0	4	0	33	6	108	3
Gilmour	5	3	4	0	4	0	29	0
Chappell					16	7	29	1
Walters					3	2	7	0

FALL OF WICKETS

	A	E	A	E
Wkt	1st	1st	2nd	2nd
1st	11	19	33	28
2nd	13	30	40	113
3rd	23	34	53	279
4th	45	40	132	290
5th	51	40	187	346
6th	102	61	244	369
7th	114	65	277	380
8th	117	78	353	385
9th	136	86	407	410
10th	138	95	—	417

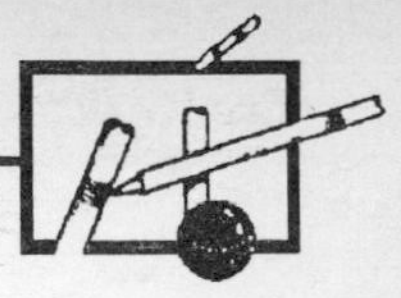

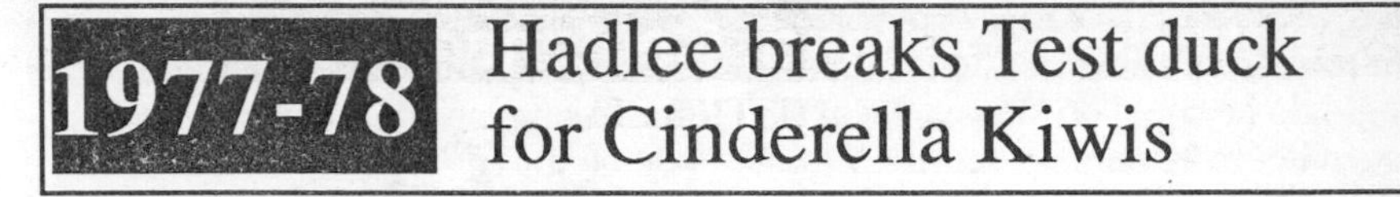

1977-78 Hadlee breaks Test duck for Cinderella Kiwis

Match: New Zealand v England, First Test
Venue: Basin Reserve, Wellington **Date:** February 10, 11, 12, 14, 15

THE SETTING: In 47 Test matches in 48 years New Zealand had never had the satisfaction of beating England. Comparing the two teams on paper, there seemed little prospect of the Kiwis breaking their duck when they faced each other for the 48th time in a gale force wind that whipped around the Basin Reserve ground in Wellington.

England, skippered by the redoubtable Geoff Boycott, had Bob Willis and Ian Botham in their bowling attack and Derek Randall was there to support Boycott and Botham in the run gathering business. Behind the stumps was the wicket-keepers' wicket-keeper Bob Taylor.

New Zealand had a solid side, but not one that anybody would have backed with good money to beat Boycott's England. The one trump card they had was Richard Hadlee, son of former Kiwis skipper Walter and one of the few world-class players in the team. He was a more than useful batsman, and a fast bowler who could stand comparison with the best in the game.

When Boycott won the toss and put New Zealand in to bat, few could have guessed that the gale rocking the stumps was almost a symbol of the wind of change that was about to blow through international cricket. Suddenly the New Zealanders were to prove that they were no longer to be considered the Cinderella country of cricket. They were ready to have a ball...at England's expense.

THE MATCH: Derbyshire left-hander John Wright, making his Test debut, laid the foundation to a respectable New Zealand first innings total of 228 with a Boycott-style exhibition of tormentingly slow but sure scoring. He survived a confident appeal for a catch behind off the first ball of the match, and spent 47 minutes seeking his first run. Wright was still at the wicket at the close of the first day's play with a painstaking 55 runs to his name.

Bev Congdon (44) and Richard Hadlee (27 not out) played enterprising knocks, and though Wright was out without adding to his score on the second day he had done a fine holding-together job for his team in rainy, wind-swept conditions that made concentration difficult for all the players.

Chris Old, bowling into the jaws of the biting gale-force wind, was the most penetrative of the England bowlers and finished with the excellent figures of six for 54 off 30 overs. In one nine-over spell he took four wickets for 11 runs and the acrobatic Taylor held a quartet of superb catches as New Zealand lost four wickets for five runs. Boycott, as if showing that anything John Wright could do he could do slower, spent seven hours 22 minutes scoring 77 runs. The England skipper was continually aggravated by the swirling wind and occasionally had to hold up play while he removed grit from behind his contact lenses.

None of the other England batsmen could match Boycott's staying power against tight bowling by Richard Hadlee (four for 74), Richard Collinge (three for 42) and Congdon (two for 14), who had a spell of seven successive maidens.

England were all out for 215, with Graham Roope (37) giving a middle-order lift to an otherwise uninspired batting performance.

Wright (19) and Robert Anderson (26) gave New Zealand a solid start to their second innings with an opening stand of 54, but then Bob Willis moved up a gear and sent four wickets tumbling for 14 in 31 deliveries. Botham (two for 13) joined in the blitz and the Kiwis suddenly found themselves staring defeat in the face when all out for 123 after at one stage being 82 for one.

England were left with what looked a modest victory target of 137, but they were demolished in one of the most sensational collapses in the history of English Test cricket. In the final two hours of play on the fourth day the tourists lost eight wickets for 53 runs and opener Brian Rose had retired with a bruised arm.

Collinge (three for 35) started the rot when he bowled Boycott off his pads for one, the second time he had dismissed him in the match on his way to his 100th wicket in Test cricket. Richard Hadlee then produced some inspired bowling against a demoralised England team for whom only Botham (19) and Phil Edmonds (11) reached double figures.

Rain on the final morning caused a frustrating delay of 40 minutes before Richard Hadlee fittingly took the last two wickets to finish England off at 64 and to clinch a famous victory that provided New Zealand's finest hour.

Hadlee finished with exceptional figures of six for 26 off 13.3 overs and a match analysis of ten for 100. He and Collinge bowled unchanged apart for one over from Hadlee's older brother Dayle.

THE WITNESSES: Geoff Boycott: 'They were the most aggravating conditions that I have ever encountered. There was a gale blowing on most of the days and it was continually changing direction. The wind was crucifying my eyes. But the conditions were the same for both sides and I offer New Zealand my heartiest congratulations.'

Richard Hadlee: 'This is the greatest day of my cricketing life. We have waited a long time for this, and I believe it will be the start of New Zealand becoming established as a team to be reckoned with.'

FOR THE RECORD: England won the second Test and drew the third of a three-match series. The highlight of England's 174-runs victory was Botham's maiden Test century and his eight wickets in the match.

Richard Hadlee pointed the way to an historic victory for New Zealand

New Zealand v England, First Test, 1977-78

NEW ZEALAND

J.G. Wright	lbw b Botham	55	— c Roope b Willis	19
R.W. Anderson	c Taylor b Old	28	— lbw b Old	26
G.P. Howarth	c Botham b Old	13	— c Edmonds b Willis	21
M.G. Burgess*	b Willis	9	— c Boycott b Botham	6
B.E. Congdon	c Taylor b Old	44	— c Roope b Willis	0
J.M. Parker	c Rose b Willis	16	— c Edmonds b Willis	4
W.K. Lees†	c Taylor b Old	1	— lbw b Hendrick	11
R.J. Hadlee	not out	27	— c Boycott b Willis	2
D.R. Hadlee	c Taylor b Old	1	— c Roope b Botham	2
R.O. Collinge	b Old	1	— c Edmonds b Hendrick	6
S.L. Boock	b Botham	4	— not out	0
Extras	(B 12, LB 3, W 1, NB 13)	29	(B 2, LB 9, W 2, NB 13)	26
Total		**228**		**123**

ENGLAND

B.C. Rose	c Lees b Collinge	21	— not out	5
G. Boycott*	c Congdon b Collinge	77	— b Collinge	1
G. Miller	b Boock	24	— c Anderson b Collinge	4
R.W. Taylor†	c and b Collinge	8	— run out	0
D.W. Randall	c Burgess b R.J. Hadlee	4	— lbw b Collinge	9
G.R.J. Roope	c Lees b R.J. Hadlee	37	— c Lees b R.J. Hadlee	0
I.T. Botham	c Burgess b R.J. Hadlee	7	— c Boock b R.J. Hadlee	19
C.M. Old	b R.J. Hadlee	10	— lbw b R.J. Hadlee	9
P.H. Edmonds	lbw b Congdon	4	— c Parker b R.J. Hadlee	11
M. Hendrick	lbw b Congdon	0	— c Parker b R.J. Hadlee	0
R.G.D. Willis	not out	6	— c Howarth b R.J. Hadlee	3
Extras	(LB 4, NB 13)	17	(NB 3)	3
Total		**215**		**64**

ENGLAND	O	M	R	W	O	M	R	W
Willis	25	7	65	2	15	2	32	5
Hendrick	17	2	46	0	10	2	16	2
Old	30	11	54	6	9	2	32	1
Edmonds	3	1	7	0	1	0	4	0
Botham	12.6	2	27	2	9.3	3	13	2

NEW ZEALAND	O	M	R	W	O	M	R	W
R.J. Hadlee	28	5	74	4	13.3	4	26	6
Collinge	18	5	42	3	13	5	35	3
D.R. Hadlee	21	5	47	0	1	1	0	0
Boock	10	5	21	1				
Congdon	17.4	11	14	2				

FALL OF WICKETS

Wkt	NZ 1st	E 1st	NZ 2nd	E 2nd
1st	42	39	54	2
2nd	96	89	82	8
3rd	114	108	93	18
4th	152	126	93	18
5th	191	183	98	38
6th	193	188	99	38
7th	194	203	104	53
8th	196	205	116	53
9th	208	206	123	63
10th	228	215	123	64

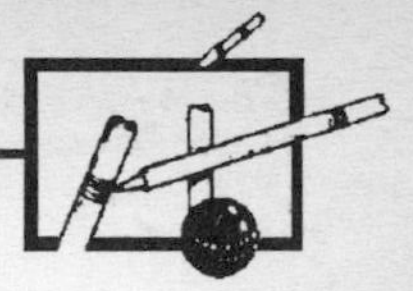

1978-79 Sarfraz stuns Aussies with seven wickets for one run

Match: Australia v Pakistan, First Test
Venue: Melbourne **Date:** March 10, 11, 12, 14, 15

THE SETTING: This was Pakistan's 100th Test match and they celebrated it with an astonishing win over Australia. Of all the victories recorded in this selection of the world's greatest cricket matches, this was the most improbable of them all.

The player who turned almost certain defeat into victory for Pakistan was Sarfraz Nawaz, a bowler of many moods who on his day was capable of destroying the best batting line-ups.

On the final day of the first Test against Australia in Melbourne he was in the right mood and the day certainly belonged to him as he produced one of the most amazing bowling spells in the history of Test cricket.

THE MATCH: Australian skipper Graham Yallop won the toss and put Pakistan in to bat in the hope that his battery of fast bowlers could squeeze out what little life there was in the wicket. He was happy with his decision when Rodney Hogg, in a blistering opening spell, removed the first three Pakistani batsmen for just nine runs.

Captain Mushtaq Mohammad (36), Imran Khan (33) and Sarfraz (35) did their best to repair the damage and managed to boost the final total to 196 after they had been 99 for six. There were two freak moments in an otherwise undistinguished Australian reply of 168. Openers Graeme Wood and Andrew Hilditch collided in mid-wicket when chasing for a run. Wood sprained his wrist and had to retire hurt, not resuming his innings until nine wickets were down. Rodney Hogg angrily knocked down his stumps with his bat when he was given run out after leaving his crease before the ball was 'dead'. Mushtaq sportingly recalled him but the umpire Clarence Harvey—elder brother of Neil—refused to change the decision.

Davenall Whatmore, making his Test debut, was Australia's top scorer with a carefully compiled 43. Imran Khan (four for 26) was the most successful of the Pakistani bowlers, with Sarfraz taking two for 39 off 21.6 overs.

Majid Khan unwrapped a glorious innings of 108, sharing a sparkling second-wicket stand of 135 with Zaheer Abbas (59) during which they played shots all round the wicket against an overworked Australian attack that then took punishment from Asif Iqbal (44) before Mushtaq declared at 353 for nine.

Whatmore substituted for Wood as opener in Australia's second innings and he and Hilditch put on 49 before Sarfraz bowled each of them.

At the close of play on the fourth day Australia were 117 for two and needed 265 runs to win.

Yallop was needlessly run out early on the final morning, but then Allan Border (105) and Kim Hughes (84) shared a fourth-wicket partnership of 177 that put Australia within reach of what appeared to be a comfortable victory.

At 4.30 pm on the final day the Aussies were just 77 runs short of their target and had seven wickets standing. Then Sarfraz stepped into the history books with a remarkable display of seam bowling that left the Australians shell-shocked.

His figures were fairly modest at two for 85, but in the space of only 33 deliveries Sarfraz took all the remaining seven Australian wickets at a cost of just one run.

From thinking of victory at 305 for three, the Australians suddenly found themselves rushed out for 310.

Sarfraz's match figures were 11 wickets for 125, and he had become the only Pakistani bowler to take nine Test wickets in an innings.

THE WITNESSES: Sarfraz Nawaz: 'I don't know who was more shocked—me or the Australians. To get the best out of the conditions I shortened my run-up and bowled with the seam up. I managed to get movement in the air and off the ground and I was able to hit the stumps five times. It was the most amazing day of my career.'

Mushtaq Mohammad: 'We were getting a little desperate when Sarfraz produced his incredible performance. It was one of the most astonishing things I have ever seen on a cricket field. It seemed like there was a never-ending procession of Australian batsmen going to and from the pavilion. It was a wonderful occasion for Sarfraz in particular and for Pakistan cricket in general.'

Graham Yallop: 'We were all speechless in the dressing-room and just could not believe what had happened to us. In all my time in cricket I had never seen anything quite like it. At tea-time on the final day we were convinced we had the game wrapped up. An hour later we were wondering how we had lost. It was a performance in a million by Sarfraz.'

FOR THE RECORD: It was a two Test series, and two weeks later in Perth Australia got some consolation when they won by seven wickets. Javed Miandad (129) and Asif Iqbal (134) scored an unbeaten century in each innings but had little support. Sarfraz took two for 112 in the first innings and nought for 85 in the second. He was severely criticised during Australia's second innings when he got Andrew Hilditch out for 'handling the ball.' Hilditch was at the non-striker's end and innocently fielded a wayward return and handed the ball to Sarfraz, who was the bowler. Sarfraz appealed to the umpire who had to go by the rule-book and he gave Hilditch out. It followed the run-out of Sikander in Pakistan's second innings when bowler Alan Hurst (five for 94) removed his bails when he was backing up from the non-striker's end. Allan Border was top scorer for Australia in both of their innings, hitting 85 and then 66 not out.

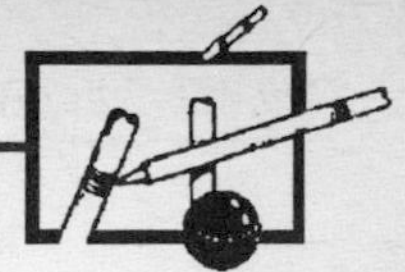

Australia v Pakistan, First Test, 1978-79

PAKISTAN

Majid Khan	c Wright b Hogg	1	— b Border	108
Mohsin Khan	c Hilditch b Hogg	14	— c and b Hogg	14
Zaheer Abbas	b Hogg	11	— b Hogg	59
Javed Miandad	b Hogg	19	— c Wright b Border	16
Asif Iqbal	c Wright b Clark	9	— lbw b Hogg	44
Mushtaq Mohammad*	c Wright b Hurst	36	— c sub b Sleep	28
Wasim Raja	b Hurst	13	— c Wright b Hurst	28
Imran Khan	c Wright b Hurst	33	— c Clark b Hurst	28
Sarfraz Nawaz	c Wright b Sleep	35	— lbw b Hurst	1
Wasim Bari†	run out	0	— not out	8
Sikander Bakht	not out	5		
Extras	(B 2, LB 7, W 1, NB 10)	20	(B 4, LB 6, NB 9)	19
Total		**196**	(9 wickets declared)	**353**

AUSTRALIA

G.M. Wood	not out	5	— c Wasim Bari b Sarfraz	0
A.M.J. Hilditch	c Miandad b Imran	3	— b Sarfraz	62
A.R. Border	b Imran	20	— b Sarfraz	105
G.N. Yallop*	b Imran	25	— run out	8
K.J. Hughes	run out	19	— c Mohsin b Sarfraz	84
D.F. Whatmore	lbw b Sarfraz	43	— b Sarfraz	15
P.R. Sleep	c Wasim Bari b Imran	10	— b Sarfraz	0
K.J. Wright†	c Imran b Wasim Raja	9	— not out	1
W.M. Clark	c Mushtaq b Wasim Raja	9	— b Sarfraz	0
R.M. Hogg	run out	9	— lbw b Sarfraz	0
A.G. Hurst	c and b Sarfraz	0	— c Wasim Bari b Sarfraz	0
Extras	(B 1, LB 5, W 2, NB 8)	16	(B 13, LB 13, NB 9)	35
Total		**168**		**310**

AUSTRALIA	O	M	R	W	O	M	R	W
Hogg	17	4	49	4	19	2	75	3
Hurst	20	4	55	3	19.5	1	115	3
Clark	17	4	56	1	21	6	47	0
Sleep	7.7	2	16	1	8	0	62	1
Border					14	5	35	2

PAKISTAN	O	M	R	W	O	M	R	W
Imran	18	8	26	4	27	9	73	0
Sarfraz	21.6	6	39	2	35.4	7	86	9
Sikander	10	1	29	0	7	0	29	0
Mushtaq	7	0	35	0	11	0	42	0
Wasim Raja	5	0	23	2	3	0	11	0
Majid					9	1	34	0

FALL OF WICKETS

	P	A	P	A
Wkt	1st	1st	2nd	2nd
1st	2	11	30	49
2nd	22	53	165	109
3rd	28	63	204	128
4th	40	97	209	305
5th	83	109	261	305
6th	99	140	299	306
7th	122	152	330	308
8th	173	167	332	309
9th	177	167	353	310
10th	196	168	—	310

1979-80 Jubilation as Botham and Taylor eclipse the Indians

Match: India v England, Golden Jubilee Test
Venue: Wankhede Stadium, Bombay **Date:** February 15, 17, 18, 19

THE SETTING: There has never been a game of cricket quite like this one. It was staged to celebrate the Golden Jubilee of the formation of the Board of Control for Cricket in India. At the end of an extraordindary Test it was the England cricketers who had reason to jubilate after world record performances by all-rounder Ian Botham and wicket-keeper Bob Taylor.

The rest day was brought forward because of the eclipse of the sun, and then it was the Indian cricketers who found themselves totally eclipsed to end a sequence of 15 Test matches without a single defeat.

For England the victory came as a welcome morale-booster after a tour to Australia in which they had taken three successive hammerings. This was the springtime of Botham's eventful career, and he stamped his mark on almost every session in the match.

THE MATCH: Botham's first impact on the match was with the ball. With a heavy cloud cover and the pitch, by Indian standards, unusually grassy, the conditions suited him down to the ground. He swung merrily away and unleashed the occasional cutter as he haunted the Indian batsmen with bowling that was as unpredictable and explosive as the man delivering the ball. After Sunil Gavaskar and Anglo-Indian Roger Binny had shared an opening stand of 56, Botham went into overdrive and in 22.5 overs removed six batsman for 58 runs. Wicket-keeper Bob Taylor, all smoothness and efficiency behind the stumps, held five catches off the bowling of Botham and another two off Graham Stevenson, who was making his Test debut. These seven dismissals by the Derbyshire 'keeper equalled the world record for a Test innings set by Wasim Bari for Pakistan in New Zealand a year earlier.

It was another wicket-keeper, Syed Kirmani, who brought some order to India's disintegrating innings with an unbeaten 40 that raised the total to 242.

England struggled in the early stages of their innings against the bowling of Kapil Dev (three for 64) and Karsan Ghavri (five for 52) before Botham and Taylor combined again—this time with the bat. In what was virtually a match-winning stand, they put on 171 for the sixth wicket after England had stumbled to 58 for five.

The slim-line Botham—this was before his 'Beefy' days—powered the ball to the boundary 17 times on his way to 114 in 260 minutes. Taylor (43) was content to play a supporting role that seemed curtailed with their

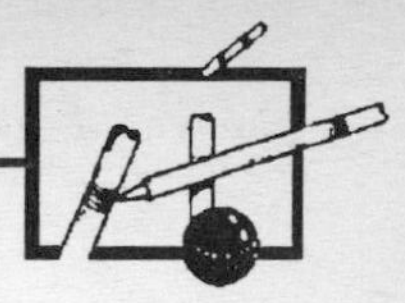

partnership at 85. Umpire Hanumantha Rao raised his finger to signal that Taylor was out following an appeal for a catch behind the wicket by Kirmani.

It was obvious to all neutral onlookers that Taylor had not got a touch, and he protested at the decision—an act that was out of character for a player renowned for his sportsmanship, but on this occasion he had a lot of sympathy including that of Indian skipper Gundappa Viswanath. He was fielding at slip and cooled what could have been an explosive situation by confirming to the umpire that Taylor had not touched the ball, and the decision was revoked.

Boosted by late-order hitting from Stevenson (27 not out) and John Lever (21), England managed to total 296 and had a lead of 54 which was remarkable considering their early slump.

On the third day Botham was back dominating the stage again with the ball. He was still extracting sufficient bounce and movement to trouble all the Indian batsmen and during the course of the second innings England were able to celebrate two world records.

Taylor held on to three catches—all off Botham—to set a world record of ten catches in a Test match. When Botham took his fourth wicket of the second innings he became the first player in the history of Test cricket to score a century and take ten wickets in one match.

India looked in danger of being beaten inside three days when their innings lay in ruins at 58 for six, but then Kapil Dev produced a Botham-style knock before he ran out of partners at 45 not out and with the Indian total at 149.

Botham finished the innings with seven wickets for 48 off 26 overs, and a match analysis of 13 for 106—an incredible performance when put alongside the 114 runs he had gathered with the bat. What made it even more remarkable is the fact that the Bombay pitch was an infamous graveyard for medium and pace bowlers. It was the slow bowlers who normally reaped a harvest, and the England selectors picked two specialist spinners in Derek Underwood and John Emburey. They finished up with little more than a walk-on role in what was the Botham and Taylor show. Underwood bowled just seven overs and Emburey did not get to turn over his arm at all.

There was one more amazing cameo to come, this time without the involvement of either Botham or Taylor.

Geoff Boycott and Graham Gooch opened the second innings with England needing just 96 runs for victory and with a day and a half in which to collect them. Boycott was given out by the umpire following another appeal for a catch behind by Kirmani. It was clear to everybody else that Boycott had not touched the ball, and there were no protests when he ignored the umpire's raised finger and continued his innings.

India used seven bowlers in a desperate bid to make a breakthrough, but Gooch (49) and Boycott (43) played with coolness and control and steered England to victory by ten wickets with a full day to spare.

THE WITNESSES: Bob Taylor: 'This was my most memorable match behind the stumps. Ian Botham joked that I had superglue on my gloves because everything stuck. It was an unbelievable performance by Both. He has the energy of two men and is world-class with the bat and the ball. One thing's for certain, nothing is ever dull when he is on the field. He is a bundle of energy and is always making something happen.'

Mike Brearley, England skipper: 'It was a herculean performance from Ian. Despite all his efforts, he never once showed signs of tiredness and wanted to be involved in everything. The only problem I had with him was getting the ball off him! He is now firmly established as one of the great all-rounders.'

Gundappa Viswanath: 'The Golden Jubilee game came at a bad time for us. We had played 17 Test matches in seven months and were worn out. But that must not be allowed to diminish an extraordindary performance by Ian Botham. He is such a powerful man that I predict he will be giving many teams trouble with the bat and the ball in the years to come.'

FOR THE RECORD: There were two performances in the Golden Jubilee match to brighten the gloom of India's defeat. Viswanath completed his 5,000th run in 69 Tests and Kirmani still became the first Indian wicket-keeper to make 100 Test dismissals despite his two 'phantom' catches being turned down.

Bob Taylor catches Sunil Gavaskar off the bowling of Ian Botham

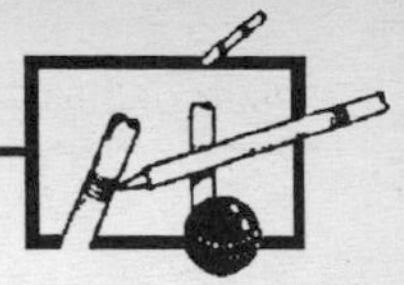

India v England, Golden Jubilee Test, 1980

INDIA

S.M. Gavaskar	c Taylor b Botham	49	— c Taylor b Botham	24
R.M.H. Binny	run out	15	— lbw b Botham	0
D.B. Vengsarkar	c Taylor b Stevenson	34	— lbw b Lever	10
G.R. Viswanath*	b Lever	11	— c Taylor b Botham	5
S.M. Patil	c Taylor b Botham	30	— lbw b Botham	0
Yashpal Sharma	lbw b Botham	21	— lbw b Botham	27
Kapil Dev	c Taylor b Botham	0	— not out	45
S.M.H. Kirmani†	not out	40	— c Gooch b Botham	0
K.D. Ghavri	c Taylor b Stevenson	11	— c Brearley b Lever	5
N.S. Yadav	c Taylor b Botham	8	— c Taylor b Botham	15
D.R. Doshi	c Taylor b Botham	6	— c and b Lever	0
Extras	(B 5, LB 3, NB 9)	17	(B 4, LB 8, W 1, NB 5)	18
Total		**242**		**149**

ENGLAND

G.A. Gooch	c Kirmani b Ghavri	8	— not out	49
G. Boycott	c Kirmani b Binny	22	— not out	43
W. Larkins	lbw b Ghavri	0		
D.I. Gower	lbw b Kapil Dev	16		
J.M. Brearley*	lbw b Kapil Dev	5		
I.T. Botham	lbw b Ghavri	114		
R.W. Taylor†	lbw b Kapil Dev	43		
J.E. Emburey	c Binny b Ghavri	8		
J.K. Lever	b Doshi	21		
G.B. Stevenson	not out	27		
D.L. Underwood	b Ghavri	1		
Extras	(B 8, LB 9, NB 14)	31	(B 3, LB 1, NB 2)	6
Total		**296**	(0 wickets)	**98**

ENGLAND	O	M	R	W	O	M	R	W
Lever	23	3	82	1	20.1	2	65	3
Botham	22.5	7	58	6	26	7	48	7
Stevenson	14	1	59	2	5	1	13	0
Underwood	6	1	23	0	1	0	5	0
Gooch	4	2	3	0				

INDIA	O	M	R	W	O	M	R	W
Kapil Dev	29	8	64	3	8	2	21	0
Ghavri	20.1	5	52	5	5	0	12	0
Binny	19	3	70	1				
Doshi	23	6	57	1	6	1	12	0
Yadav	6	2	22	0	6	0	31	0
Patil					3	0	8	0
Gavaskar					1	0	4	0
Viswanath					0.3	0	4	0

FALL OF WICKETS

	I	E	I	E
Wkt	1st	1st	2nd	2nd
1st	56	21	4	—
2nd	102	21	22	—
3rd	108	45	31	—
4th	135	57	31	—
5th	160	58	56	—
6th	160	229	58	—
7th	181	245	102	—
8th	197	262	115	—
9th	223	283	148	—
10th	242	296	149	—

Botham and Willis perform a miracle at Headingley

Match: England v Australia, Third Test
Venue: Headingley **Date:** July 16, 17, 18, 20, 21

THE SETTING: England had gone 12 Tests without a victory since the triumph in the Golden Jubliee Test in Bombay. All the matches had been played under the captaincy of Ian Botham who had emerged as one of the most charismatic yet at the same time controversial characters on the cricket circuit.

After England had lost the first Test and drawn the second against an Australian team skippered by Kim Hughes, Botham resigned as captain—a decision that saved the selectors from what was looming as an inevitable sacking.

They recalled the outstanding field marshal Mike Brearley, who had stepped down in the summer of 1980 after helping to build a team, both in stature and spirit, that was a match for the best in the world. The side he led into the third Test against Australia at Headingley included Botham, who was suddenly free from the shackles of responsibility that had anchored his performances in recent months.

THE MATCH: Australia batted throughout the first two days that produced fairly pedestrian cricket that matched the greyness of the skies. Thanks to a patient maiden Test century by opener John Dyson (102) and enterprising knocks by Kim Hughes (89) and Graham Yallop (58), the tourists built a formidable total of 401. Botham toiled through 39.2 overs and was suddenly rewarded for all his effort during a spell after tea on the second day when he took five wickets for 35 runs. He finished with figures of six for 95.

England had a nightmare third day that saw them swept out for 174 and, forced to follow on, they lost Graham Gooch without a run on the board. At one stage the betting odds offered against an England victory drifted to 500 to 1—and there were few takers.

Botham was top scorer for England in their pitiful first innings with an aggressive 50 before he fell to the pace of Dennis Lillee, giving a catch behind to Rodney Marsh to become the Australian wicket-keeper's 264th victim in Test matches—one more than Alan Knott's world record.

Australia needed to use only three bowlers, with Lillee (four for 49), Terry Alderman (three for 59) and Geoff Lawson (two for 32) maintaining a pace attack that unhinged a procession of England batsmen.

Following the dismissal of Gooch for a duck by Lillee at the start of England's second innings, the umpires abandoned play for the day because of bad light. It was a decision that caused uproar among the spectators. But there were those who saw it

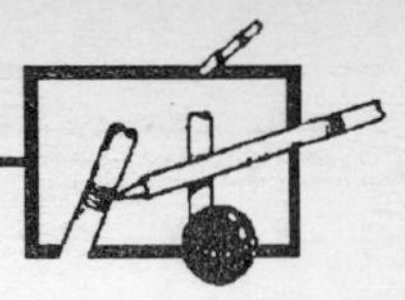

as just a delaying of the execution for England's backs-to-the-wall batsmen.

By late afternoon on the fourth day England were still 92 runs in arrears and struggling to keep the game alive at 135 for seven against the sustained pace of Lillee, Alderman and Lawson. Boycott had battled valiantly for three and a half hours before becoming the sixth wicket to fall for 46 runs and when Bob Taylor followed two runs later the England players were congratulating themselves on the sense they had shown in packing their bags and checking out of their hotel before the morning's play commenced.

It was at this point of seeming hopelessness that Botham turned the match and the series on its head with an heroic and quite astounding innings. It led to a queue forming at the England squad's hotel three hours later as players, officials and media men re-booked their rooms.

With Graham Dilley as an inspired comrade in arms, Botham scattered the Australian fielders with a barrage of attacking shots that took him hurtling to a hundred off only 87 balls. Together they put on 117 in 80 minutes for the eighth wicket before Dilley departed with 56 priceless runs to his name.

Chris Old then joined Botham and took over where Dilley left off with a succession of powerful blows that took him quickly to 29 before he was bowled by Lawson with the England total looking much healthier at 319 for nine. At the close of play England were 124 ahead and Botham and Bob Willis were together as last-wicket partners. Botham then joined the rush

Bob Willis on the run at Headingley after taking his eighth wicket

to re-book hotel rooms.

He increased his score to 149 the next morning before Willis was caught by Allan Border off the bowling of Alderman, who was having an exceptional first Test series and finished with figures of six for 135 off 35.3 overs. His analysis had looked much better before Botham started his bombardment.

Australia were left with 130 runs for victory and remained favourites, but England were suddenly sniffing an outside chance of winning a game that had seemed dead and buried the previous day. Botham's batting had electrified the England team in general and Bob Willis in particular.

Willis performed Botham-type heroics after the tourists had navigated the score to a comfortable 56 for one. Skipper Mike Brearley gave him the opportunity to change ends so that the strong wind was at his back. He responded with the finest bowling performance of his life and he took eight of the nine Australian wickets that fell for 55 runs. Bob Taylor hung on to seven catches to overtake John Murray's world record of 1,270 catches in first-class cricket.

Willis finished with his best-ever figures of eight for 43 off 15.1 overs to clinch a fantastic England victory by 18 runs. It was the first time this century that a team had won a Test match after following-on and was like something out of the pages of *The Wizard* rather than *Wisden*.

THE WITNESSES: Ian Botham: 'When Graham Dilley joined me in the middle I said to him, "Come on, let's give it a bit of humpty." We knew it was pointless trying to play it safe and so we went for our shots. We had a lot of luck but we grew in confidence as the Australians started to show signs of desperation. Graham deserves a lot of the credit for our recovery because he matched me stroke for stroke.'

Bob Willis: 'It did not sink in what we had achieved until I was on my way home miles from Headingley. I was concentrating too hard on the job in hand to take in anything that happened on the pitch. All I was thinking of was the next ball.'

FOR THE RECORD: Botham transformed the fourth Test with the ball just as emphatically as he had with the bat at Headingley. England looked doomed to defeat after totalling 189 and 219 against the swing of Alderman and the spin of Ray Bright. In a match in which no batsman reached 50, Australia needed just 142 to win with nine second innings wickets standing. Botham took five wickets for one run as they lost their last six wickets for 16 runs in 47 minutes. Botham was at it again in the fifth Test at Old Trafford when—after getting a duck in the first innings— he included an Ashes record of six sixes in a hurricane innings of 118 that pointed England towards victory by 103 runs over the shell-shocked Aussies for whom Yallop (114) and Border (123 not out) scored centuries. In a drawn sixth Test Border scored his second undefeated century, Botham took ten wickets, Lillee returned his best-ever figures of 11 for 159 and Geoff Boycott collected his 21st Test century.

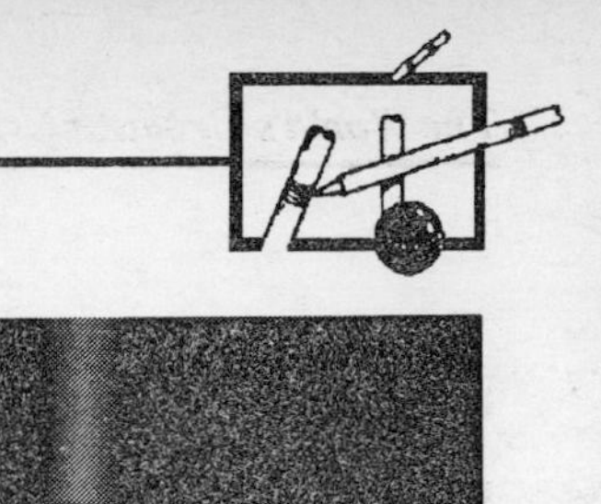

Ian Botham in full flow at Headingley with Rodney Marsh as a spectator

England v Australia, Third Test, 1981

AUSTRALIA

J. Dyson	b Dilley	102	— c Taylor b Willis	34
G.M. Wood	lbw b Botham	34	— c Taylor b Botham	10
T.M. Chappell	c Taylor b Willey	27	— c Taylor b Willis	8
K.J. Hughes*	c and b Botham	89	— c Botham b Willis	0
R.J. Bright	b Dilley	7	— b Willis	19
G.N. Yallop	c Taylor b Botham	58	— c Gatting b Willis	0
A.R. Border	lbw b Botham	8	— b Old	0
R.W. Marsh†	b Botham	28	— c Dilley b Willis	4
G.F. Lawson	c Taylor b Botham	13	— c Taylor b Willis	1
D.K. Lillee	not out	3	— c Gatting b Willis	17
T.M. Alderman	not out	0	— not out	0
Extras	(B 4, LB 13, W 3, NB 12)	32	(LB 3, W 1, NB 14)	18
Total	(9 wickets declared)	**401**		**111**

ENGLAND

G.A. Gooch	lbw b Alderman	2	— c Alderman b Lillee	0
G. Boycott	b Lawson	12	— lbw b Alderman	46
J.M. Brearley*	c Marsh b Alderman	10	— c Alderman b Lillee	14
D.I. Gower	c Marsh b Lawson	24	— c Border b Alderman	9
M.W. Gatting	lbw b Lillee	15	— lbw b Alderman	1
P. Willey	b Lawson	8	— c Dyson b Lillee	33
I.T. Botham	c Marsh b Lillee	50	— not out	149
R.W. Taylor†	c Marsh b Lillee	5	— c Bright b Alderman	1
G.R. Dilley	c and b Lillee	13	— b Alderman	56
C.M. Old	c Border b Alderman	0	— b Lawson	29
R.G.D. Willis	not out	1	— c Border b Alderman	2
Extras	(B 6, LB 11, W 6, NB 11)	34	(B 5, LB 3, W 3, NB 5)	16
Total		**174**		**356**

ENGLAND	O	M	R	W	O	M	R	W
Willis	30	8	72	0	15.1	3	43	8
Old	43	14	91	0	9	1	21	1
Dilley	27	4	78	2	2	0	11	0
Botham	39.2	11	95	6	7	3	14	1
Willey	13	2	31	1	3	1	4	0
Boycott	3	2	2	0				

AUSTRALIA	O	M	R	W	O	M	R	W
Lillee	18.5	7	49	4	25	6	94	3
Alderman	19	4	59	3	35.3	6	135	6
Lawson	13	3	32	3	23	4	96	1
Bright					4	0	15	0

FALL OF WICKETS

	A	E	E	A
Wkt	1st	1st	2nd	2nd
1st	55	12	0	13
2nd	149	40	18	56
3rd	196	42	37	58
4th	220	84	41	58
5th	332	87	105	65
6th	354	112	133	68
7th	357	148	135	74
8th	396	166	252	75
9th	401	167	319	110
10th	—	174	356	111

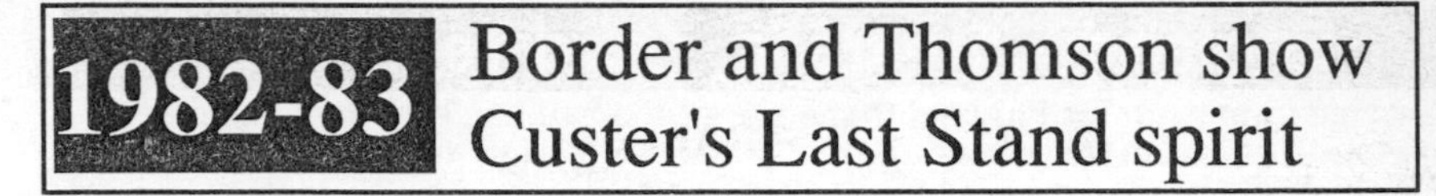

1982-83 Border and Thomson show Custer's Last Stand spirit

Match: Australia v England, Fourth Test
Venue: Melbourne **Date:** December 26, 27, 28, 29, 30

THE SETTING: A measure of the excitement generated by the climax of this 250th Ashes Test is that a crowd of 18,000 gathered at the Melbourne Cricket Ground on the final morning to witness what could be little more than an hour's play.

The fact that they were allowed in free of charge is of no consequence, for every one of them would willingly have paid to see one of the most thrilling and tense finales in the history of Test cricket.

They were drawn to the ground by a last-wicket partnership between Allan Border and Jeff Thomson that is talked about Down Under with the same sort of respectful tones as Custer's Last Stand is recounted in the United States.

But it wasn't the Indians who were surrounding Border and Thomson. It was England skipper Bob Willis and his men battling desperately to gain their first Test win of the tour and so level the series.

THE MATCH: Skipper Greg Chappell won the toss and gambled on putting England in on unknown territory. The MCG square had only recently been relaid and nobody knew how it would play. There was enough dampness in the pitch to encourage pacemen Rodney Hogg (four for 69) and Jeff Thomson (two for 49) and openers Geoff Cook and Graeme Fowler were hustled out for 25, quickly followed by David Gower at 56. Chris Tavaré (89), in uncharacteristic adventurous mood, set the pace as he and Allan Lamb (83) added 161 in a sparkling fourth wicket partnership that covered just 32 overs. Spinner Bruce Yardley (four for 89) made a mess of England's middle-order and they tottered from 217 for four to 284 all out.

Each of the first three days featured one full innnings. It was Australia's turn to fall apart on the second day, with only Kim Hughes (66), David Hookes (53), Rodney Marsh (53) and Kepler Wessels (47) getting into any sort of batting rhythm. It was fast bowler Norman Cowans who first put the Aussies in trouble when he took the wickets of John Dyson and Greg Chappell with successive balls. At the end of the innings England trailed by just three runs.

England were in trouble at 43 for three in their second innings, but steady batting by Fowler (65) mixed with the belligerence of Botham (46) and the determination of Derek Pringle (42) and Bob Taylor (37) lifted the total to a reasonable 294 on a pitch that was unpredictable and on which Australia did not relish the thought of batting last.

Cowans produced the best performance of his career in Australia's second innings to lift England to the brink of victory. He finished with figures of six for 77 off 26 overs and in one spell took the wickets of top scorer Hookes (68), Marsh, Yardley and Hogg at a cost of 19 runs and in the space of seven overs.

Australia were all but out for the count when Thomson joined the bold Border at the wicket at 218 for nine. By the close of play on the fourth day they had edged the total up to 255 for nine in a stand that had grabbed the attention of the nation as well as thousands of English cricket fanatics half a world away with their ears stuck to radios listening to the ball-by-ball broadcasts in the early hours of the morning. The Aussies finished the day needing 37 runs to win.

They continued to defy the England bowlers in the opening hour of the final day and pushed their partnership to 70 runs in 128 minutes. They had declined to run 29 comfortable singles. Every run that they did take was greeted with the sort of roar you hear when a Cup Final goal is scored.

When Botham began the 18th over of the session Australia were just four runs away from a sensational victory. His first ball was going through shoulder-high wide on the leg side and Thomson, unbeaten on 21, could have let it go harmlessly by. But he made a half-hearted lunge at it to present what looked an easy catch to Tavaré at second slip. He clutched at the ball but managed only to parry it and it flew away behind first slip Geoff Miller, who was fielding a yard or two deeper than Tavaré. Miller turned as nimbly as an Astaire on grass, did a quick two-step in pursuit of the ball and bent and caught it 12 inches off the ground. It was a dramatic end to a dramatic last stand.

For Botham it was a milestone wicket. It made him only the second Englishman after Wilfred Rhodes to have taken 100 wickets and scored 1,000 runs against the Australians.

THE WITNESSES: Allan Border, not out on 62: 'We almost made the impossible possible. The longer we stayed out there the more rattled the England fielders were becoming. It's easy now to say we should not have turned down so many singles, but we just did not want to give England the slightest encouragement.'

Jeff Thomson: 'It was heartbreaking to get so near to our target and then have it snatched away from us. I've never known so much excitement before. The crowd went crazy every time we put a run on the board.'

Bob Willis: 'It was a magnificent effort by Border and Thomson, particularly Jeff who is not a recognised batsman. We were trying to get him down the bowling end and were almost inviting them to run singles. But they were very cagey.'

FOR THE RECORD: England's victory by three runs equalled the narrowest runs margin in Test cricket which was set when Australia beat England in 1902. The fifth Test in which Kim Hughes scored 137 was drawn, enabling Australia to retain the Ashes. Rodney Marsh set a new record for an Ashes series by holding 28 catches.

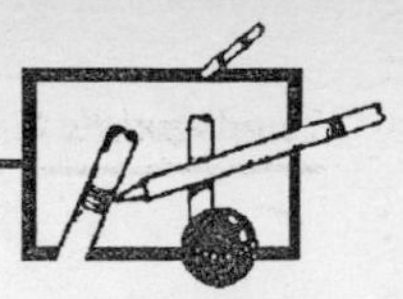

Allan Border in high and mighty mood during his stand with Jeff Thomson

Australia v England, Fourth Test, 1982-83

ENGLAND

G. Cook	c Chappell b Thomson	10	— c Yardley b Thomson	26
G. Fowler	c Chappell b Hogg	4	— b Hogg	65
C.J. Tavare	c Yardley b Thomson	89	— b Hogg	0
D.I. Gower	c Marsh b Hogg	18	— c Marsh b Lawson	3
A.J. Lamb	c Dyson b Yardley	83	— c Marsh b Hogg	26
I.T. Botham	c Wessels b Yardley	27	— c Chappell b Thomson	46
G. Miller	c Border b Yardley	10	— lbw b Lawson	14
D.R. Pringle	c Wessels b Hogg	9	— c Marsh b Lawson	42
R.W. Taylor†	c Marsh b Yardley	1	— lbw b Thomson	37
R.G.D. Willis*	not out	6	— not out	8
N.G. Cowans	c Lawson b Hogg	3	— b Lawson	10
Extras	(B 3, LB 6, W 3, NB 12)	24	(B 2, LB 9, NB 6)	17
Total		**284**		**294**

AUSTRALIA

K.C. Wessels	b Willis	47	— b Cowans	14
J. Dyson	lbw b Cowans	21	— c Tavare b Botham	31
G.S. Chappell*	c Lamb b Cowans	0	— c sub b Cowans	2
K.J. Hughes	b Willis	66	— c Taylor b Miller	48
A.R. Border	b Botham	2	— not out	62
D.W. Hookes	c Taylor b Pringle	53	— c Willis b Cowans	68
R.W. Marsh†	b Willis	53	— lbw b Cowans	13
B. Yardley	b Miller	9	— b Cowans	0
G.F. Lawson	c Fowler b Miller	0	— c Cowans b Pringle	7
R.M. Hogg	not out	1	— lbw b Cowans	4
J.R. Thomson	b Miller	1	— c Miller b Botham	21
Extras	(LB 8, NB 19)	27	(B 5, LB 9, W 1, NB 3)	18
Total		**287**		**288**

AUSTRALIA	O	M	R	W	O	M	R	W
Lawson	17	6	48	0	21.4	6	66	4
Hogg	23.3	6	69	4	22	5	64	3
Yardley	27	9	89	4	15	2	67	0
Thomson	13	2	49	2	21	3	74	3
Chappell	1	0	5	0	1	0	6	0

ENGLAND	O	M	R	W	O	M	R	W
Willis	15	2	38	3	17	0	57	0
Botham	18	3	69	1	25.1	4	80	2
Cowans	16	0	69	2	26	6	77	6
Pringle	15	2	40	1	12	4	26	1
Miller	15	5	44	3	16	6	30	1

FALL OF WICKETS

	E	A	E	A
Wkt	1st	1st	2nd	2nd
1st	11	55	40	37
2nd	25	55	41	39
3rd	56	83	45	71
4th	217	89	128	171
5th	227	180	129	173
6th	259	261	160	190
7th	262	276	201	190
8th	268	276	262	202
9th	278	278	280	218
10th	284	287	294	288

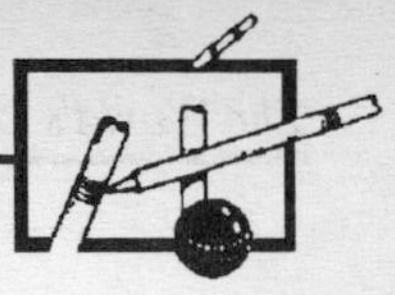

1983-84 Hadlee rattles skeletons in the England cupboard

Match: New Zealand v England, Second Test
Venue: Lancaster Park, Christchurch **Date:** February 3, 4, 5

THE SETTING: If England's cricketers could drop a veil on a Test match performance this would be the one they would most like to hide from view. Recording it here is like rattling skeletons in the cupboard.

They managed to get themselves beaten by an innings in an embarrassing match that lasted a total of less than 12 hours.

But the Test deserves its place in this catalogue of cricket's greatest games because for New Zealand it represents the most spectacular victory in their history.

Saddest of all the England players was Sussex all-rounder Tony Pigott, who was in New Zealand playing for Wellington when injury problems led to his surprise call into the England team at the last minute for his one and only Test appearance. He postponed his wedding to achieve his lifetime's ambition of playing in a Test match. He took a wicket with his seventh ball, but must have soon wished he'd gone on his honeymoon instead.

THE MATCH: New Zealand batted first in conditions that would have suited England's seam bowlers if they had been in anything like their best form, but they were loose and lackadaisical with their deliveries. Norman Cowans (three for 52) was briefly successful and skipper Bob Willis (four for 51) bowled intelligently once he realised he was best advised to come in off a shortened run to get the most of the seaming conditions. But the evidence that the rest of England's bowling was not up to par showed in a scorebook that revealed that New Zealand's batsmen helped themselves to 42 fours during the first innings.

Richard Hadlee made the most of the slackness in the England attack and hammered 99 off 81 balls in 111 minutes before being caught by Bob Taylor off the bowling of Willis.

New Zealand averaged 4.2 an over to total 307, with Jeff Crowe (47) and Jeremy Coney (41) both playing with huge enthusiasm and enterprise.

Botham, the hero of the hour in so many matches for England, produced his least impressive Test figures with a return of one wicket for 88 runs off 17 overs. He bowled so many long hops that somebody suggested he should be nicknamed the Kangaroo Kid rather than Guy the Gorilla. The joker did not say it to his face. Everybody is entitled to an off day. This was Botham's.

If anything, England's batting was even worse than their bowling. Mike Gatting, with an undefeated 19, was the top scorer in a feeble first innings reply of 82. Hadlee (three for 16),

Lance Cairns (three for 35), Ewen Chatfield (three for 10) and Stephen Boock (one for 12) shared the wickets between them. Graeme Fowler was bowled by slow left-armer Boock in the last over of the opening day. Rain delayed play until after tea on the second day and by the time of the close England had lost seven wickets for 53.

They were all out 45 minutes before lunch on the third day after the determined Gatting had run out of partners. England were forced to follow on for the first time in 59 Tests against the Kiwis and with cracks showing in the pitch it was obvious that batting was not going to get any easier.

Needing 225 runs to avoid the ignominy of an innings defeat, England openers Fowler and Chris Tavaré showed some resistance at the start by hanging on until lunch. An hour after the interval New Zealand had made a meal of the England batsmen. Six were out for 33 in the face of speed from Hadlee (five for 28) and spin from Boock (three for 25).

Derek Randall and Bob Taylor added a spirited 39 for the sixth wicket after Boock had dismissed both Gatting and Botham for ducks. At the end of England's innings for 93 at 4.31 p.m. on the third afternoon newcomer Pigott was left not out on eight and wondering how his dream match had managed to turn into a nightmare.

England's defeat by an innings and 132 runs was their heaviest loss for ten years, and for the first time this century an England team had failed to total 100 in either innings.

THE WITNESSES: Bob Willis: 'We had the worst of the pitch, but it is no good hiding behind excuses. We played badly throughout the match. Our bowling was some of the worst I have ever seen in Test cricket.'

Geoff Howarth, New Zealand skipper: 'This is one of my proudest moments in cricket. Some people might consider it a freak result, but we worked hard for it and once we had England on the hook we refused to let them off. Richard Hadlee proved yet again that he is without question one of the greatest all-rounders in the world. Our objective must now be to try to win the series.'

FOR THE RECORD: The first Test in Wellington was drawn. Botham showed his true form with a century and five wickets in an innings in the same Test for a record fifth time. He and Derek Randall (164) put on 232 in 201 minutes in a sixth-wicket partnership in England's first innings of 463. Lance Cairns took England's first six wickets and finished with figures of seven for 143. Martin Crowe and Jeremy Cooney both scored maiden Test hundreds in New Zealand's second innings total of 537. The Kiwis clinched their first ever win in a series over England when they drew the third Test in Auckland. John Wright (130) and Jeff Crowe (128) shared a fourth-wicket partnership of 154, and wicket-keeper Ian Smith (113 not out) scored his maiden Test century in a New Zealand total of 496. England replied with 439, with Randall (104), Chris Smith (91) and Botham (70) the top scorers.

N. Zealand v England, Second Test, 1983-84

NEW ZEALAND

J.G. Wright	c Taylor b Cowans	25
B.A. Edgar	c Randall b Pigott	1
G.P. Howarth*	b Cowans	9
M.D. Crowe	c Tavare b Botham	19
J.J. Crowe	lbw b Cowans	47
J.V. Coney	c Botham b Pigott	41
R.J. Hadlee	c Taylor b Willis	99
I.D.S. Smith†	not out	32
B.L. Cairns	c Taylor b Willis	2
S.L. Boock	c Taylor b Willis	5
E.J. Chatfield	lbw b Willis	0
Extras	(B 8, LB 11, W 2, NB 6)	27
Total		**307**

ENGLAND

G. Fowler	b Boock	4	— c Howarth b Boock	10
C.J. Tavare	c J.J. Crowe b Hadlee	3	— c Smith b Hadlee	6
D.I. Gower	lbw b Hadlee	2	— c Cairns b Hadlee	8
A.J. Lamb	c Smith b Chatfield	11	— c Coney b Chatfield	9
D.W. Randall	c Coney b Hadlee	0	— c Cairns b Hadlee	25
I.T. Botham	c Chatfield b Cairns	18	— c M.D. Crowe b Boock	0
M.W. Gatting	not out	19	— c Hadlee b Boock	0
R.W. Taylor†	c J.J. Crowe b Cairns	2	— run out	15
A.C.S. Pigott	lbw b Cairns	4	— not out	8
R.G.D. Willis*	b Chatfield	6	— c Howarth b Hadlee	0
N.G. Cowans	c Coney b Chatfield	4	c Smith b Hadlee	7
Extras	(LB 6, NB 3)	9	(LB 2, NB 3)	5
Total		**82**		**93**

ENGLAND	O	M	R	W
Willis	22.1	5	51	4
Botham	17	1	88	1
Pigott	17	7	75	2
Cowans	14	2	52	3
Gatting	2	0	14	0

NEW ZEALAND	O	M	R	W	O	M	R	W
Hadlee	17	9	16	3	18	6	28	5
Cairns	19	5	35	3	9	3	21	0
Boock	6	3	12	1	13	3	25	3
Chatfield	8.2	3	10	3	11	1	14	1

FALL OF WICKETS

	NZ	E	E
Wkt	1st	1st	2nd
1st	30	7	15
2nd	42	9	23
3rd	53	10	25
4th	87	10	31
5th	137	41	31
6th	203	41	33
7th	281	47	72
8th	291	58	76
9th	301	72	80
10th	307	82	93

1984 Revived Greenidge buries England under tons of runs

Match: England v West Indies, Second Test
Venue: Lord's **Date:** June 28, 29, 30, July 2, 3

THE SETTING: Lord's celebrated its centenary with this Test, and West Indies marked a special occasion with a special performance. For four days England were allowed to deceive themselves into thinking they were going to win the match, a dream that was demolished in just four hours on the final day.

England were still bearing the scars of a physical and psychological mauling in the the first Test at Edgbaston two weeks earlier when the tourists powered to victory by an innings and 180 runs. Skipper David Gower led a team that included one newcomer in Nottinghamshire opening batsman Chris Broad. This meant for the first time England were starting their innings with three left-handers.

West Indies skipper Clive Lloyd won the toss and English hearts missed a beat when he invited England to bat against a pace attack that was missing the injured Michael Holding but included, in the menacing Malcolm Marshall, the latest off the Carribean conveyor belt of fast bowlers.

THE MATCH: Graeme Fowler and Broad, the seventh different openers paired by the selectors in eight matches, gave England a marvellous send-off. New boy Broad batted as to the Test manner born and in one spell of 12 balls found the boundary five times as the West Indies allowed him to feast on his favourite stroke through mid-wicket. Meantime, Graeme Fowler was progressing quietly towards what was to be one of the most satisfactory centuries of his career. Their stand was broken at 101 when Broad (55) was caught down the leg side by wicket-keeper Jeff Dujon to give Marshall the first of his six wickets for 85.

Fowler continued to peck away and was rewarded with 109 runs off 259 deliveries. It was a triumph as much for his powers of concentration as his strokeplay because he had to play himself in six times owing to aggravating stoppages for bad light.

Apart from a powerfully struck 30 by Botham and a defiant unbeaten 23 by Paul Downton, England failed to build on the foundation provided by Broad and Fowler. There was one piece of extraordinary fielding when Geoff Miller was run out by a spectacular 75-yard throw by Eldine Baptiste that uprooted the middle stump.

It was Ian Botham who yet again put England in command with a Trojan effort with the ball. He took three wickets for 21 in his opening spell on the second evening as West Indies set out to reply to the England total of 286. He got his outswinger

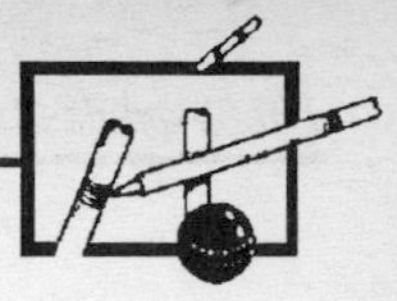

working to perfection the following day and worried all the West Indian batsmen. He finished with the excellent figures of eight for 103 off 27.4 overs, and became the first England bowler to take eight wickets in an innings against the West Indies. The one scalp he did not feel he deserved on his belt was that of his great friend and rival Vivian Richards. A swerving inswinger struck Richards on the pad and Botham started and then stifled an appeal. Umpire Barrie Meyer shocked everybody by raising his finger. Richards, then on 72 and looking set to improve his average of 92 in Tests against England, could not keep the disbelief off his face as he sauntered back to the pavilion. Meyer later took the unusual step of publicly admitting he felt he had made an error of judgement, and he revealed that he had apologised to Richards for what was an honest mistake. It was one of a record-equalling 12 lbw decisions given during the match.

West Indies were all out for 245, and Allan Lamb (110) and Botham (80) led such an assault and battery in the second innings that Gower had what he considered was the luxury of being able to declare at 300 for nine. It left the tourists a victory target of 341. On paper it looked a tall order, but out on the pitch Gordon Greenidge and Larry Gomes made it look as easy as knocking down sandcastles.

They came together when Desmond Haynes was run out at 57, the first time that West Indies had lost a second innings wicket in seven matches. They were still together 300 minutes later with victory in their pockets. Greenidge was the chief partner, hitting two sixes and 29 fours as he became the first West Indian batsman to score a double century at Lord's. He was undefeated on 214 at the finish, with Gomes cruising along at 92 not out. It was the first time since 1948 that England had lost after declaring closed their second innings.

THE WITNESSES: David Gower: 'We really fancied our chances of bowling the West Indies out, but this was not taking into account the possibility of Gordon Greenidge suddenly finding his best form. He had not been among the runs during the tour to date and I just wish he had waited a little longer before producing his brilliant knock. The highlight for me was once again seeing Ian Botham confounding and silencing his critics. Those who thought he could no longer produce top-class swing bowling were made to eat their words.'

Gordon Greenidge: 'This was my first double century in Test cricket. To have achieved it in the Lord's centenary match made it all the more memorable. I knew I was due some runs, and I could not have found a better occasion for them.'

FOR THE RECORD: West Indies completed what was then a unique 'blackwash' with a 5-0 win in the series. Greenidge scored a second double century in the fourth Test, and Marshall took five wickets for 35 in England's first innings in the fifth Test to lift his total for the series to 24 wickets, this despite missing the fourth Test through injury. Allan Lamb scored three successive Test centuries for England.

Gordon Greenidge moves four runs nearer his double century at Lord's

England v West Indies, Second Test, 1984

ENGLAND

Batsman	1st innings		2nd innings	
G. Fowler	c Harper b Baptiste	106	— lbw b Small	11
B.C. Broad	c Dujon b Marshall	55	— c Harper b Garner	0
D.I. Gower*	lbw b Marshall	3	— c Lloyd b Small	21
A.J. Lamb	lbw b Marshall	23	— c Dujon b Marshall	110
M.W. Gatting	lbw b Marshall	1	— lbw b Marshall	29
I.T. Botham	c Richards b Baptiste	30	— lbw b Garner	81
P.R. Downton†	not out	23	— lbw b Small	4
G. Miller	run out	0	— b Harper	9
D.R. Pringle	lbw b Garner	2	— lbw b Garner	8
N.A. Foster	c Harper b Marshall	6	— not out	9
R.G.D. Willis	b Marshall	2		
Extras	(B 4, LB 14, W 2, NB 15)	35	(B 4, LB 7, W 1, NB 6)	18
Total		**286**	(9 wickets declared)	**300**

WEST INDIES

Batsman	1st innings		2nd innings	
C.G. Greenidge	c Miller b Botham	1	— not out	214
D.L. Haynes	lbw b Botham	12	— run out	17
H.A. Gomes	c Gatting b Botham	10	— not out	92
I.V.A. Richards	lbw b Botham	72		
C.H. Lloyd*	lbw b Botham	39		
P.J.L. Dujon†	c Fowler b Botham	8		
M.D. Marshall	c Pringle b Willis	29		
E.A.E. Baptiste	c Downton b Willis	44		
R.A. Harper	c Gatting b Botham	8		
J. Garner	c Downton b Botham	6		
M.A. Small	not out	3		
Extras	(LB 5, W 1, NB 7)	13	(B 4, LB 4, NB 13)	21
Total		**245**	(1 wicket)	**344**

WEST INDIES	O	M	R	W	O	M	R	W
Garner	32	10	67	1	30.3	3	91	3
Small	9	0	38	0	12	2	40	3
Marshall	36.5	10	85	6	22	6	85	2
Baptiste	20	6	36	2	26	8	48	0
Harper	8	0	25	0	8	1	18	1

ENGLAND	O	M	R	W	O	M	R	W
Willis	19	5	48	2	15	5	48	0
Botham	27.4	6	103	8	20.1	2	117	0
Pringle	11	0	54	0	8	0	44	0
Foster	6	2	13	0	12	0	69	0
Miller	2	0	14	0	11	0	45	0

FALL OF WICKETS

Wkt	E 1st	WI 1st	E 2nd	WI 2nd
1st	101	1	5	57
2nd	106	18	33	—
3rd	183	35	36	—
4th	185	138	88	—
5th	243	147	216	—
6th	248	173	230	—
7th	251	213	273	—
8th	255	231	290	—
9th	264	241	300	—
10th	286	245	—	—

1985 Match-winner Gower gets caught in a controversy

Match: England v Australia, Fifth Test
Venue: Edgbaston **Date:** August 15, 16, 17, 19, 20

THE SETTING: England and Australia were locked together at 1-1 with two Tests drawn when the cricketing circus moved to Edgbaston where brilliant play by England— mixed with controversy and shaken and stirred by some outspoken comment— produced an explosive cocktail of a match.

The Aussies were battling to save themselves from an innings defeat on the final day when a defiant stand by Wayne Phillips was ended in a freak manner. He flashed at a delivery from spinner Phil Edmonds and the ball cracked against the instep of Allan Lamb, who was fielding at silly point. Lamb performed a hitch-kick as he tried to take avoiding action and this resulted in the ball bobbing up off his boot to be caught by his neighbour David Gower.

The England players appealed for a catch and umpire David Shepherd consulted with David Constant, his colleague at square-leg, who ruled it a fair catch. It was a decision that caused anger in the Aussie dressing-room, and they made no secret of the fact that they thought Phillips should have been given the benefit of the doubt. It dropped a cloud of controversy over a match that had been rainbow bright for England from the moment that David Gower won the toss and put Australia in to bat.

THE MATCH: The Australians, with Kepler Wessels (83) showing the way, made good progress on the first day before rain washed out the second session. Richard Ellison, fighting off a heavy cold that threatened to force his withdrawal from his Ashes debut, exploited a low cloud cover on the second morning and ripped the heart out of the Aussie batting with a spell of four wickets for 15. The tourists seemed almost hypnotised by his swing bowling and he finished with figures of six for 77 off 31.5 overs.

Replying to the Australian total of 335, England gave one of their finest batting performances of the decade. It was skipper David Gower who led by example with the sort of commanding yet graceful batting of which he is a master. He shared a record second wicket partnership of 331 with Tim Robinson (148) and then added another 94 with Mike Gatting before holing out to rival skipper Allan Border at point. Gower's artistically compiled 215 runs brought him the highest score of his career and his second double century in the Test arena.

By tea on the fourth day England were 545 for three, with Gatting and Lamb (46) carrying on the merciless chase for runs. Then Botham struck mighty sixes off the first and third

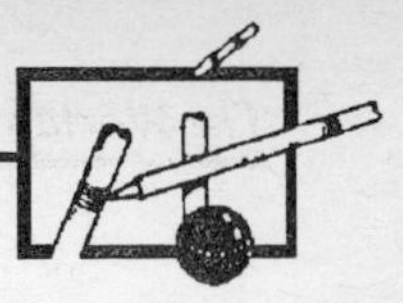

balls that he received from Craig McDermott. Gatting was undefeated on 100 when Gower put the Australian bowlers out of their misery by declaring at 595 for five.

It was then Ellison back in the spotlight, this time with an incredible spell of four wickets for one run in 15 balls. It came after Botham had removed Andrew Hilditch for ten and the tourists crumbled to 36 for five.

Australia once again looked to the rain gods. Rain had saved them from defeat at Old Trafford and it washed out the morning's play on the final day of this fifth Test.

Phillips fought a noble rearguard action when play resumed in the afternoon until his controversial dismissal for 59. Botham whipped out the final two batsmen as he took over as England's leading wicket taker in Tests against Australia. England were winners by an innings and 118 runs.

THE WITNESSES: Allan Border: 'It was a diabolical decision to give Phillips out. Nobody could possibly have told whether the ball had touched the ground before it came off Lamb's foot. The benefit of doubt in such instances must always go to the batsman. It cost us the match.'

David Gower: 'I had no doubt whatsoever that the catch was a fair one, and umpire David Constant was perfectly placed to get a clear view. The memory of Richard Ellison's performance will keep him contented in old age. It was a stunning exhibition of swing bowling.'

FOR THE RECORD: England regained the Ashes by beating Australia by an innings and 94 runs in the sixth Test at The Oval. The highlight was a second wicket stand of 351 between Graham Gooch (196) and Gower (157).

David Gower dispatches Jeff Thomson to the boundary at Edgbaston

England v Australia, Fifth Test, 1985

AUSTRALIA

G.M. Wood	c Edmonds b Botham	19	— c Robinson b Ellison	10
A.M.J. Hilditch	c Downton b Edmonds	39	— c Ellison b Botham	10
K.C. Wessels	c Downton b Ellison	83	— c Downton b Ellison	10
A.R. Border*	c Edmonds b Ellison	45	— b Ellison	2
G.M. Ritchie	c Botham b Ellison	8	— c Lamb b Emburey	20
W.B. Phillips†	c Robinson b Ellison	15	— c Gower b Edmonds	59
S.P. O'Donnell	c Downton b Taylor	1	— b Botham	11
G.F. Lawson	run out	53	— c Gower b Edmonds	3
C.J. McDermott	c Gower b Ellison	35	— c Edmonds b Botham	8
J.R. Thomson	not out	28	— not out	4
R.G. Holland	c Edmonds b Ellison	0	— lbw b Ellison	0
Extras	(LB 4, W 1, NB 4)	9	(B 1, LB 3, NB 1)	5
Total		**335**		**142**

ENGLAND

G.A. Gooch	c Phillips b Thomson	19
R.T. Robinson	b Lawson	148
D.I. Gower*	c Border b Lawson	215
M.W. Gatting	not out	100
A.J. Lamb	c Wood b McDermott	46
I.T. Botham	c Thomson b McDermott	18
P.R. Downton†	not out	0
J.E. Emburey		
R.M. Ellison		
P.H. Edmonds		
L.B. Taylor		
Extras	(B 7, LB 20, NB 22)	49
Total	(5 wickets declared)	**595**

ENGLAND	O	M	R	W	O	M	R	W
Botham	27	1	108	1	14.1	2	52	3
Taylor	26	5	78	1	13	4	27	0
Ellison	31.5	9	77	6	9	3	27	4
Edmonds	20	4	47	1	15	9	13	2
Emburey	9	2	21	0	13	5	19	1

AUSTRALIA	O	M	R	W
Lawson	37	1	135	2
McDermott	31	2	155	2
Thomson	19	1	101	1
Holland	25	4	95	0
O'Donnell	16	3	69	0
Border	6	1	13	0

FALL OF WICKETS

	A	E	A
Wkt	1st	1st	2nd
1st	44	38	10
2nd	92	369	32
3rd	189	463	32
4th	191	572	35
5th	207	592	36
6th	208	—	113
7th	218	—	117
8th	276	—	120
9th	335	—	137
10th	335	—	142

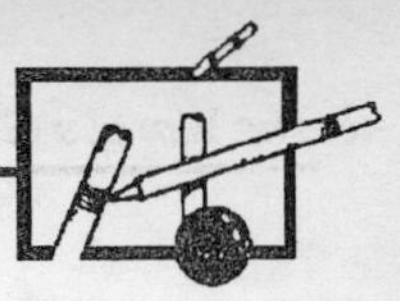

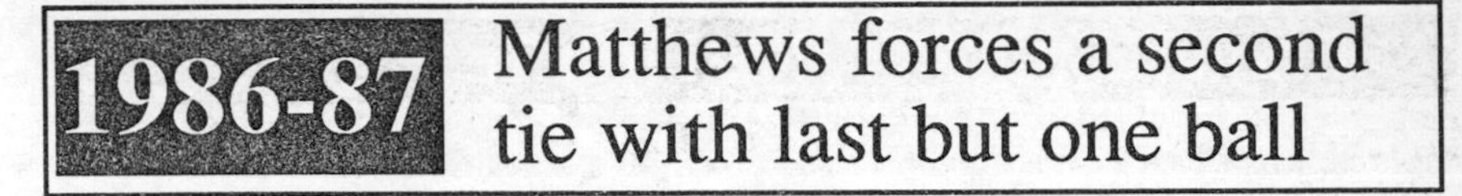

1986-87 Matthews forces a second tie with last but one ball

Match: India v Australia, First Test

Venue: Chidambaram, Madras **Date:** September 18, 19, 20, 21, 22

THE SETTING: It took 498 matches to produce the first tie in Test history (see the 1960-61 chapter, page 55) and it was another 554 matches before this Test delivered tie number two. As in the famous Brisbane Test, this match ended with one ball left to bowl. Where it differed from the classic first tie is that there was none of the sportsmanship and adventurous spirit that made the Brisbane Test the game that could be held up as representing cricket at its very best.

This match in Madras was marred by petty squabbling and gamesmanship, particularly on the final day when the players on both sides were walking a tightrope of tension.

THE MATCH: Australian skipper Allan Border won the toss and elected to bat on a sterile, comfortably paced wicket. The tourists occupied the crease throughout the first two days and for 37 minutes into the third morning before Border declared with a whopping 574 for seven on the scoreboard. Vice-captain David Boon laid the foundation with a patiently composed opening innings of 122, his third century in four Tests against India. Dean Jones and Border then put on 178 for the fourth wicket after the Aussie captain had been dropped off the first ball he faced. The conditions were so humid that during his marathon stay at the wicket Jones had to receive treatment for heat exhaustion and leg cramps. He was so dehydrated after he was bowled by Yadav for 210 that he was put on a saline drip and detained overnight in hospital. In his heroic innings he faced 330 balls in 503 minutes and struck 27 fours and two sixes.

Border reached 106 and Greg Matthews chipped in with a quickly struck 44 before the declaration with all the Indian bowlers looking thoroughly demoralised.

India made a rocketing start to their reply when Srikkanth reached 50 in 55 minutes, but Armanath and then Srikkanth were out off successive balls and only a spirited knock by Shastri (62) and then a stirring captain's innings by Kapil Dev (119) saved India from being asked to follow on. They totalled 397 against an Australian attack in which Greg Matthews (five for 103) was outstanding with his off-spin.

Australia made a quick dart for runs and Border declared at stumps on the fourth day at 170 for five, 49 of which had come from the bat of Boon. It was a generous, even risky, declaration and India went into the final day needing 348 for a win that had seemed beyond their reach when Australia were dominating the wicket in the first innings. Sunil Gavaskar

(90), piloted India to 94 for one at lunch. Gavaskar and Armarnarth (50) continued the careful accumulation of runs in the afternoon session and at the tea interval India were nicely poised for a spurt at 193 for two.

There were 30 overs left and India picked up their run rate in the final session as they set out in search of the 155 runs still required. Azharuddin (42) and Shastri started to pepper the boundary against Australia's all-spin attack of Matthews and Ray Bright.

Tempers began to fray and there were several squabbles between batsmen and fielders which, after the match, led to accusations of games-manship and intimidation.

Padit (39) was the sixth man out at 331 and there were just 17 runs needed for victory. Bright then hit a purple patch and removed three batsmen in quick succession to leave India down to their last man, Maninder Singh, who came in to join the unbeaten Shastri.

Matthews, who sent down 40 consecutive overs in the second innings, bowled the final over with India needing four runs to win. Shastri scrambled two runs, and then a single to leave Maninder facing Matthews. The scores were level. Three balls left.

With the 30,000 spectators holding their breath, Maninder failed to score off the fourth ball. Matthews sent down the penultimate ball of the match and Maninder played back, failed to make contact and it rapped him on the pads. There was a chorus of appeals from the Australian fielders and when the umpire raised his finger to signal leg before wicket they descended on Matthews and carried him around in triumph. It was his tenth wicket of the match and—for only the second time in history—a Test had finished tied.

THE WITNESSES: Allan Border: 'As Greg started the final over I told him to make sure he zeroed the ball in at those stumps. It was really nerve-racking, but in the end we got the perfect result. I was a kid in short pants when the last tied Test was played, and now I've had the pleasure of playing in one. It's almost better than winning!'

Kapil Dev: 'It got quite tense out in the middle and we did not take kindly to some of the Australian tactics. There was a lot of gamesmanship going on. At the end of the day, though, the spectators got terrific value and we very nearly pulled off a fantastic victory.'

Bobby Simpson, Australian manager: 'I played in the first tied Test, and while this one did not quite reach the heights of the Brisbane game it was still one heck of a match. I thought Greg Matthews was a real hero the way he kept plugging away, and Dean Jones showed the sort of courage for which medals are awarded.'

FOR THE RECORD: The second Test was drawn after rain had washed out the first three days. The third and final Test was also drawn. Ravi Shastri (121) and Dilip Vengsarkar (164) shared an unbroken sixth-wicket stand of 298 after Gavaskar had scored 103. Graham Marsh scord 101 for Australia.

India v Australia, First Test, 1986-87

AUSTRALIA

Batsman	1st innings		2nd innings	
D.C. Boon	c Kapil Dev b Sharma	122	— lbw b Maninder	49
G.R. Marsh	c Kapil Dev b Yadav	22	— b Shastri	11
D.M. Jones	b Yadav	210	— c Azharuddin b Maninder	24
R.J. Bright	c Shastri b Yadav	30		
A.R. Border*	c Gavaskar b Shastri	106	— b Maninder	27
G.M. Ritchie	run out	13	— c Pandit b Shastri	28
G.R.J. Matthews	c Pandit b Yadav	44	— not out	27
S.R. Waugh	not out	12	— not out	2
T.J. Zoehrer†				
C.J. McDermott				
B.A. Reid				
Extras	(B 1, LB 7, W 1, NB 6)	15	(LB 1, NB 1)	2
Total	(7 wickets declared)	**574**	(5 wickets declared)	**170**

INDIA

Batsman	1st innings		2nd innings	
S.M. Gavaskar	c and b Matthews	8	— c Jones b Bright	90
K. Srikkanth	c Ritchie b Matthews	53	— c Waugh b Matthews	39
M. Armanath	run out	1	— c Boon b Matthews	51
M. Azharuddin	c and b Bright	50	— c Ritchie b Bright	42
R.J. Shastri	c Zoehrer b Matthews	62	— not out	48
C.S. Pandit	c Waugh b Matthews	35	— b Matthews	39
Kapil Dev*	c Border b Matthews	119	— c Bright b Matthews	1
K.S. More†	c Zoehrer b Waugh	4	— lbw b Bright	0
C. Sharma	c Zoehrer b Reid	30	— c McDermott b Bright	23
N.S. Yadav	c Border b Bright	19	— b Bright	8
Maninder Singh	not out	0	— lbw b Matthews	0
Extras	(B 1, LB 9, NB 6)	16	(B1, LB 3, NB 2)	6
Total		**397**		**347**

INDIA	O	M	R	W	O	M	R	W
Kapil Dev	18	5	52	0	1	0	5	0
Sharma	16	1	70	1	6	0	19	0
Maninder	39	8	135	0	19	2	60	3
Yadav	49.5	9	142	4	9	0	35	0
Shastri	47	8	161	1	14	2	50	2
Srikkanth	1	0	6	0				

AUSTRALIA	O	M	R	W	O	M	R	W
McDermott	14	2	59	0	5	0	27	0
Reid	18	4	93	1	10	2	48	0
Matthews	28.2	3	103	5	39.5	7	146	5
Bright	23	3	88	2	25	3	94	5
Waugh	11	2	44	1	4	1	16	0
Border					3	0	12	0

FALL OF WICKETS

Wkt	A 1st	I 1st	A 2nd	I 2nd
1st	48	62	31	55
2nd	206	65	81	158
3rd	282	65	94	204
4th	460	142	125	251
5th	481	206	165	253
6th	544	220	—	291
7th	574	245	—	331
8th	—	330	—	334
9th	—	387	—	344
10th	—	397	—	347

1987-88 Qadir conjures a victory in the land of the rising finger

Match: Pakistan v England, First Test
Venue: Gaddafi Stadium, Lahore **Date:** November 25, 26, 27, 28

THE SETTING: What appeared to be one of the greatest bowling performances of all time by Pakistani leg spinner Abdul Qadir was soured by a series of disputed decisions that left the England team complaining bitterly about the standard of umpiring.

Qadir took 13 wickets in the match, including nine for 56 in the first innings. It was claimed by the incensed tourists that five of Qadir's lbw victims were not out, and that in the second innings at least two batsmen were given out caught without having made contact with the ball.

But after taking into account the protests of the England players, there still has to be admiration for Qadir's skill. Bowling the ball from out of the back of his hand, he baffled and bewildered a procession of batsmen with a variation of mystifying and mesmerising leg-breaks, googlies, top-spinners and flippers.

Qadir claimed the wicket of every England batsman once, and he twice dismissed skipper Mike Gatting and Tim Robinson.

THE MATCH: Mike Gatting was pleased to win the toss and bat first on a pitch notorious for making life difficult for any team batting last. But the England captain's pleasure quickly gave way to anxiety as Qadir started to deceive the batsmen from the moment he joined the attack 45 minutes after the start. England were four down for just 50 runs at lunch. Gatting was one of the players sent back by Qadir for a duck, but the leg before wicket decision against him was one of those that certainly looked dubious.

Only a determined 41 by Chris Broad and a late-order stand of 57 between Neil Foster (39) and Bruce French (38 not out) saved England from total collapse. Qadir took his nine wickets in 37 overs and he included 13 maidens in his prodigious performance.

England were all out for 175 in 83 overs. David Capel was the only batsman to avoid the curse of Qadir. He was alleged to have been caught for a duck off the bowling of Tauseef Ahmed. He completed a pair in the second innings, but again it was clear to most neutral onlookers that he had not laid a bat on the ball.

At the end of the second day Pakistan were powerfully placed on 272 for four, the bulk of their runs being compiled in a third-wicket partnership of 142 between Mudassar Nazar (120) and skipper Javed Miandad (65) against some loose and untidy bowling.

England played with greater efficiency on the third day and dismissed the last six Pakistan bats-

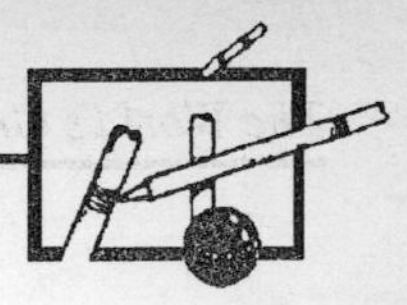

Abdul Qadir had England in a spin

men for 120, with Wasim Akram (40) boosting their score with a savage attack on Capel who conceded 28 runs in just three overs. Ironically, Qadir was the victim of a disputed umpiring decision when stumped by French off the bowling of Nick Cook (three for 87). Qadir lost his temper and argued with Gatting and the umpire.

He was soon back worrying the England batsmen with his wizardry as they attempted to cut back their arrears of 217 runs. Chris Broad was his first victim in the second innings, a dismissal that triggered one of the most blatant exhibitions of dissent ever seen in a Test match. Broad stood his ground when given out caught by wicket-keeper Ashraf Ali. Broad was convinced he had not touched the ball and refused to walk until his partner Graham Gooch quietly coaxed him to return to the pavilion where he was 'reprimanded' for his behaviour. Gooch followed soon after in a replica of the Broad dismissal, again not appearing to have touched the ball.

England were now thoroughly depressed and only John Emburey (38 not out) put up a fight as they tumbled all out for 130, teased and tormented by the Pakistani spinners and infuriated by the umpires. Qadir finished with match figures of 13 for 101 and England were beaten by an innings and 87 runs.

THE WITNESSES: Mike Gatting: 'I've never seen such blatant umpiring. If the umpiring is going to be the same as this in the next two Tests it doesn't matter what we do, we shan't win. It is a complete farce.'

Javed Miandad: 'It was a marvellous display of bowling by Qadir, particularly in the first innings. His figures speak for themselves. He had the England batsmen tied in tangles.'

FOR THE RECORD: The drawn second Test was scarred by an angry and ugly confrontation between Mike Gatting and umpire Shakoor Rana just before the close of play on the second day. Their verbal dispute led to the third day being postponed while Rana waited for a written apology from the England captain. Broad (116) scored a century in England's first innings. England salvaged a draw from the third Test in which Qadir had match figures of 10 for 186. Capel (98), Gooch (93) and Emburey (70 and 74 not out) saved England from defeat.

Pakistan v England, First Test, 1987-88

ENGLAND

G.A. Gooch	b Qadir	12	— c Ashraf b Qasim	15
B.C. Broad	c Mujtaba b Qadir	41	— c Ashraf b Qasim	13
R.T. Robinson	c Ashraf b Qadir	6	— lbw b Qadir	1
M.W. Gatting*	lbw b Qadir	0	— lbw b Qadir	23
C.W.J. Athey	lbw b Qadir	5	— c Ashraf b Tauseef	2
D.J. Capel	c Mujtaba b Tauseef	0	— c Miandad b Qadir	0
P.A.J. DeFreitas	lbw b Qadir	5	— c Tauseef b Qasim	15
J.E. Emburey	b Qadir	0	— not out	38
N.A. Foster	lbw b Qadir	39	— c sub b Tauseef	1
B.N. French†	not out	38	— lbw b Qadir	9
N.G.B. Cook	c Miandad b Qadir	10	— b Tauseef	5
Extras	(B 4, LB 14, NB 1)	19	(B 4, LB 4)	8
Total		**175**		**130**

PAKISTAN

Mudassar Nazar	lbw b Foster	120
Rameez Raja	b Emburey	35
Salim Malik	b Emburey	0
Javed Miandad*	c Gooch b Cook	65
Ijaz Ahmed	b DeFreitas	44
Asif Mujtaba	b Foster	7
Ashraf Ali†	b Emburey	7
Wasim Akram	c Broad b Cook	40
Abdul Qadir	st French b Cook	38
Iqbal Qasim	run out	1
Tauseef Ahmed	not out	1
Extras	(B 18, LB 8, NB 4)	30
Total		**392**

PAKISTAN	O	M	R	W	O	M	R	W
Akram	14	4	32	0	2	0	6	0
Mudassar	5	3	9	0	1	0	4	0
Qadir	37	13	56	9	36	14	45	4
Tauseef	23	9	38	1	20.2	7	28	3
Qasim	4	0	22	0	20	10	39	3

ENGLAND	O	M	R	W
DeFreitas	29	7	84	1
Foster	23	6	58	2
Emburey	48	16	109	3
Cook	31	10	87	3
Capel	3	0	28	0

FALL OF WICKETS

	E	P	E
Wkt	1st	1st	2nd
1st	22	71	23
2nd	36	71	24
3rd	36	213	38
4th	44	272	43
5th	55	290	66
6th	70	301	70
7th	81	328	73
8th	94	360	105
9th	151	370	116
10th	175	392	130

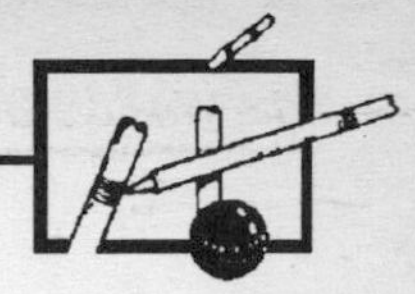

1988 'Tom Thumb' Logie has a big hand in England's fall

Match: England v West Indies, Second Test
Venue: Lord's **Date:** June 16, 17, 18, 20, 21

THE SETTING: Mike Gatting was sensationally sacked as England captain following the first Test against the all-conquering West Indies after the tabloid press had blown out of all proportion a tittle-tattle scandal involving a barmaid.

His county colleague John Emburey was appointed in his place for this second Test, and at lunchtime on the first day the Middlesex spinner could have been forgiven for thinking that he was going to celebrate his first match as captain with a famous victory.

The might of the West Indies batting lay in ruins, and the England players looked forward to finishing off their decimated innings in the afternoon session.

By tea-time, England were back at the bottom of the mountain.

THE MATCH: West Indies skipper Viv Richards won the toss and then deliberated for five minutes before deciding to bat first on a Lord's pitch that he eyed with suspicion. His fears prove well founded when Graham Dilley's hostile opening spell brought him the valued wickets of Desmond Haynes, Gordon Greenidge, Richie Richardson and, the most prized of all, Viv Richards. Gladstone Small pitched in with the scalp of Carl Hooper, who presented wicket-keeper Paul Downton with one of his three victims in this West Indies-style opening blast by England. The tourists were reduced to 54 for five, and it could have been six wickets down when Gus Logie edged a catchable ball to Derek Pringle off the bowling of Dilley. The Essex man failed to hold on to it and after lunch Logie gave him continual reminders of how expensive the miss had been.

Labelled Trinidad's Tom Thumb by the media, the tiny Logie left his fingerprints all over the England bowling returns as he helped himself to a half century that included a record 12 boundaries. His accomplice in the raid on the scoreboard was Jeff Dujon, who is one of the most gifted wicket-keeper batsmen of all time. He followed Logie's lead and started to stroke the ball around the Lord's field with a pleasing-to-the-eye elegance. Their sixth wicket partnership lasted from lunch until tea during which they repaired the West Indies total with the addition of 130 runs. Dujon, dropped by Gooch at 42, played on to Emburey 22 runs later, and then the England skipper caught Logie off Small for 81. Gooch made no mistake when given a catching chance by the dangerous Malcolm Marshall off the energetic bowling of Dilley.

Small disposed of Curtley Ambrose (spectacularly caught by Gower) and Patrick Patterson for ducks and the West Indies were all out for 209, which by their run-mountain standards was a molehill of a score. Dilley finished with five wickets for 55 off 23 overs, and Small's figures were four for 64 off 18.5 overs.

England lost an unhappy Chris Broad—leg before to Marshall for a duck—in the closing session before poor light forced an early finish. They had moved carefully to 88 for two by lunch the following morning, but then Marshall revealed why he had become recognised as the world's number one purveyor of pace. He bowled with terrifying speed, making the ball climb off a length and he hustled England out for 165 off 59 overs. Only Gower (46) and a gallant but out-of-touch Gooch (44) approached reasonable scores. Marshall's six for 32 was the best analysis by a West Indies bowler in a Lord's Test, eclipsing the six for 67 by Michael Holding in 1980.

Downton caught Haynes for five off the bowling of Dilley early on the third day, but English hopes of a repeat of the first innings downfall died on the bat of Gordon Greenidge who chose this match to come out of an unproductive spell. He and Richie Richardson saw West Indies through to lunch at 104 for one and in the afternoon session the England bowlers got the sort of pounding that breaks hearts and wrecks averages.

Richards unwrapped a rapid 72, and Greenidge marked the arrival of his 15th Test century with a crashing straight-drive off Small. Logie and Dujon (52) then gave the England bowlers a touch of *déjà vu* with a repeat of their sixth wicket stand in the first innings, this time going one run better with a partnership of 131

Malcolm Marshall strikes and Chris Broad departs for a duck at Lord's

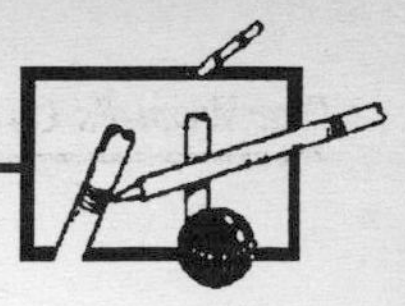

runs. By the close of play on the Saturday evening West Indies were 398 runs ahead at 354 for five and the rest day talk was of how soon Richards would declare on the Monday. But the West Indies captain allowed the innings to run its full course and Logie was left not out five runs short of a deserved century when Dilley (four for 73) and Paul Jarvis (four for 107) polished off the tail.

England were left with 442 runs to win in 172 overs. It looked a bridge too far, and when Marshall whipped out openers Gooch and Broad in the space of two runs soon after lunch there seemed no route open to them apart from to a heavy defeat.

It was odds-on England being beaten inside four days. But this did not take into account the fighting spirit of Allan Lamb, who on his 34th birthday produced an heroic innings that extended his Test career after a procession of uninspiring performances. He grafted away in the face of some always lively and often hostile bowling, and at stumps he was not out on 99 in an England score of 214 for seven.

The final day's play was into its 25th minute before Lamb scored the single that brought him his hard-earned century. Hooper and Walsh combined to run him out for 113, and Marshall took his tenth wicket of the match when he had Small caught by Richards. Jarvis (29 not out) and Dilley (28) put together a valiant last-wicket stand but then Patterson ended the innings on 307 when he persuaded Dilley to give a catch to Richardson after a stay at the wicket of 52 minutes. West Indies had won by 134 runs and with half a day to spare. Trevor Bailey had the unenviable task of having to select the Man of the Match, and he gave the nod to the diminutive Logie ahead of Marshall, who had bowled petrifyingly fast despite having his damaged ribs heavily strapped.

THE WITNESSES: Vivian Richards:'We still haven't got it quite right as a team, and I think you will see that the best is yet to come from this side. We are having to rely on individual brilliance at the moment and Gus Logie, Gordon Greenidge, Jeff Dujon and Malcolm Marshall all had their special moments.'

John Emburey: 'On the first morning of the match when we had West Indies at 54 for five I thought what a great job it is captaining England. By the time Monday had rolled on I was not so sure!'

FOR THE RECORD: West Indies won the series 4-0 after a draw in the first Test. Marshall took seven for 22 in the second innings of the third Test and finished the series with a record 35 wickets. Gus Logie led the batting averages with 364 runs at an average 72.80. Gooch was the leading runmaker for England with a total 459 at an average 45.90. Dilley was England's most successful bowler with 15 wickets, average 26.87. England called on four captains during the series—Gatting, Emburey, Chris Cowdrey and Graham Gooch. West Indies had now won 14 of their last 15 Tests against England, whose sequence of matches without a win stretched to 18.

England v West Indies, Second Test, 1988

WEST INDIES

C.G. Greenidge	c Downton b Dilley	22	— c Emburey b Dilley	103
D.L. Haynes	c Moxon b Dilley	12	— c Downton b Dilley	5
R.B. Richardson	c Emburey b Dilley	5	— lbw b Pringle	26
I.V.A. Richards*	c Downton b Dilley	6	— b Pringle	72
C.L. Hooper	c Downton b Small	3	— c Downton b Jarvis	11
A.L. Logie	c Emburey b Small	81	— not out	95
P.J.L. Dujon†	b Emburey	53	— b Jarvis	52
M.D. Marshall	c Gooch b Dilley	11	— b Jarvis	6
C.E.L. Ambrose	c Gower b Small	0	— b Dilley	0
C.A. Walsh	not out	9	— b Dilley	0
B.P. Patterson	b Small	0	— c Downton b Jarvis	2
Extras	(LB 6, NB 1))	7	(LB 19, W 1, NB 5)	25
Total		**209**		**397**

ENGLAND

G.A. Gooch	b Marshall	44	— lbw b Marshall	16
B.C. Broad	lbw b Marshall	0	— c Dujon b Marshall	1
M.D. Moxon	c Richards b Ambrose	26	— run out	14
D.I. Gower	c sub b Walsh	46	— c Richardson b Patterson	1
A.J. Lamb	lbw b Marshall	10	— run out	113
D.R. Pringle	c Dujon b Walsh	1	— lbw b Walsh	0
P.R. Downton†	lbw b Marshall	11	— lbw b Marshall	27
J.E. Emburey*	b Patterson	7	— b Ambrose	30
G.C. Small	not out	5	— c Richards b Marshall	7
P.W. Jarvis	c Haynes b Marshall	7	— not out	29
G.R. Dilley	b Marshall	0	— c Richardson b Patterson	28
Extras	(LB 6, NB 2)	8	(B 5, LB 20, W 2, NB 14)	41
Total		**165**		**307**

ENGLAND	O	M	R	W	O	M	R	W
Dilley	23	6	55	5	27	6	73	4
Jarvis	13	2	47	0	26	3	107	4
Small	18.5	5	64	4	19	1	76	0
Pringle	7	3	20	0	21	4	60	2
Emburey	6	2	17	1	15	1	62	0

WEST INDIES	O	M	R	W	O	M	R	W
Marshall	18	5	32	6	25	5	60	4
Patterson	13	3	52	1	21.5	2	100	2
Ambrose	12	1	39	1	20	4	47	1
Walsh	16	6	36	2	20	1	75	1

FALL OF WICKETS

	WI	E	WI	E
Wkt	1st	1st	2nd	2nd
1st	21	13	32	27
2nd	40	58	115	29
3rd	47	112	198	31
4th	50	129	226	104
5th	54	134	240	105
6th	184	140	371	161
7th	199	153	379	212
8th	199	157	380	232
9th	199	165	384	254
10th	209	165	397	307

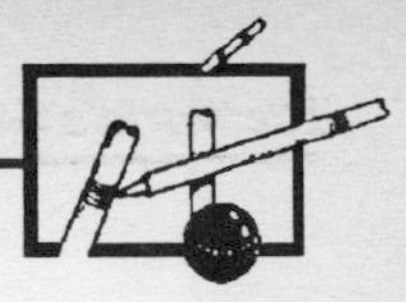

1988-89 Hughes takes 13 wickets but Aussies are bumped off

Match: Australia v West Indies, Second Test
Venue: WACA, Perth **Date:** December 2, 3, 4, 5, 6

THE SETTING: Mervyn Hughes, digging deep to discover the dragon fire of his Welsh ancestors, produced the bowling performance of a lifetime for Australia against the West Indies on a spiteful pitch at Perth.

Hughes, a beetle-browed Victorian who is built like a Welsh second-row forward, set a new record for the Australia-West Indies Tests by taking 13 wickets.

That was the good news for Australia. The bad news was that the wickets cost Hughes 217 runs as the Aussies caved in to their second defeat in the series against a West Indian team that was reaching the supreme standards predicted by skipper Viv Richards.

It was a game scarred by ill feeling between the two teams after a third day bouncer from Curtly Ambrose had fractured the jaw of Australian fast bowler Geoff Lawson, who was making his comeback to the Test arena after two years on the sidelines.

THE MATCH: It was master blaster Richards, playing in his 101st Test match, who laid the foundation for victory after Allan Border had won the toss and put the tourists in to bat on a moist, lively pitch. Border had reached the milestone of his 99th Test, but Richards made him feel like a man weighed down by a millstone as he cut loose on the first day. He shared an unbeaten fifth-wicket stand of 100 with Gus Logie to push the West Indies total to 280 for four before bad light forced a premature end to the day's play with Richards not out on 95.

The Australians were left wondering what a series of dropped catches had cost them. Each of the tourists' first five batsmen had been given a second life, three of the missed chances coming off the bowling of the unfortunate Lawson.

Richards wasted no time reaching his century during the first over of the second morning. He and Logie took their partnership to 163 before Logie went for 93. The West Indies skipper followed soon after for 146, a hurricane innings that contained 21 fours and three sixes.

The last five West Indian wickets folded for 28. Hughes dismissed Ambrose with the last ball of his 36th over and then had last man Patrick Patterson caught off the first ball of his 37th over. They were successive wickets that were to have a special significance late on the third day.

Australia, replying to a formidable total of 449, had reached 119 for one by stumps on the second day, with David Boon 65 not out. Graeme

Wood (111) and Steve Waugh (93) staged a magnificent resistance movement after Australia had slipped to 167 for four on the third morning.

Australia were within sight of the West Indies total, and the tourists responded by unleashing a barrage of wicked bouncers in a bid to unsettle the home batsmen. Lawson, facing his second ball against Ambrose, was struck on the jaw and collapsed on to his wicket. It was a horrifying moment and medical staff rushed out to the middle where Lawson lay motionless. He was taken off on a stretcher and treated in hospital for a multiple cheekbone fracture.

It was of little interest to Allan Border that the umpires had decided not to give Lawson out, ruling that the ball was dead when he fell on his wicket. The tight-lipped Australian skipper declared the innings closed 54 runs short of the West Indies total and there were muttered threats about the Aussies getting their own back for what had happened to the luckless Lawson.

There was time for just four overs, and with his first ball a fired-up Hughes trapped Gordon Greenidge leg before for a duck to complete a hat-trick spread over two innings and three overs. Remarkably, in the first Test at Brisbane, Courtney Walsh had completed the first Test hat-trick for 12 years, and his feat was also spread over two innings.

The talk was of an all-out bumper war, and officials on both sides appealed for calm and for common-sense to prevail. Interviewed after his hospital treatment, Lawson summed up the feelings of the players when he said: 'They bowl short at us, so we'll bowl short at them. They started it.'

Bobby Simpson, Australian manager, commented: 'There are too many bouncers being bowled, particularly at the tail-enders.'

There was a tense atmosphere for the remainder of the match, and on the fourth day Hughes produced some hostile, West Indian-style pace bowling that brought him six more wickets. He might have had a better return but for more slack fielding. A century by opener Desmond Haynes with solid supporting knocks by Carl Hooper (64) and Richie Richardson (48) put the tourists in a powerful position at 331 for eight at the close.

Hughes took his haul to eight wickets for 87 on the final morning before Viv Richards declared at 349 for nine. Mervyn's best-ever match figures of 13 for 217 set a new record for the series between Australia and West Indies.

The Australians never really recovered after losing both openers with the score on 14 and with a huge total of 404 needed for victory. Brave Geoff Lawson, his swollen jaw protected by padding, went into the nets to practise in case he was needed in the closing stages.

But only Wood (42) and wicket-keeper Ian Healy—who hit a maiden Test half-century—put up any real defiance, and it was soon clear that it would be pointless Lawson risking further injury in what was a lost cause.

At one stage it seemed the best chance Australia had of reaching their target was by the tourists inflicting defeat on themselves. They conceded

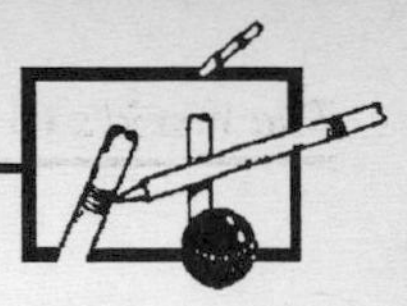

no fewer than 87 runs off no balls. Malcolm Marshall was their chief culprit, bowling wildly in his quest for the 300th Test wicket of his career. He took four wickets in the match to finish on a total of 299 wickets.

West Indies finally cruised to victory by 169 runs with 25 overs to spare. Ambrose claimed three wickets to take his match figures to eight for 138.

THE WITNESSES: Allan Border: 'The consolation for us is that we played much better than in the first Test at Brisbane. In fact we were a hell of a lot better. Don't forget we were without one of our main strike bowlers throughout the second innings. Mervyn Hughes did a magnificent job for us and thoroughly deserved his success. We were all sickened by what happened to Geoff Lawson. He volunteered to bat in the second innings, but I decided there was no point in him risking further injury. There were such big cracks in the pitch on the final day that you could have fallen down one of the holes and got lost!'

Geoff Lawson: 'There's no excuse for what happened to me. I should have been wearing a helmet with a face mask. There is no ill feeling between Curtly Ambrose and me. He didn't set out to deliberately hurt me.'

Mervyn Hughes: 'I can't believe that I've taken 13 wickets and am on the losing side. I'm proud of my achievement, but I would have been much happier if we had won.'

Viv Richards: 'We're sorry about the injury to Geoff Lawson. It's just one of those things that happen in cricket. The Australians gave us a tough battle, but I thought we had the upper hand most of the time.'

FOR THE RECORD: West Indies won the first Test in Brisbane by nine wickets. The match highlights were a 13th century opening partnership by Gordon Greenidge (80) and Desmond Haynes (40), a powerfully struck 81 by Richie Richardson and a gallant 90 by Steve Waugh. Viv Richards celebrated his 100th Test by taking his 100th catch in Test cricket. Allan Border got a duck and 20 in 150 minutes in his 100th Test appearance in the third Test at Melbourne, won by the West Indies by 285 runs. The match was again marred by an overdose of short-pitch bowling. Border, with his rarely used left-arm spin, took seven wickets for 44 on the first day of the fourth Test to send West Indies tumbling from 144 for one to 224 all out. He then scored 75 in support of David Boon (149) in Australia's reply of 401, and he took another four wickets as West Indies collapsed to 256 all out despite a century by Haynes (143). Australia reached the 80-run target for the loss of three wickets, and it was Border who struck the winning runs to send West Indies toppling to their first defeat in 11 Tests. Dean Jones (216) and Mike Whitney (seven for 89) produced personal bests for Australia in a final Test that fizzled out into a draw after the tourists had declined to chase a last day victory target of 371. Desmond Haynes scored a West Indian record 536 runs during the series.

Australia v West Indies, Second Test, 1988-89

WEST INDIES

C.G. Greenidge	b Lawson	40	— lbw b Hughes	0
D.L. Haynes	lbw b Hughes	11	— c Healy b Hughes	100
R.B. Richardson	c Boon b Hughes	66	— c Healy b Hughes	48
C.L. Hooper	c Boon b Lawson	26	— c Dodemaide b Hughes	64
I.V.A. Richards*	c Dodemaide b Lawson	146	— lbw b Hughes	5
A.L. Logie	c Waugh b May	93	— b Hughes	30
P.J.L. Dujon†	c Veletta b May	32	— c Dodemaide b Hughes	9
M.D. Marshall	c Veletta b Hughes	4	— c Healy b Dodemaide	23
C.E.L. Ambrose	c Healy b Hughes	8	— c Wood b Hughes	15
C.A. Walsh	not out	0	— not out	17
B.P. Patterson	c Dodemaide b Hughes	1	— not out	6
Extras	(B 1, LB 12, NB 9))	22	(B 14, LB 9, NB 9)	32
Total		**449**	(9 wickets declared)	**349**

AUSTRALIA

G.R. Marsh	c Richardson b Walsh	30	— c Logie b Marshall	6
D.C. Boon	c Logie b Ambrose	80	— b Patterson	4
M.R.J. Veletta	run out	11	— c Dujon b Marshall	13
G.M. Wood	c Richardson b Ambrose	111	— c Greenidge b Walsh	42
A.R. Border*	c Dujon b Ambrose	6	— b Hooper	26
S.R. Waugh	c Dujon b Ambrose	91	— c Hooper b Patterson	26
I.A. Healy†	lbw b Marshall	8	— c Logie b Ambrose	52
A.I.C. Dodemaide	not out	7	— lbw b Ambrose	11
T.B.A. May	c Richards b Ambrose	2	— not out	8
G.F. Lawson	retired hurt	0	— absent hurt	—
M.G. Hughes			— c Logie b Ambrose	0
Extras	(B 6, LB 8, NB 35)	49	(B 5, LB 4, NB 37)	46
Total	(8 wickets declared)	**395**		**234**

AUSTRALIA	O	M	R	W	O	M	R	W
Lawson	32	7	97	3				
Hughes	36.1	7	130	5	37	9	87	8
Dodemaide	17	1	79	0	24	2	101	1
Waugh	28	3	90	0	23	1	70	0
May	10	3	40	2	14	1	68	0

WEST INDIES	O	M	R	W	O	M	R	W
Marshall	23	3	84	1	12	0	50	2
Patterson	16	1	95	0	14	2	58	2
Walsh	19	3	58	1	15	1	46	1
Ambrose	23.3	3	72	5	17	1	66	3
Richards	14	0	43	0				
Hooper	5	0	29	0	5	2	5	1

FALL OF WICKETS

Wkt	WI 1st	A 1st	WI 2nd	A 2nd
1st	16	83	0	14
2nd	82	139	103	14
3rd	126	152	216	46
4th	180	167	236	93
5th	343	367	246	138
6th	421	374	259	140
7th	426	388	300	190
8th	440	395	310	232
9th	448	—	341	234
10th	449	—	—	—